A DESIGN FOR POLITICAL SCIENCE:
SCOPE, OBJECTIVES, AND METHODS

This monograph is the sixth in a series published by The American Academy of Political and Social Science. Monographs previously issued in this series are:

Monograph 1: October 1962   THE LIMITS OF BEHAVIORALISM IN POLITICAL SCIENCE

Monograph 2: June 1963   MATHEMATICS AND THE SOCIAL SCIENCES: THE UTILITY AND INUTILITY OF MATHEMATICS IN THE STUDY OF ECONOMICS, POLITICAL SCIENCE, AND SOCIOLOGY

Monograph 3: August 1963   ACHIEVING EXCELLENCE IN PUBLIC SERVICE

Monograph 4: April 1964   LEISURE IN AMERICA: BLESSING OR CURSE?

Monograph 5: February 1965   FUNCTIONALISM IN THE SOCIAL SCIENCES: THE STRENGTH AND LIMITS OF FUNCTIONALISM IN ANTHROPOLOGY, ECONOMICS, POLITICAL SCIENCE, AND SOCIOLOGY

A DESIGN FOR POLITICAL SCIENCE: SCOPE, OBJECTIVES, AND METHODS

108021

Monograph 6 in a series sponsored by The American
Academy of Political and Social Science

Edited by James C. Charlesworth

PHILADELPHIA
DECEMBER 1966

Issued by The American Academy of Political and Social Science at Prince and Lemon Sts., Lancaster, Pennsylvania.

Editorial and Business Office, 3937 Chestnut Street, Philadelphia, Pennsylvania 19104.

CONTENTS

FOREWORD

Although the officers of this Academy were aware of published approaches to the study of political science by Hyneman, Lasswell, Young, Van Dyke, de Grazia, Easton, Rankin, Waldo, and Dimock, *et al.*, we believed that there have been some rapid developments since some of these studies were made and that a new synthesis or selective appraisal would be currently useful. Accordingly, we organized a conference, which met in Philadelphia on 28 and 29 December, 1965, and addressed itself to creating "A Design for Political Science: Scope, Objectives, and Methods."

Twenty scholars accepted our invitation to participate:

Alfred de Grazia	New York
Karl W. Deutsch	Yale
David Easton	Chicago
Harry Eckstein	Princeton
Heinz Eulau	Stanford
Lee S. Greene	Tennessee
Alan P. Grimes	Michigan State
Harold Guetzkow	Northwestern
Louis Hartz	Harvard
Alpheus T. Mason	Princeton
Hans J. Morgenthau	Chicago
Norman D. Palmer	Pennsylvania
Robert V. Presthus	Cornell
David Spitz	Ohio State
Vernon Van Dyke	Iowa
Frederick M. Watkins	Yale
Paul N. Ylvisaker	Ford Foundation
Roland Young	Northwestern

The chairman and vice-chairman were James C. Charlesworth and Stephen B. Sweeney, President and first Vice President of this Academy, respectively. Karl von Vorys of the University of Pennsylvania, who is a consultant with the Academy, assisted in the planning of the conference.

Unfortunately Professors Easton, Eckstein, Greene, Mason, and Presthus were prevented by illness or other imperative from attending.

Three principal papers were prepared in advance of the meeting and distributed to all of the participants—one on Scope by Van Dyke, one on Objectives by Morgenthau, and one on Methods by Deutsch. Critiques of each of these papers were contributed by three members of the conference—Greene, Hartz, and Watkins on Scope; de Grazia, Palmer, and Ylvisaker on Objectives; and Eulau, Guetzkow, and Young on Methods. Most of these papers were also distributed before the meeting opened.

The conference opened in a mood to make a bold and synoptic approach to the discipline of political science. The conferees soon evinced a desire to integrate all of its substantive and procedural aspects. They set out on a project designed to transcend the teaching of political science in American colleges and the writing of guides and textbooks, and sought to measure the importance of political science in a broad philosophic context and to consider whether it is an adornment of the mind as well as a practical instrument of government.

The officers of the Academy were encouraged by the results of this conference to make plans to organize similar meetings dealing with sociology, international relations, public administration, and social psychology.

This monograph will be distributed free to all professional political scientists in the United States.

JAMES C. CHARLESWORTH

The Optimum Scope of Political Science *

By Vernon Van Dyke

WE can think of scope in terms of the kinds of questions we try to answer—the kinds of problems that we attack—and in terms of the kinds of data that we bring to bear. In these terms, no one would contend that the scope of political science is fixed very sharply or that any boundaries are at all sacrosanct. We have somewhat different conceptions of the subject of our inquiries, variously describing it as politics or government or the policy process or the political system; and each label carries with it some probable implications for the scope of our work. Moreover, we pursue various purposes, are guided by different theories, and employ various approaches and methods; and again the choices that we make are interrelated with the selection of questions and data, and so affect scope.[1]

Since so many factors are involved, a discussion of scope could be organized in various ways. I propose to focus mainly on conceptions of our field of inquiry and their probable implications. I might note that a very large volume—I think an ever increasing volume—of material on political science is being published, and that we do not have any very reliable classificatory or mapping system by which to tell what terrain is being covered or left unexplored. This means that it is difficult to say what the actual scope of political science is; we have to rely on our impressions. Impressions that our coverage is inadequate have led to recommendations for expanding the scope of the field, and I propose to take up some of them.

* For comments and suggestions elicited by an earlier draft of this paper I wish to thank Karl von Vorys of the University of Pennsylvania and my colleagues at Iowa, especially G. Robert Boynton, Lane Davis, Samuel C. Patterson, and Joseph Tanenhaus.

[1] Charles S. Hyneman, *The Study of Politics* (Urbana: University of Illinois Press, 1959), p. 21.

1

THE IMPLICATIONS OF A FOCUS ON POLITICS

It is common to say that *politics* is the subject of political science. More to the point, perhaps, is the fact that it is often simply taken for granted that *politics* is the subject. I am among those who have done this. This means that a definition of politics at least suggests the outer limits of the field, whether or not everything within those limits actually gets covered.

Edward C. Banfield's definition of politics and one that I have advanced can both be cited to serve our present purposes. Banfield's focus is on "actors (both persons and formal organizations) who are oriented toward the attainment of ends." When actors pursue conflicting ends, an issue exists. And "politics is the activity (negotiation, argument, discussion, application of force, persuasion, etc.) by which an issue is agitated or settled." [2] Without at the time knowing of Banfield's definition, I advanced one in 1960 that is somewhat similar. In its short version it is that politics consists of struggle among actors pursuing conflicting desires on public issues. [3] The principal differences are that whereas Banfield's stress is on "activity," mine is on a particular kind of activity, struggle; and whereas he does not say what kind of issues are political, I specify that they must be "public"— that is, that they must have to do with group policy, group organization, group leadership, or the conduct or regulation of intergroup relationships.

These definitions seem to me to imply, with respect to the scope of political science, that we should try, among other things, to identify political actors; to identify and clarify the goals that they seek, and perhaps recommend alternatives or at least call attention to them; to analyze interrelationships among ends; to describe and assess the means that are or might be employed in the pursuit of ends; to determine the reasons and causes influencing the choice of ends and means; and, in general, to find out why political issues arise, how the struggle over them is conducted, what governs the outcome, and what the effects of the struggle are or may be. Studies pursued under this conception can be

[2] Martin Myerson and Edward C. Banfield, *Politics, Planning and the Public Interest* (Glencoe, Ill.: Free Press, 1955), pp. 304–305.

[3] Vernon Van Dyke, *Political Science: A Philosophical Analysis* (Stanford, Calif.: Stanford University Press, 1960), p. 134.

either particular or general. In fact, some focus on specific actors and issues and are more or less policy-oriented; others, though perhaps achieving their ultimate justification in their contribution to policy-making, aim directly at general knowledge relating to classes of actors or kinds of problems.

Though these definitions have merit, they lead to certain difficulties and do not give an entirely satisfying answer to the question of the optimum scope of political science. My definition has been attacked for the focus on struggle. Banfield's wording is less open to question on this score, though the difference is not very great. His focus is also on issues, which implies that controversy, if not struggle, is an essential feature of politics. This, in fact, suggests one of the important questions about both his conception and mine—whether political scientists do or should restrict themselves to issues. It also suggests the question which issues are political and whether all political issues automatically fall within the scope of political science. Perhaps I should add that I am not raising the question whether we as scholars should always address ourselves to precisely the issues faced by practitioners; this would be an absurd rule. The question is whether we should define our field of inquiry in terms of issues, tackling whatever intellectual problems we choose within that field.

One of the obvious implications of a focus on politics defined in terms of issues or controversy is that a very substantial portion of the activities of government are placed beyond the purview of political science. A great deal that goes on in government, and in intergovernmental relations, occurs on the basis of consent. A United States Senator once told me that 90 per cent of the matters that the Senate concerned itself with were nonpolitical; he meant, I am sure, that there was no real controversy over them. The "struggle," if there was one, was to ascertain the relevant facts and perhaps to induce the appropriate persons or agencies to give the problem attention; once this was done, there would likely be consensus on the appropriate action to take. Whether or not 90 is the correct percentage, it is obvious that there is considerable truth in what the Senator said. Congress devotes a significant portion of its time to overseeing, in a nonpolitical way, activities of the executive branch of the government that are themselves generally regarded as nonpolitical. Issues may arise, but many of them relate to questions of fact or judgment rather than to political demands. The same kind of thing happens at the state and local level—probably to an even greater extent. The development and operation of the public educational system are major activities of state and local governments; as the struggle over integration attests, political issues sometimes arise in this field, but still the general record is one of the nonpolitical treatment of educational problems. In the little suburban municipality in which I live, elections are nonpartisan and frequently noncompetitive, and votes on the town council are ordinarily unanimous. Similarly, many aspects of county government are managerial or administrative; politics may determine who holds the offices, but not what they do once they are elected.

Schattschneider points out another difficulty in the notion that political science is the study of politics and that politics centers on issues. To be sure, he takes the view that "the central problem in politics is the management of conflict," but he reminds us that conflict can sometimes be forestalled by preventing issues from arising or by getting them subordinated, obscured, or rendered obsolete. "Some issues are organized into politics while others are organized out." [4] Bachrach and Baratz elaborate on the point: "To the extent that a person or group—consciously or unconsciously—creates or reinforces barriers to the public airing of policy conflicts, that person or group has power." They go on to speak of the possibility that a political actor may have less to do with decision-making than with nondecision-making; that is, he may "limit decision-making to relatively noncontroversial matters, by influencing community values and political procedures and rituals." [5] Of course, action to prevent issues from arising is itself, in a sense, a form of struggle, but the definitions of politics in question are much more likely to suggest open and direct struggle and controversy than subtle strategies that keep issues from coming to the fore.

[4] E. E. Schattschneider, *The Semisovereign People* (New York: Holt, Rinehart and Winston, 1960), p. 71.
[5] Peter Bachrach and Morton S. Baratz, "Two Faces of Power," *American Political Science Review,* 56 (December 1962), p. 949.

Apart from the question whether we as political scientists should restrict ourselves to the study of struggle over issues is the question which issues are political and whether all political issues automatically fall within the scope of political science. Suppose, for example, we think of the practice of political scientists concerning research on crime, rioting, revolutions, and war. Most of us, I believe, do not regard it as part of our job to explain crime on the part of private individuals or to try to find out how to deter or to combat it, even though crime is a challenge to law and order and even though the effort to repress it is an important part of governmental activity. In contrast, we do regard it as part of our job to explain war and to try to find out how to deter or combat it. Further, we tend to ignore rioting and to neglect grossly revolutions and civil wars.

What is the rationale of our behavior? One of the rules has just been discussed: that we are commonly not much concerned in the absence of a public issue. And ordinarily there is no public issue about crime on the part of private individuals. The relevant laws are ordinarily not in dispute; and neither are the duties of the police or of the court. So we concede the study of crime to sociologists, lawyers, and others. But the rule concerning the presence or absence of a public issue does not provide a full answer. The question of capital punishment, for example, has sometimes become a minor political issue; but even so, political scientists give it little or no attention, except perhaps in connection with the study of the more general problems relating to the governmental process. My supposition is that we have tacitly added a rule to the one regarding controversy: that where we have conceded a subject to another discipline because it is generally nonpolitical, we tend to maintain the division of labor even when the subject enters the political arena.

No problem arises, of course, about the reason for our concern with war; it is obviously a struggle among actors pursuing conflicting desires on public issues.

Why do we neglect rioting and revolution? The rule that we concern ourselves only with actual or prospective public issues provides part of the answer. Many riots and many mob actions belong in the same category with crime in that no public issue is involved. But this can scarcely be a full explanation.

Some riots are clearly the work of actors engaged in struggle on public issues, and all civil wars and revolutions are in this category. I suspect that our neglect of the subject should be treated in part as a lapse. Those who take their cues from the provisions of the Constitution and from our institutional arrangements have not been guided to the subject of riots and revolutions. Moreover, political life in the United States has been so stable for so long that the subject has not come urgently to our attention. Greater national involvement in the life of other countries is changing this situation; and so, perhaps, is the racial problem that we confront at home.

I should note that problems relating to riots and revolutions can be turned around and stated so as to call for inquiry into the conditions making for the establishment and preservation of stable and effective government. In fact, this is a broader way of stating the problem, for it encompasses studies of such subjects as nation-building, socialization, and political mobilization. As long as American political scientists were focusing their efforts on the United States and western Europe, these subjects got little attention, but developments in the world in the last decade or so have brought significant expansion in the area of our concern.[6]

The question which issues are political, and which ones come within the scope of political science, is somewhat complicated by such adjectives as economic, legal, and military. Obviously, economic, legal, and military issues may also be political, but even so the use of these adjectives suggests that study of them calls for a special expertise that political scientists may not have. We are especially inclined to concede economic issues to economists. We rarely take up questions concerning tax and fiscal policy, except perhaps where budgets and budget-making are directly involved. We provide very little of the knowledge on which the Council of Economic Advisers has to draw. When governments go more and more into the planning of their economies, thus expanding the scope of their activities, we do not expand the scope of political science accordingly. In so far as gov-

---

[6] One of the more recent and novel studies on this subject is Karl von Vorys, *Political Development in Pakistan* (Princeton, N.J.: Princeton University Press, 1965).

ernment and economic life are concerned, the scope of political science is about the same whether the political system studied is that of Spain, the Soviet Union, or the United States. Some political scientists are unhappy about this situation, but few are doing anything to change it. I might note incidentally that several years ago when I was working on the rationale of the American space program, I ran on to a lively controversy on the subject of United States patent policy. The National Aeronautics and Space Administration (NASA) was contracting out research to private firms. When the private firm, using government money, made a patentable discovery, who was or should have been entitled to the patent? Congressional hearings occurred on the question; administrative rulings were made; and legislation was debated. By all the definitions of *political* that I know, the issue was political. But I still wonder whether it fits within the scope of political science and by what overriding criterion it is included or excluded.

Political scientists have not been quite so much inclined to steer clear of a question because it is called legal or judicial, probably because constitutional law has been part of the field from the first. The overlapping of the fields is recognized and accepted. But where the overlapping does or should end is somewhat uncertain. Is jurisprudence, for example, an appropriate part of political science? Is administrative law?

In recent years political scientists—especially some of those concerned with international politics—have been less and less intimidated by the adjective *military*. From our ranks come some of the leading students of such problems as deterrence and limited war. But still there are problems. We have not so far given an unqualified affirmative answer to the question whether all aspects of military strategy come within our field. We have begun to study military strategy when it has a bearing on "political" objectives; but this very way of thinking about the subject implies that some questions of strategy are outside the scope of political science. Perhaps the answer is to be found in our attitude toward crime and criminals. When the goal and the kind of methods to use are both agreed upon, we are willing to leave the subject to others. And in the case of many questions relating to military affairs and military strategy, this means leaving the subject without an academic home, save in a very few institutions.

Questions arise in the field of human rights that illustrate the problem further. The United States and most other countries have endorsed a Declaration of Human Rights, and the question of concluding one or more international covenants has been debated for many years. Undoubtedly, the general issue of human rights and of national and international action with regard to them comes within the scope of political science. But human rights are said to include the rights of persons of full age to marry and to found a family, the right to equal pay for equal work, the right to periodic holidays with pay, and many other rights. Then do the laws and practices of various countries regarding these rights become suitable subjects for political scientists to inquire into? Should political science journals carry articles on attitudes in various countries concerning the "full age" for marriage and concerning the policies of Liberia relating to forced labor recruitment? Along the same line, consider legislation in the United States concerning marriage and divorce, and concerning birth control. These are areas in which political issues arise, and it would undoubtedly be appropriate for a political scientist to study the kinds of activities in which people engage in order to get the issue resolved as they wish. But would it be appropriate to engage in studies of the age at which marriage occurs, the conditions giving rise to divorce, and the moral and religious questions on birth control?

Analogous problems come up in connection with the study of motives of political behavior and of the psychological effects of political practices and legal rules. Those who try to explain why people vote as they do, or to explain why some people seek political careers, or why governmental leaders follow policies that precipitate or avert war sometimes find psychological or psychiatric data useful. Similarly, in interpreting constitutional provisions bearing on racial discrimination, the Supreme Court has considered the relationship between discrimination and personality development. Does this mean, then, that political scientists should join psychologists and psychiatrists in experiments concerning human motivation and in analyses of the factors that help shape personality?

One of the facts that we are facing here is contained in the extreme statement that everything is related to everything else. We can start out examining what is undoubtedly a political question and undoubtedly a part of political science. But if we pursue the subject very far we may soon find ourselves in the midst of another discipline—or simply in unclaimed territory. And I am not aware of any clear-cut rule for determining whether or at what point we have crossed the outer limits of political science. Even if we say that our central concern is with the struggle over issues, we, in fact, seem to add a rule of convenience or expediency: that we should concede even political issues to scholars in other disciplines—especially to economists—whenever their expertise is especially relevant. Moreover, except where the issue concerns the rules, procedures, and methods of political struggle, we tend to leave it to scholars in other disciplines to supply the data—sociological, economic, psychological—that explain why the issue arose and what consequences follow from any settlement that is reached.

I should, perhaps, add two final notes on the question of the implications for scope of a focus on politics. The first is that the definition of politics with which one starts is obviously of crucial significance. If, instead of using the definitions that I have cited, we were to say, for example, that politics is a struggle for power or a clash of interest groups, somewhat different consequences would ensue. I believe that the difficulties would be greater. The second is that when we talk about politics we pretty regularly mean the politics associated with public government—the kind of government that goes with sovereignty. We may speak of the politics of private groups, but only in exceptional cases is this the kind of politics with which we are concerned.

THE IMPLICATIONS OF A FOCUS ON GOVERNMENT

If we object to a focus on politics in part because it leaves such a wide range of governmental activity beyond our purview, one possible solution would be to jump the other way and say that our concern is with government. Charles S. Hyneman thinks that, in fact, this is our prime concern. "The central point of attention in American political science . . . is that part of the affairs of the state which centers in government, and that kind or part of government which speaks through law." [7]   For short, he speaks of "legal government" as the focus, meaning public as distinct from private government.

Hyneman himself stresses the magnitude of our tasks if we commit ourselves to the idea that legal or public government is the terrain that we should explore.

Certain controversial subjects of domestic policy in the United States, especially agricultural policy, water resources policy, and a number of matters generally entitled government-labor-business, have come in for increased attention in recent years.   But relatively little effort has been made by American political scientists to describe policies adopted in many other highly important areas of public concern, such as health, education, marriage and divorce, crime, and conduct which lies at the edges of legality. . . . As yet there has not appeared a rationale that seems to guide political scientists in the selection of policies to be described.[8]

At other points Hyneman names still other subjects associated with government that political scientists have not explored.

Obviously, the statement that we do or should focus on public government eliminates some of the difficulties that attend a focus on issues.   At the same time, it does not eliminate them all; for example, it does not eliminate the problem of determining how far into related disciplines political scientists should go in providing the substantive knowledge on which various kinds of decisions should be based.   Moreover, it introduces some new difficulties.   Though permitting attention to consensual politics, it suggests no limit to the kinds of questions relating to government with which political scientists should be concerned.   The United States Weather Bureau, the Food and Drug Administration, the National Institutes of Health, the Tennessee Valley Authority, the Government Printing Office, and the Foreign Service Institute of the Department of State are all parts of public government.   If public or legal government is our subject, with what questions concerning these agencies should political scientists deal, and what questions concerning them are outside the optimum scope of our field?

[7] Hyneman, *op. cit.*, pp. 26–27.
[8] *Ibid.*, p. 39.

If a focus on legal government opens up too vast a terrain, on the one hand, it traditionally has had connotations that are too narrow, on the other. Traditionally, it has connoted a description of institutional arrangements and of governmental policies and functions, offered with a minimum of attention to theory; too often the descriptions have been formal and legalistic, neglectful of the informal processes and channels through which influence is brought to bear; and too often they have been associated with reformist zeal. Further, those who have accepted government as their focus have tended pretty regularly to neglect international politics, and such attention as they have given to the subject has tended to go to international law and organization. Even today, given the traditional outlook that goes with a focus on government, public law usually means domestic law. The legislative process is usually assumed to be purely domestic. Comparative politics calls for the comparison of domestic political systems, not the comparison of the domestic and the international. The subdivision of political science called political theory concerns itself almost entirely with government within states and with relationships between government and individuals or groups; from the days of Plato and Aristotle on down, political theorists have given very little attention to international politics. Obviously, I think there is too much of a tendency to put international politics off in a compartment by itself, and this leads me to question the use of *government* as the defining term for political science, for the term is associated with the practice of compartmentalization. I might add that those who focus on international politics have not always promoted their own integration into political science. The very fact that they speak of international *relations* creates problems, for many relationships are nonpolitical. I wonder what we would include in the study of domestic politics if we said that the subject encompassed domestic relations.

IMPLICATIONS OF A FOCUS ON THE POLICY PROCESS

Rather than focus on issues or on government, some political scientists choose to focus on the policy process; or they say that

political science is or should be a policy science.[9] Like almost
all our terms, these are rather vague, and different scholars
construe them differently.   Reference to the policy process may
mean the process by which issues are resolved—the decision-
making process. If an issue arises, the object of those focusing
on the policy process is to identify the actors and interests, the
legal and institutional arrangements, and the conditions, methods, and procedures that relate to the outcome, and to analyze
and perhaps assess their relative roles or influence in shaping the
outcome.   General knowledge of the nature of the process and
the factors affecting its functioning is what is sought.   The reasons why the issue arose, the relative merits of different solutions,
and the consequences of the decision that is made are, I assume,
put on or beyond the periphery of the field of political science.

The notion that our focus should be on the policy process has
a good deal in common with the notion that it should be on politics, defined as a struggle over issues, and many of the comments
already made apply again.   In addition, the term *policy process*
connotes a narrower range of interest than the term *politics,*
pretty much excluding concern for the substance of policy.   A
political scientist who says that his concern is with the policy
process could probably answer my question whether NASA's
patent policy is really within our field; he would not concern
himself directly with the problem of equity that is involved or
with the relationship between patent policy and technological
progress; but he would concern himself with the actors engaged
in the struggle—including their claims regarding equity and
progress—and the methods and procedures by which the struggle is resolved.   Similarly, the student of the policy process
would be unlikely to study the substance of the foreign policies
pursued by a government, or the actual or probable effect of
armaments or disarmament on the relationship of states.   If he
gives any attention at all to international politics, his concern
is likely to be with the formulation of policies by governments
and with the formulation of policies in international organizations.

The term *policy science* has a broader connotation than the
term *policy process,* permitting various kinds of studies—descriptive and prescriptive, if not normative—relating to politics.   It

[9] *Ibid.,* pp. 100–108, 165–173.

does very little, however, to indicate limits. It might, for example, suggest a study of the rules and principles followed by the National Science Foundation (NSF) and the National Institutes of Health (NIH) in making grants. For that matter, it is not at all clear that the term *policy process* would exclude such matters.

THE IMPLICATIONS OF A FOCUS ON THE POLITICAL SYSTEM

The term *the political system* is so thoroughly identified with David Easton that we should focus on his conceptions and contributions. They are distinctive and impressive, but at the same time they do not resolve all difficulties. It would be too much to expect this of any approach or analytical framework. When Easton says that our concern is with "that system of interactions in any society through which . . . binding or authoritative allocations are made and implemented,"[10] he does a good deal to indicate an appropriate scope for political science. This way of conceptualizing the field reduces the difficulties that attend a focus on politics defined as struggle over issues, for the authoritative allocations of values could be tacit, unattended by current struggle. Easton's definition encompasses the politics of consent as well as the politics of struggle. But it also seems to encompass economic decisions and policies that allocate values authoritatively, and leaves the political scientist uncertain what the division of labor between him and the economist is or should be. More generally, Easton's conceptual scheme does not do much to resolve the question of the extent to which political scientists must also be economists, sociologists, psychologists, and military strategists.

One of the merits of Easton's framework for analysis is the effort to make it applicable to politics at every level. As is already clear, I consider this highly desirable, and I suppose that his scheme could, in fact, be applied to international as well as to domestic politics. At the same time, the fact shows up pervasively in his books that he writes with domestic politics primarily in mind, and the question comes up persistently whether

[10] David Easton, *A Framework for Political Analysis* (Englewood Cliffs, N.J.: Prentice-Hall, 1965), p. 50.

his formulations are as apt or as suitable as they might be for inquiry into the international field. I am fearful that his scheme will, in practice, prove much more readily suitable to the study of domestic politics and that it will thus perpetuate if not accentuate the tendency to treat the two fields separately and differently.

Proposals to Expand the Scope of Political Science

Neither Easton's conceptual scheme nor the definitions cited above call clearly for any change in the present vague but widely accepted attitudes about the scope of political science. Some suggestions along this line have been made, however, most of them relating to the border region between political science and economics. One argument is that as the role of government in economic life expands, the scope of political science should also expand. Another is that we should pay attention to some of the interactions that Easton describes as parapolitical; more specifically, that we should pay attention to private government as well as to public government, that is, to the great corporations which, in American life, make or share in making decisions that have widespread effects.

Michael Reagan makes both of these arguments. With the United States in mind, he speaks of the "merger of the public and private," which manifests itself in several forms: in the Communication Satellite Corporation which is, in part, government-owned; in the insertion in government contracts of terms giving effect to public policy, for example, fair employment practices; in interrelationships between federal regulatory agencies and the industries that they are supposed to regulate; and in the fact of public political pressures (perhaps through congressional hearings) on private business practices.[11] A number of other developments might also be cited that confuse the distinction between the public and the private. When the United States Mediation Service plays a prominent role in negotiations between management and labor—and when the President of the United States becomes personally involved—are the negotiations

[11] Michael D. Reagan, *The Managed Economy* (New York: Oxford University Press, 1963), pp. 190–210.

private and nonpolitical or public and political? When scientific research is paid for pretty largely by the government, to what extent does the determination of its nature and direction become a matter of public policy? These questions pertain to the United States, but we might note that in some other countries—above all in those that have collectivized their economies—the merger of the private and the public has gone much farther. Reagan's admonition is that "the skills of the political scientist and those of the economist must be fused if adequate analysis of the system and the appropriate prescriptions for public policy are to be developed."

Reagan also points to the widespread effects of decisions made by some of our great private corporations. What General Motors does in the pursuit of its interests clearly affects the public interest. Reagan is even concerned about the sense of social responsibility that some great corporations have developed and about the philanthropy in which they engage, suggesting that we may be heading into a paternalistic system where leading roles are played by benevolent feudal lords. And he urges that political scientists concern themselves with these matters. "The rise of the managed economy reunites politics and economics into a truly political economy." [12] We should be "concerned with popular control over economic decisions affecting the public, whether these are made in the public sector or by the private 'governments' of the corporations." "Public decisions," he argues, are not only those made by government, but those that affect the public; and concern for public decisions, so defined, requires "consideration of the relationship of business management to the people, as well as the relationship of government and the people." [13]

Robert Dahl raises somewhat similar questions. He thinks that it would be an "arid enterprise" to debate the question whether political science should or should not encompass the politics of business firms and of relationships between such firms, but he surveys the state of our knowledge about these questions nevertheless. And he does the same for questions concerning

[12] *Ibid.*, p. 19.
[13] *Ibid.*, p. 214.

relationships between public government and business.[14] Further, he calls attention to a no man's land that has grown up between political science and economics, and argues that if a theory is to be developed that will help provide answers to questions arising from "the diversity and complexity of contemporary economic orders," economists are likely to have to give more attention to political science, and political scientists are likely to have to give more attention to economics.[15]

Apart from the question of the relationship between political science and economics, other questions have been raised, explicitly or implicitly, about the traditional scope of political science. Oliver Garceau went beyond it when he wrote about *The Political Life of the American Medical Association*. Masters, Salisbury, and Eliot have concerned themselves with *State Politics and the Public Schools*. And in recent years various studies of organizations, organizational behavior, and leadership have proceeded without much regard for a distinction between the political and the parapolitical. Grant McConnell has discussed "The Spirit of Private Government," [16] focusing on trade unions; but the distinctions that he finds between private and public government are so great as to raise the question whether worth-while analogies and comparisons can be made.

CONCLUSION

Obviously, this review does not lead to a clear-cut conclusion either about the actual scope of political science or about its optimum scope. I have dwelt on some of the different conceptions of the nature of the subject that we study, and I think it is clear that each conception carries somewhat different implications for scope. I doubt whether it would be justifiable to describe any of them as either wrong or right. I accept Easton's view that no one way of conceptualizing any major area of human behavior will do full justice to all its variety and complexity. Each type of theoreti-

[14] Robert A. Dahl, "Business and Politics: A Critical Appraisal of Political Science," *Social Science Research on Business: Product and Potential*, ed. Robert A. Dahl, Mason Haire, and Paul F. Lazarsfeld (New York: Columbia University Press, 1959), p. 5.

[15] *Ibid.*, pp. 16–17.

[16] *American Political Science Review*, 52 (September 1958), pp. 754–770.

cal orientation brings to the surface a different set of problems, provides unique insights and emphases, and thereby makes it possible for alternative and even competing theories to be equally and simultaneously useful.[17]

Further, optimum scope is determined not only by conceptions of the subject of inquiry but also by the kinds of purposes that the scholar pursues and the kinds of methods that he is willing to employ. It would thus be inappropriate for me to make a recommendation concerning optimum scope until questions pertaining to purpose and method have been resolved.

[17] Easton, *op. cit.*, p. 23.

Comments on Professor Van Dyke's Paper

By Lee S. Greene

THE concluding paragraphs of Professor Van Dyke's paper, including an approved quotation of Professor Easton, suggest either that the time for recommending an optimum scope of political science is not at hand or possibly that no limitation of scope ought to be attempted at all. If this represents the feeling of the principal paper for this session, it is certainly not the role of a commentator to essay setting such a scope. In any event, I could not, even under the impulsion to start an argument, disagree with these conclusions of Professor Van Dyke and Professor Easton. It seems to me that any attempt to prescribe a scope for a discipline may well end in failure in a society such as ours, and, in any event, ought to fail. Indeed, I think it is in the interest of our discipline to resist any influences which might have the effect of limiting or directing the interests of scholars in our field. It has recently been decided that political science may be considered for some of the moneys made available by the National Science Foundation (NSF). Small amounts of these funds may be allocated to equipment which can be of use only to certain kinds of political scientists. So far as I am aware, other NSF grants may be more widely used, but the danger exists, perhaps only to a small degree, that the presence of such money exerts a limiting pressure on us.

Certainly I do not detect in Professor Van Dyke's paper any spirit of limitation or exclusiveness. Indeed, the announced purpose of the paper is for further expansion of the field. I am in complete accord with this view, assuming only one other point, which I presume is implicit in the paper, namely, that scope should be left entirely up to the individual scholar. Heresy should be no ground for excommunication in this society.

Professor Van Dyke has suggested a focus on struggle, and prescribes that such struggle should be public. He admits in answer to earlier comments that this approach leaves out much nonpolitical activity of political figures who act a good deal of the time by consent.   I think two points might be made about this: first, that action by consent is often the result of past struggles, as, for example, those between a representative body and a single executive (a history which political scientists cannot neglect, particularly as such agreements may always come apart) and, second, that the focus on struggle, if at all precisely determined, would leave out extensive areas which do interest some political scientists.   The oversight by Congress of the executive branch, even if it could at times be described as nonpolitical, is of interest to some of our colleagues because it describes a system of operations which, part of the time, permits a peaceful day-to-day operation.   That these operations are also of interest to the industrial engineer, the lawyer, or the sociologist does not disturb me in any way.   At the same time, I would agree that a number of small-town decisions and such county operations as the register of deeds and the county library have little chance of providing fodder for the political scientist.

Perhaps the basic difficulty met by anyone who tries to reach a definition is that the definition itself can be shifted around. Thus, Professor Van Dyke recognizes that struggle can be defined so as to include action to prevent issues from arising.   But a definition which can be indefinitely stretched loses something of its usefulness.

Professor Van Dyke suggests several study areas which we have ordinarily left to other scholars, such as crime, rioting, and revolution.   At the same time he cites a growing interest in problems of military organization and civilian-military relations.   Apparently, war is not the only subject which cannot safely be left to the generals.   It could have been argued here, I suppose, that political scientists have no special competence.   Some of our colleagues have shown by thoughtful study that competence can be acquired.   Presumably a novelist could do something of the same thing, and some of them have.   The novelist, however, has a different aim, and will justifiably fit his data to the aim.   Presumably the political scientist will try to follow where evidence leads.

But I would not agree that political scientists have completely conceded revolutions and civil wars to others.   The problems presented by revolution have surely interested political theorists for a long time, and the resurgence of civil disobedience should force us to consider again not only the nature of a political struggle but the moral issues which bring once more into question the very basis of the state. I would suggest that political scientists traffic particularly in insoluble problems.

An increasing number of political scientists now concern themselves with the problems of developing countries, where rioting, civil disturbance, and revolution are a way of life. And I know at least one American political scientist who has an interest in the causes and prevention of crime.

I was somewhat puzzled by the suggestion that politics had been neglected in the study of international affairs. I had always thought that students in the international sphere were quite seriously concerned with international politics, and that if any areas were being neglected it was rather those of organization and law—particularly, in recent years, international law. The history of political theory includes figures, such as Grotius, whose studies I had thought were motivated by concerns with international politics, even though the works were not. As a minor point, I was struck by the inclusion of the Tennessee Valley Authority (TVA) in a group of agencies of somewhat less colorful history, such as the Weather Bureau and the Government Printing Office. The weather in TVA has often been more turbulent than in the Weather Bureau; in fact, the Authority has been under a fair amount of scrutiny by political scientists for some thirty years and still offers opportunities. Our own staff has recently explored in some depth the quiet conflicts between the Authority and the municipalities.

Professor Van Dyke reiterates criticisms of a traditional kind of legalistic political science which neglected theory and informal processes, and engaged in reform. I cannot help thinking that these criticisms were overdone by certain members of our profession, although Professor Van Dyke is moderate indeed. For one thing, I think it rather absurd to criticize one study because it is not another. In the field of municipal government, for example, a certain attention has focused lately around the fact, often related with surprise, that chief administrators engage in "political" activity. In truth, this has been perfectly evident to any informed student—and certainly to the practitioners—for at least thirty years.   Current studies add to our detailed knowledge of this situation; they do not justify a feeling that one has landed on the moon.   I would not wish to dispute what I believe is the warning implicit in Professor Van Dyke's statements that these matters should not be neglected.   I am only suggesting a degree of humility towards an older—and mostly now retired—generation.   And I may be expressing a feeling that I cannot always avoid: namely, the present rechurning of old buttermilk may suggest that formidable difficulties lie in the way of any further advance.   I am comforted by this remark of Dahl's:

> However, many of the political scientists who occupied themselves with regulation were primarily concerned with administrative activities rather than "politics" (*if I may be permitted a distinction that is widely regarded as passé, and may therefore be due for revival*).[1]

In somewhat the same way, it seems to me that the "discovery" of the importance of corporative decisions for political study is no more than a rediscovery.   And, again, surely the political science student who has spent some time examining medieval theory will be immersed in church politics.   The separation of church and state is no more than a culture-bound and time-bound concept, which for much of history is not valid.   The politics of the Late Roman Empire could scarcely be sorted out from the theological arguments of that time, nor indeed from the personal ambitions and characters of ecclesiastical politicians.   Even in our time the separation is made with difficulty.   Moreover, the government of churches furnishes interesting material for study, and the long continued conflict of the individual conscience and loyalty to a demanding state is again resuming major significance.

I take it that one of the reasons that some of our colleagues try to concentrate on the political process is that this offers an area which, hopefully, other disciplines could not pirate.   Such a hope may, of course, be a forlorn one—sociologists have found the political process intriguing.   For me, the acceptance of process as the proper scope of political science presents the serious difficulty that more important and significant matters are ex-

[1] Robert Dahl, Mason Haire, and Paul F. Lazarsfeld (eds.), *Social Science Research on Business* (New York: Columbia University Press, 1959), p. 20 (italics mine).

cluded.   The processes by which the courts make decisions and by which those decisions are accepted are of undoubted interest and significance, but the decisions themselves are at least equally so.   Process, by itself, is simply too limiting.

I suppose that all scholars find keeping up with cognate fields a difficult matter.   It has always seemed to me that the political scientist occupies a particularly difficult spot, for he might be legitimately expected to know some anthropology, sociology, some law, a bit of psychology, some economics, a smattering of mathematics, and several languages, unhappily now including African and Oriental tongues.   Unfriendly remarks about political scientists who know little law are common (note some of K. C. Davis' remarks), and no doubt some of us make foolish statements on economic questions.   I am bothered by the suspicion that when some of our colleagues borrow from psychology they may pick a discredited school or scholar.   And the reviews of the mathematics of sociologists and political scientists by mathematicians are often fearfully devastating.   (I ought to add, of course, that this is not always so!)

In any event, I believe that we should not be scared off by supposed expertise held by others.   Professor Van Dyke has asked whether administrative law is properly political science. I am indifferent to such an inquiry.   Kenneth Culp Davis, who at times is sharply contemptuous of the unverified assumptions of political scientists, offers judgments based on his own ideas, and perhaps states some for which evidence cannot be found. (Such unsupported judgments hold little danger for the wary reader.)   Indeed, it is only when lawyers become judges that they deny themselves jurisdiction.   I would insist on similar liberties for the political scientist.

Professor Norman Wengert suggested at my institution a year or so ago that political scientists should concern themselves with the content of public policy from the point of view of judging that policy.   He claims that the abandonment of that approach by the economists has left the area unoccupied.   I suppose several objections might be made to this idea, one being that no "scientific" means may be available, and another that we have no especial competence in such matters.   I confess that neither objection worries me particularly.

For many years the traditional doctrines of public administration, as discussed by White, Gulick, and Urwick, on earlier foundations, have been under attack by Hyneman, Simon, and many others. It is interesting to me to note something of a conservative reaction again in the literature. In any case the old doctrine is still being heavily used by practitioners. I do not suggest that the researchers need pay much attention to the practitioners, but a number of political scientists (so-called at any rate) have, either by necessity or choice, stood rather close to day-to-day administration in action.

We have lived through a period—and perhaps are still in it— when hopes were high for more precision, measurement, and perhaps some degree of predictability. I cannot rid myself of the fear that these hopes are exaggerated and altogether likely to be partially disappointed. The portion of the subject matter of our field which lends itself to measurement covers only a part of the area with which political scientists may justifiably concern themselves. No matter how interesting this aspect of behavior is to some of our colleagues, others remain who do not find these investigations inviting for themselves. I would not wish to read either group out of the field. If one writer wishes to spend a portion of his time in an attempt to play games with the Supreme Court and another prefers to take a more traditional approach, I would not deny to either a respected place in the curriculum.

Since 1900, the growing profession, like others, has had its full share of trends—perhaps fads. How can one be sure that a current trend is definitive? Even if all such movements are treated as serious attempts to advance, we should not forget that human behavior has defeated some formidable minds of the past, including Descartes and many equally ambitious but less gifted scholars. It is perfectly possible that political science may reach a final boundary; such an end would not be unique in human experience.

Comments on Professor Van Dyke's Paper

By Louis Hartz

I AGREE wholeheartedly with Professor Van Dyke's conclusion that no single concept of political science can exhaust its scope, that every view of the field includes certain things and excludes others. There is a relativity here which is beyond question. And yet why does the battle over the "true scope" of political study continue? Why are we forever searching for the Platonic idea in this respect? Certainly, in part, the answer lies in a matter which is more sociological than it is intellectual: in the fact that a very considerable group of people belong to the profession of political science and that what interests them, what they work on, gains an enormous access of strength. What we are really arguing about when we search for the methodological absolute is where our collective energy is to go. Even purely rationalistic enthusiasms, which hold that a given approach will finally produce "objectivity" or "progress" in the field, are associated with the idea of a group of scholars each supplementing the work of the other. And, in fact, progress or not, any approach gains enormously from collective support. It is these considerations which, as a matter of professional fact, make Professor Van Dyke's relativistic wisdom hard to maintain.

The wisdom itself, as I have said, seems to me beyond doubt. Nor is it alone because we can easily locate, as Professor Van Dyke points out, what is "left out" in any given formulation of the field. It is true that if we concentrate on issues we obviously underplay the phenomena associated with consensus. It is also true that if we concentrate on the policy process we clearly omit or minimize the substance of policy measures themselves. But the fact is that when we elevate a single scheme to the rank of an absolute, we do not even know how much we "leave out." Every field, in addition to being an intellectual problem, is a historical matter. It is in the process of "becoming," responding to new pressures both empirical and intellectual. The case against a single view of "scope" is not merely that it eliminates things that interest some of us. In a deeper sense, it is that it eliminates things we have not yet thought of, that it closes down the future.

It is true, of course, that any substantive achievement in a field at any time involves a narrowing of focus. Thus, whatever may be the omissions involved in a study of issues the study itself is perfectly defensible. So is a concern with "process" or with "government," regardless of the contraction of perspective these orientations involve. This is not to say, of course, that a man can forget the data, wherever it is, which contradicts his generalizations. It is merely to argue that to study any subject one must cut into it from some point of view and that this involves an arbitrary partiality. And yet is this not, from another angle, merely to restate the case for diversity? If we could indeed seize the "political" as a whole, seize it once and for all, the variety for which Professor Van Dyke pleads would be unnecessary. It is the very fact that we cannot even think about the subject without selecting a part of it which forces upon us the humility involved in tolerance.

It is even true that we cannot make significant headway in terms of any approach unless a considerable number of scholars agree to the contraction of focus it involves. One may argue for the "right" of every scholar to approach his subject in his own way, and perhaps, within the limits of rational consistency and documentary accuracy, Professor Van Dyke's position comes down to precisely this sort of anarchy. But it is useless to believe that a single man working alone can do all the work that is necessary to implement any fundamental view of a field. We must not confuse this issue with the issue of the lone and seminal genius. That personality may, in fact, appear, but he does not do his own work or, at any rate, he does not do very much of it. It is only because he gains adherents that his perspective is developed. Freud without the Freudians would have made a far less significant contribution; or to shift to our own subject and to a possibly more dramatic case, Bentley without our pressure-group students might well be completely forgotten.

It is, of course, this collective necessity for significant advance which produces the "sociological" problem involved in the matter of the scope of the field. It is easy, when a trend

is riding high, for its proponents to claim at last to have found
"political science." I am not underrating, when I stress the
scholarly need of collaboration here, an element of crowd psychology which also may be involved. It is perhaps a sad fact
that men, neither in political science nor in other fields, yearn
to assert the Thoreauvian rights which the inscrutability of the
universe offers them. Ordinarily, the collective endeavor required to exploit a given line of inquiry is nourished by something which closely resembles, on the academic level, Tocqueville's "tyranny of opinion."

And yet, issues of courage and psychology apart, the paradox
which we basically face here is that at any moment the development of a scholarly field requires a simultaneous contraction of
view by a considerable number, perhaps a majority, of the men
working in it, whereas the future development of the field depends on the capacity of others to challenge precisely that contraction, precisely that collective concentration. Ideally, there
need be no problem here. A thousand legalists, developing the
approach of Lieber or Burgess, could keep reminding themselves
that the approach was relative, so that when a realist like Steffens
or H. J. Ford appeared he could instantly be given an academic
haven. But we know that this does not ordinarily happen.
Some form of exclusive claim to "political science" is advanced
by the majority, which hurls the challenger himself into a counter-
claim of the same sort. It is no accident that significant shifts
of substantive perspective in political science, as in other fields,
have always involved sharp methodological flareups.

Actually I do not believe that the issue of "scope" itself, however interesting, could generate a great deal of polemical heat
or intensity. It is the substantive concerns behind it, and the
human investments they involve, which produce the energy we
see. Indeed, I wonder whether the scope of fields ordinarily
changes as a result of the wholesale methodological reflection
which, by right, ought to change it. Is it not usually an actual
thrust, as when evolution reorients biology, or the study of the
political machine destroys constitutional legalism, which produces
the new sense of the field as a whole? In any case, the concept
of "scope" does become the vehicle for the competition of frag-
mentary perspectives. And in that competition, in part because

the collaboration of many workers on a single line is a real need, the absolute notion of "true scope" inevitably appears. The relativistic insight of Professor Van Dyke tends to go by the board.

I am not sure that there is a solution to this problem, any more than there is a solution to the problem of hyperbole in electoral campaigns. Political scientists may be no more political than other scholars, but they are not less so. And the issue here is an issue of their human interaction in actual work. But this very fact, perhaps, holds out a final consolation. What is it which ultimately yields the challenge to tyrannical orthodoxy, ultimately thrusts forward the work based on the neglected view? Usually it is not a logical matter, but a matter of experience. It was the Progressive movement with all of its reform passion which first produced political "realism" in America. It was the Depression and the New Deal which fostered the economic view of politics. Today it is the impact of world events which is shattering the parochialism of political science and producing the new cosmopolitan field of "political development." As an ordinary social group, in other words, the political science community not only engages in ordinary hyperbole but responds to the impact of ordinary experience. What logic might not be able to accomplish in the face of social pressure, other types of social pressure themselves can. So long as the historic milieu in which the political scientist moves changes, no concept of "scope" will be able to remain absolute, and the relativity which analysis justifies will be imposed by historic experience. This may seem like a pathetic reliance to enunciate before a professional conference. But I for one would not care to do without it.

Comments on Professor Van Dyke's Paper

By Frederick M. Watkins

WE must be grateful to Professor Van Dyke for his comprehensive critical survey of this subject. The current literature in the field is both extensive and confusing. In mapping it so successfully the author of this paper has done us an invaluable service.

Where, then, do we go from here? The paper as it stands is short on conclusions. Each proposed definition of the scope of political science has been exposed in turn to so searching a criticism that the reader is left with the impression that there is little to choose between them, all being basically untenable. Without going quite so far as this, Professor Van Dyke himself concludes by quoting Easton's warning that "no one way of conceptualizing any major area of human behavior will do full justice to all its variety and complexity" and by pointing out that any attempt to go beyond a listing and critique of possible alternatives would be, to say the least of it, distinctly premature.

My own reading of the situation is much less negative. Of all the definitions of optimum scope presented here, there is one which seems to me to stand head and shoulders above the rest, being subject to none of the various difficulties to which Professor Van Dyke has so acutely drawn our attention. This, paradoxically enough, is the definition suggested by Professor David Easton, the very man who is cited, at the end of the paper, in support of the skeptical proposition that the problem of providing *any* generally acceptable definition is almost certainly insoluble.

What, then, is the matter with most of the proposed definitions? A number of different things, of course. There is one difficulty, however, which reappears throughout the paper in so many different forms and contexts that it clearly stands out as the one most urgently in need of consideration.

This difficulty, stated in its most general form, is that a large proportion, at least, of the proposed definitions fail to provide any really comprehensible limits to the possible scope of political science. No matter how politics is conceived, there can be no doubt that a large and increasing proportion of political decisions are concerned with economic questions; does it not then follow that political scientists ought to be fully trained economists? Some of the most crucial political issues have to do with the optimum deployment of military forces; how can a political scientist venture to speak on the subject unless he is an expert on military science? Law enforcement, public health, race relations, and a variety of other hot topics challenge the skills of lawyers, doctors, sociologists, and a host of other highly specialized professionals; must political scientists, in addition to all the other claims on their time and attention, master these skills as well? Since everything is ultimately connected with everything else, it would be hard to imagine any considerable body of knowledge or experience that would be wholly irrelevant to the work of governments and of their policy advisors. No sane man doubts the necessity of drawing the line somewhere. But as Professor Van Dyke points out, and most convincingly, widely accepted and mutually divergent definitions of political science share one common defect: they provide no really useful guidance as to where the line should be drawn.

Does the fact that society itself is a seamless web condemn all social sciences to an unendingly desperate imperialism? Not at all. Consider, for a moment, how the economists have handled the problem.

Economists are concerned, in a way, about wealth, more especially, perhaps, about the "wealth of nations." Now the wealth of nations, substantively considered, is affected by practically everything: family systems, natural resources, science and technology, politics, what have you. Do economists, then, feel called upon to master engineering, science, medicine, climatology and all the rest? Not at all.

Why not? Because they have been content to study a particular aspect of the complex social whole. Their specialty is the allocation of rare resources. How those resources are created is none of their business, except insofar as it may be affected by the allocation process itself. No one would dream of asking them to decide on the merits of specific fertilizers and pesticides, important as such decisions may be from the standpoint of agricultural productivity. Their concern is with the rational (that is, economical) allocation of such rare resources as the society in question may be able to produce and with summing up the consequences in terms of meaningful general concepts, such as gross national product. This keeps them fully occupied as experts in a useful branch of the social sciences.

The lesson to be drawn from this is fairly obvious. A viable social science cannot afford to take as its province the study of any substantive social entity (the economy, the government, public policy) in all of its aspects. Restricted as that entity may be in itself, the fact that everything is connected with everything else will soon lead to an infinite proliferation of responsibilities. Instead, it must select some *one* significant aspect which is common to social life in all of its manifestations (like the allocation of rare resources) and try to understand that one aspect as thoroughly as possible.

What, then, is the aspect of social life that is distinctively the concern of political science? I have already expressed a preference for the position of Professor Easton. He believes that our interest as political scientists should be in "that system of interactions in any society through which . . . binding or authoritative allocations are made and implemented." Although it is tempting to challenge this formula in some of its phrasing, there is no real point in doing so, since it goes, as it stands, to the heart of the matter. Some arrangements for authoritative decision-making are an indispensable aspect of any society. Who makes those decisions, and the processes by which they are communicated and implemented, have always been, and must always be, the essential subject matter of political science.

Professor Van Dyke is by no means insensitive to the merits of this position. He tells us:

This way of conceptualizing the field reduces the difficulties that attend a focus on politics defined as struggle over issues, for the authoritative allocations of values could be tacit, unattended by current struggle. Easton's definition encompasses the politics of consent as well as the politics of struggle.

Since I myself, in a long unremembered day, once tried to define political science in terms of coercive power alone, I am glad to acknowledge the soundness of a position that recognizes the complex interactions of coercion and consent that go into the composition of any sort of public (that is, social) authority.

Where Professor Van Dyke goes wrong, in my opinion, is in his failure to recognize the all-important ways in which this definition serves to distinguish the science of politics from the other social (and natural) sciences. "Easton's conceptual scheme does not do much to resolve the question of the extent to which political scientists must also be economists, sociologists, psychologists, and military strategists." I could not disagree with him more.

The important thing to be noted here is the necessary distinction between the *process* of decision-making and the *content* of the decisions made. If economics were the science of wealth-production, all knowledge would be its proper concern. If political science were the science of determining public policies, it would need to be at least as comprehensive. But political science, like economics, has a less ambitious purpose. It is concerned not with the potentially infinite content of all public decisions, but with the process by which those decisions are reached.

Using this as a guideline, I would like to consider a few of the difficulties that Professor Van Dyke finds so oppressive. It is not easy to know where to start, from a point where every prospect seems equally unpromising. At the risk of seeming arbitrary, I will proceed on the hunch that he is worried, above all, by the possibility that political science might some day be absorbed in economics. For his comfort, and my own, may I suggest that the present, tangential, relationship between the two disciplines is essentially correct?

Political scientists from antiquity onward have seldom been deterred from observing that economics (the allocation of rare resources) and politics (the allocation of public authority) have a good deal to do with each other. In recent times they have tended to concentrate on the ways in which wealth, however derived, can affect politics and vice versa (elections, *coups d'état*, revolutionary movements, budgets, pressure politics, propaganda). Economists, in the meanwhile, have been trying to understand the ways in which the allocation of rare resources can be most rationally achieved. Although both disciplines are concerned with a common phenomenon, wealth, they are clearly engaged in studying it from quite different points of view. There is no earthly reason why either group of specialists should feel called upon to reproduce the work of the other.

Another problem that Professor Van Dyke brings up again and again is the failure of political science to deal adequately with the problem of international relations. On the surface this complaint is hard to understand. Over the past half-century, in America at least, political science departments have devoted a very considerable proportion of their resources to this very topic. Reading between the lines, however, I suspect that what our author has in mind is the failure of political scientists to provide comprehensive solutions to concrete issues of foreign policy. In line with their usual preoccupation with authoritative decision-making processes, they have tended to focus on those aspects of foreign relations which lend themselves to authoritative decisions. International law, diplomacy, international organization, foreign-policy formation, ideological conflicts—these are the topics that seem most clearly to fall within the scope of political science. But there are many other things, such as military and economic potentials, which must also be taken into account in any realistic formulation of a specific foreign policy. If I understand him correctly, Professor Van Dyke believes that all these things ought also to be included within the scope of political science.

My answer to this may be taken as applying not only to the inernational relations issue, but also to a number of other issues, such as the problem of law enforcement, which are raised in this paper. Where Professor Van Dyke goes wrong, in my opinion, is in assuming, or at least hoping, that it is possible for any one discipline, presumably political science, to provide expert advice on all matters relevant to the policy decisions of government. This is neither possible nor desirable; what is actually called for in any given case is the collaboration of experts from many different fields. It is significant that most universities, when they decide to institute a special program in international relations, find it proper not to tie it in with one department only, but to bring political scientists, economists, historians, geographers and others together in a common enterprise. This is the natural and proper way of trying to cope with problems of this sort.

So far, I have been emphasizing the merits of the Easton definition as a means of establishing a reasonably restrictive view of the scope of political science. In conclusion I would like to point out that this definition also has the advantage of including an important range of political experience that tends, under the present theory and practice of the discipline, to be unreasonably excluded.

As Professor Van Dyke's summary so ably shows, most formulations of the scope of political science lead, in one way or another, to focus attention more or less exclusively on the activities of governments, that is to say, of sovereign states. He himself is rightly concerned about the ways in which this bias may inhibit political scientists from studying the politics of a much wider society, the international community. But politics, rightly considered, is an inevitable aspect not merely of governmental and of international life, but of social life in general. The common sense of ordinary language reflects this obvious fact. When we speak of campus politics, union politics, foundation politics, and the like, we are referring to the existence within these other societies of authoritative decision-making processes which are essentially identical with those that operate on the national and international scenes. As a practical matter, it may well be true that national governments, because of their greater consequence and visibility, will always be the primary concern of political scientists. But if illuminating examples of political action happen to turn up in connection with the life of lesser associations, there is no legitimate reason why political scientists should refrain from using them. It is one of the very real virtues of Professor Easton's definition that, by speaking of politics as a system of interactions "in any society," it leaves the door wide open to study of politics in its fullest possible range.

Conference Discussion on Scope

VAN DYKE: I think that the comments on my paper are excellent. All of them are thoughtful and stimulating. They can be classified on the basis of one notable consideration, and that is the extent to which they agree or disagree with me. Mr. Hartz's commentary and Mr. Greene's do not really take sharp issue with what I have to say. In contrast, however, Mr. Watkins does take sharp issue with me, and so my supposition is that one useful place where we might begin is to take up the issue as it is laid out in my presentation and his comments.

Mr. Watkins is quite correct, I think, in indicating that one of the questions that troubles me is the appropriate role of political scientists in connection with research and advice on substantive questions of policy. I do not have a satisfactory answer to this question. Mr. Watkins presents an answer. He makes a pretty sharp distinction between the process by which decisions are arrived at and the content of those decisions, and indicates that the concern of political scientists is with the process, and not with the content.

Now, I shall take issue with his position. He says that I am wrong, and I say that he is wrong. I shall put it on two bases. One, I teach a course called "American Foreign Policies." Many other political scientists in the country teach such a course. I do not in my course pay much, if any, attention to the process by which these policies are arrived at; it is the outcome of the policy-making process with which I am primarily concerned. What are our problems in relationships with particular countries or regions? What kinds of policies do we pursue in connection with those problems? The whole course is a course on policy content—on the substance of policy decisions made. Now, if Mr. Watkins really means that political science *is* concerned with process and not with content, I think the "is" puts him in a bad spot. That is a descriptive term. But, as a matter of fact, a great many political scientists, particularly in the field of international affairs, do deal with the substantive content of policy decisions. Now, I do not go to the other extreme and claim that political scientists do or should pay equal attention to all kinds of policy decisions on a substantive basis. I do not know where to draw the line. At one end of the scale in the field of foreign policy, we have political scientists paying a great deal of attention to the content of the policy pursued, and over toward the other end of the scale, we have political scientists who pay little or no attention to the substantive content of policy. Political scientists do not, in fact, confine themselves to the study of process. They are concerned with process, but they are also concerned with at least some kinds of policies.

My second reaction is this. Mr. Watkins' comment implies that one can make a meaningful and perhaps a sharp distinction between the process by which decisions are arrived at, on the one hand, and the content of those decisions on the other. Now, in my paper I am not entirely clear about this point, and would like to probe for a sound position right here. My present thought is that you cannot effectively and sensibly make a sharp contrast between the process by which a decision is arrived at and the substantive content of proposals that are to be adopted or rejected. The process itself involves a consideration of the merits of the issue. People who come out for or against a particular proposition during the process of decision-making may adopt one strategy or another, depending on their attitudes concerning the substantive content of the issue before them. In Congress, for example, those who favor a bill may be able to take procedural steps that will facilitate its enactment. Conversely, those who oppose a bill may be able to block it by resorting to parliamentary devices that do not relate directly to its merits. Furthermore, my supposition is that the outcome of the decision-making process is often influenced by the substantive arguments advanced in behalf of the proposition. So I would suppose, on this basis, that any thorough understanding of the process by which the decision is arrived at calls for an examination of the substantive content of the decision in question. At the very least, it seems to me, one needs to take into account the attitudes toward substantive content taken by people who participate in the process.

WATKINS: I do not believe that we are as sharply opposed as you think. On this last point you have raised, I would agree that the attitudes of people toward the content of a decision may have something to do with the way in which the decision-making process is carried out. I do not think that anybody has ever tried to exclude that kind of consideration from the scope of political science. Certainly, I would not.

But it is quite a different thing to say that political scientists should be concerned with all the factual and other components that go into the making of proper political decisions. A political scientist's attitude toward medical expertise, for example, has a lot to do with what he decides on public health measures, but this does not mean that he has to reproduce the work of public health experts. As a political scientist, one is not expected to have an independent judgment about how to control smallpox or yellow fever. Such judgments are the outcome of a decision-making process that ought normally to take place within the medical profession, following its time-tested procedures for the assessment of professional competence. Our problem as political scientists, or as political practitioners, is to seek the advice of properly qualified medical men, and then to translate as much of that advice as may be politically feasible into authoritative political action. Responsibility for the medical efficacy of the measures adopted rests not on us, but on the medical experts whose advice we have been following.

This is the real basis for the main point of my paper: when it comes to any question of policy it is necessary to adopt a committee approach. Any substantial policy issue involves a wide variety of expertise, which cannot possibly be encompassed, as some of Professor Van Dyke's statements would seem to require, by any one man. Thus, in considering any specific issue of foreign policy, the political scientist must put himself essentially in the position of committee chairman. If asked what we ought to do in Vietnam—and I, as a political scientist, resent very much being asked to give an authoritative answer on any such question —one has got to bring together all the best people available to throw light on all the various aspects of the problem, and then adopt some reasonable procedure to sort out all these opinions and reduce them to a single workable policy. The process of bringing diverse opinions together and using them to reach judgments which one is then prepared to enforce by public authority is the political process as I see it.

The political scientist's own contribution to this process is indicated by the traditional core of foreign-relations studies: treaty-making, diplomacy, and the foreign service as a special case of bureaucracy. The focus is always on the point at which an authoritative decision is being reached. It is there, I think, that the political scientist as political scientist has something to say about foreign relations and policies.

DE GRAZIA: I wonder whether you were not introducing another subject-matter category? The words "decision" and "decision-making" and the processes of how to decide policy or foreign policy in relation to Vietnam may seem to be subjectless categories, but are they not merely another way of slicing the same materials of political science? The fact of the weather in Vietnam is very important. Political scientists are properly afraid that, because of their training purely as political scientists, they might know nothing about the weather and therefore botch some kind of strategy for the country. You say that others ought to worry, but they do not know about decision-making, which you know something about, and, therefore, these others should call in some of your students if they are making policies involving the weather in Vietnam.

WATKINS: Somebody should know what you can get away with, with the American public.

DE GRAZIA: But is that not another species of *subject*, really?

WATKINS: Oh, yes, I am not trying to say that political science has no content; the content is the particular process by which authoritative decisions are reached and implemented.

CHARLESWORTH: I wonder if you [Watkins] would like to expand a little on the analogue you made in your paper about the economist? He is interested in the oil business, say, but he does not know anything about petrography. Why do we not also arbitrarily limit our province?

WATKINS: I think that if you will look at the actual content of the political science courses, you will find that we have limited them.

VAN DYKE: You use in your comment a statement that is

relevant here, namely, that whereas the economists deal with the allocation of rare resources, the political scientists deal with the allocation of authority, public authority. Now, this is a short-hand expression of yours, and I do not mean to hold you literally to it here. But it seems to me that this leaves a lot out. We in political science, as I see it, are not interested only in the allocation of public authority. We are interested in much more than that. We are interested, for example, in foreign-policy questions, whether or not they have much to do with the allocation of public authority in the United States. I think that our interests go beyond that. Take the whole civil rights matter. You can say that this concerns the question of who should be permitted to participate in the policy-making process, who has the vote, and the like: so you could say that it is a process question. At the same time, I think that it is also a policy question. Here it really is not a question of the allocation of public authority; it is the question of the freedom and rights and privileges of people in the political system.

EULAU: You discuss this on such a high level of generality. Let us look at the legislative process. If one studies the legislative process in terms of a single case, as Stephen Bailey did years ago and as many people have done since, then quite clearly the content of the policy and the legislative process are closely related in research. On the other hand, if one moves to a higher level of analysis, if one wants to discuss the legislative process in general, then clearly the content of any particular policy is less relevant.

VAN DYKE: But in dealing with content one can also speak in general terms, that is, the higher levels of generality may relate not only to the process, but also to the content.

EULAU: It just seems to me that how one poses the question of content versus process or of the relation between content and process depends always on the level of analysis on which one examines each case.

YOUNG: To make a general comment: first, is not the significant feature of the modern political system the fact that we have distinctive procedures for deciding different kinds of questions? This differs, certainly, from many other cultural areas, where they have not separated out the kinds of decisions which should be made by certain kinds of people. We have built up particular procedures which decide certain kinds of questions—the legislature, the judge, the judicial process, the various methods of arbitration, bureaucracy, and the like—so that it is quite easy for us to study how decisions are made. If we take this approach, we can examine the institutions in other areas without really knowing what the content of the decisions is. On the other hand, it is not possible to separate content from procedure completely, because the very fact that we have procedure means that this kind of policy or this kind of decision was made by that kind of procedure.

Take the history of law, for instance. There was a very close relationship in the writ system between content and procedure. One procured a writ, and the writ was content, but it was also procedure. And part of the difficulty even now is to develop a system for bringing cases before the courts in a neutral fashion which does not prejudge the case. Now, with regard to content, is not content at the very heart of the process in making a decision? In the legislature, for instance, they make decisions time after time on all sorts of questions, but they do have a body of professional knowledge to draw on. So it is possible to think of policy or to think of law in terms of content which is interrelated rather than segmental. So, I think that procedures and content go hand in hand, although it is possible to put the emphasis on procedure. If this were not possible, we would flounder aimlessly, and we would have to know something about all kinds of topics in which we really are not professionally interested.

Spitz: May I try to talk to the same question by a somewhat roundabout method? First, when you speak of content, the impression I get is that most of you are describing, or seeking to describe, what governments do, and not questioning what governments ought to do. Yet, if political science concerns itself with politics and governments, it is not simply concerned with how governments operate. It should make every effort to deal also with what governments ought to do. I suppose all of us have some conception of a good society. The business of government is to make decisions concerning the nature of this good society. It has to decide whether people should receive a certain type and level of education; whether people should have adequate medical care; whether people should have a certain type of housing; and the like. That governments make, and necessarily make, such decisions is a political fact; but no less important is another fact—that governments are not the only powers or devices for the making of those decisions.

Political action does not embrace the entire realm of human action. Political associations are one among several types of associations. Economic associations also are ways of achieving adequate education, adequate medical care, adequate housing, and the like. Therefore, we are confronted with a very real problem. People have alternative and complementary ways of achieving the same goals. If they cannot achieve these goals through their economic power, through economic activities, they will seek alternative ways of satisfying these demands. In the modern democratic state, such an alternative way is the political. One way, at least, of understanding government intervention is to recognize that the government has moved in to satisfy demands that cannot or will not be met through nonpolitical mechanisms; so the government provides education in the form of elementary, then secondary schools, and last by setting up state universities. The government provides, or seeks to provide, medical care. Now, this has nothing to do with procedure except, obviously, that the way in which these decisions come about determines in part the content that follows. I certainly would agree that procedure and content are interrelated, but I do not think it is enough simply to look at what governments do, whether we focus on process or on content or on both.

This leads me to a second general observation, where I must argue against Fred Watkins' notion that economics deals with the allocation of rare resources. This is one of the things that economics deals with, no doubt, and this may be what economists themselves generally advance as the prime reason for their existence. But economic organizations actually exist for a multiplicity of purposes. Every organization seeks and does more than it avowedly purports to do: it is a power system—and men seek power within an economic organization and through economic organizations. They are money-making and money-rewarding institutions—they confer wealth, and wealth, in turn, confers prestige and status; thus, men go into economic organizations not simply because they are interested in allocating rare resources, but because they want to become important people. They want to achieve a higher social or economic status or they want to move via economic organizations into positions of power in other organizations. This is a matter of horizontal as well as of vertical mobility. If one wants to become a university president or a member of a board of trustees, a very effective way is to attain eminence as a corporation director. One does not have to go up the ladder within the same field; one can go up in one area and then cross over. General Eisenhower is a good example. He rose in the military sphere, then crossed laterally, first to the head of a university, and then to the head of a state. So, if we talk of economics as simply the allocation of rare resources, what we are doing is taking one aspect of the economic life and making that the whole.

Conversely, if one takes political science, and opts (as you seem to be doing) for David Easton's definition of it as the authoritative allocation of values, I would argue that this is much too broad. It is authoritative only in the sense that it is politically binding; but obviously there are many people who do not accept it as authoritative in any moral sense, or even in a political sense. All that the political decision does is to say: this particular allocation shall take place at this time. It is in no sense authoritative for others who will continue to oppose it even though they may submit to it voluntarily or because they are compelled to do so. The question as to which values ought to be decided politically is part of the problem that we encounter in political science, and I think that Vernon Van Dyke is correct in emphasizing this. This is one of the struggles of political science: Where can you draw the line? If one says that it is the authoritative allocation of values, then, in effect, one is saying that the state has a right to decide what shall be the proper realm of the church, what shall be the proper realm of the school, and everything else. It is not so at all.

YOUNG: Why?

SPITZ: It is the authoritative allocation of values only in the realm given to the state by the community. If one accepts the distinction between a limited state and a totalitarian state, then one is saying that there are certain things outside the purview of a limited state.

YOUNG: There are authoritative values outside the state?

SPITZ: Yes, that is why I deny the adequacy of a definition of politics as the authoritative allocation of values.

WATKINS: You are forgetting one thing, though, which is how Easton puts it, and, as I emphasize at the end of my comment, this is a function of every society, not just the state.

SPITZ: Well, of course. In effect, what I am doing is stating, perhaps in a more tortured way, the old distinction between culture and civilization. We do not use that distinction very much today, but essentially a society has certain values or goals —conflicting goals, if you will—that we denote by the term "culture," and civilization consists of those means or instruments or associations which men construct in order to achieve those goals. The political association is only one of many such associations.

WATKINS: You are assuming that every organization has a political aspect.

SPITZ: I will agree, but I will still argue that there is a difference between a church and a state; there is a difference between a university and a state.

DE GRAZIA: Why do you argue that position—because there should be a distinction or because you believe that the empirical division should be perpetuated in political science by our concentrating on the state as a required subject?

SPITZ: No, I would argue that in some cases there is an empirical distinction; in other cases there ought to be such a distinction. In any event, I would not limit political science to the study of the state because, for one thing, economic organizations also have political dimensions, and I would study economic organizations insofar as they pertain to either the process or the content of the state's decisions.

WATKINS: Is not the job of getting to be the head of a trade union just the same kind of job as getting to be the head of the country?

SPITZ: Not quite the same, there is a different constituency.

WATKINS: Is that not the same kind of problem?

SPITZ: Not necessarily, because it depends on the type of organization.

GRIMES: As political scientists, should we be concerned with the struggle for power in the Ecumenical Council?

SPITZ: I would be, yes.

VAN DYKE: This is all a little odd, because the various comments made here relate to Easton's definition of politics. I am sure that Easton distinguishes between the political and the parapolitical, and, if I recall correctly, he relegates the parapolitical at least to the periphery of political science, if not beyond.

PALMER: Yes, but he is comparing the parapolitical aspects with political systems. I am not arguing about your systems approach; I am talking about Easton's systems approach. It seems to me that we have already moved well beyond the beginning of our discussion about process and content. I must say that I do not see any dichotomy here. Obviously, if someone is doing a study of the political process, he is going to be concerned with content if he is going to make any significant statements at all. I wonder, however, whether we have introduced another question with which we should be concerned, namely, the role of values in political science. This opens up some very difficult avenues of exploration, especially when the effort is being made to quantify values. Do we have to center our discussion dealing with the allocation of public authority around values, or can one study the allocation of public authority without necessarily plunging immediately into the stream of values? Related to this is a matter of the obligation, if any, which the political scientist should have toward the formulation of public policy. E. H. Carr, I believe, has said that political science is a science of not only what is but what ought to be. Now, is that so? This is something with which it is very hard to agree or disagree, but, it seems to me, it is a topic which merits some pretty hard thinking.

VAN DYKE: May I make two different kinds of comments here? Both David Spitz and Norman Palmer speak of the proper role of the political scientist in connection with "ought" questions. My belief is that we need to be concerned with "ought" questions, and I would divide them into two categories. You can use "ought" in describing the most effective means leading to a particular goal. In principle, at least, this can be arrived at on an objective, scientific basis. The other kind of "ought" statement refers to something desirable in itself. It seems to me that we should be concerned—and many of us are, in fact, concerned—with "ought" statements in both of these categories. We may not know what ought to be done in Vietnam, but many political scientists are working on the problem and hoping to find out.

Now, the other comment is of a very different sort. Fred, you speak of the allocation of authority as a shorthand way of indicating the concern of political scientists, and you also seem to endorse Easton's definition of politics as the authoritative allocation of values. Now, these terms differ. Allocation of authority does not really quite mean the same thing as the authoritative allocation of values. I wonder whether you could comment on the relationship that you see between these two terms—allocation of authority on the one hand and authoritative allocation of values on the other hand.

WATKINS: Well, "values" as Easton is using the word has nothing to do with the usual "ought" controversy. Values are something people want, comparable to values in economics. Anything, whether good or bad, that people want is a value, while the "authoritative allocation of value" concerns that part of the social process which defines what are good things or bad things.

VAN DYKE: Then, if by the authoritative allocation of values you mean the extent to which there is an authoritative response to demand, there must be a decision on whose demands will be fulfilled.

SPITZ: Does the state decide who is going to achieve salvation? There are some people who want salvation. Does the state decide that?

WATKINS: It has done so in the past.

SPITZ: It has tried, I know. But is that what we recognize today as an empirical statement? Is that what the American government does today?

WATKINS: To make an empirical statement, you would have to have some empirical evidence.

SPITZ: I am not making such a statement; I am asking you whether it is empirically true that the state decides who is to be saved. You are the one who is opting for this definition "authoritative allocation of values." I want to know who decides whether I am to be saved or not. Is it the state?

DE GRAZIA: It is appropriate to study the *extent* to which the state authoritatively allocates values. By values he means "valuing behavior."

SPITZ: No, I am taking values in the sense which, of course, you meant, as simple desires, without judging the ethical content of the desires. There are people who want to be saved. My presumption has been that the state now says that that is the business of the church; therefore, we will not allocate it; we will let the churches do it.

GRIMES: You are making a play on words here.

SPITZ: No, I am not. The problem of the political scientist is to determine the relationship between the state and these other associations.

DE GRAZIA: We may want to compete with the state for allocation.

YOUNG: Does it help to clarify anything to refer to the state? Does it not exclude nine-tenths of the things we should be interested in, not only in this country but historically and in other areas? You do not find the state in other areas as you find it here.

SPITZ: Let me say first that I agree completely. I did not mean to imply that the business of government is limited to the state, which is a relatively modern term, even though the state is limited in the range and scope of its business. Government exists even in the family—there is a relationship of authority within the family, at least within certain families.

YOUNG: In this transit strike in New York, where is the state? You have Quill and you have Lindsay; you have the transport authorities and the New York government.

SPITZ: You will know where the state is when Quill goes on strike, provided of course that the state is willing to exercise its authority.

HARTZ: I think that perhaps at this point I could intrude an observation. One of the things that one notices when considering the definitions that have been advanced here is the focus on political behavior. In consequence, for each definition one can find large numbers of people who are not doing what they should be doing and, indeed, whole territories which are not being investigated as they should be investigated by the profession. Meanwhile, other definitions concentrate on political process, and one discovers an enormous range of material that can be studied. If one concentrates on the allocation of values, or on power, then one presumably is projected into the analysis of the papacy and lesser associations, as Mr. Watkins stressed, and here, of course, the surface has scarcely been scratched.

This peculiar characteristic of definitions—that, on the one hand, they may include a large amount of activity which does take place in the profession, and, on the other, they produce enormous vistas which no one is even interested in exploring—raises in my mind one of the relevant questions that we have to consider. What is the meaning of this operational characteristic of our dilemma? I think, basically, that there is an historic dimension to it. The field of political science, as it has been organized by its membership, arose historically in a certain intellectual context in which there have been many competing tendencies and many competing processes toward development. What has happened has not been that one definition has replaced another by virtue of superior consistency, but that the field has clearly responded to major shifts in experience. Political experience will, in our time and in the future, reshape the activity of political scientists. I believe that Roland Young has raised the question of underdeveloped societies. Now, there is no question in my mind that, whatever we decide here concerning the scope of our field, substantive questions raised by the confrontation of the West with these societies will, in fact, determine a large part of the actual work which will go on in political science in the years ahead.

YOUNG: I am suggesting an improvement of the field of political science largely by way of extending the coverage of parapolitical organizations and the like; the Charles Merriam development of many years ago had many salutary effects on the field. But, in addition to that, an internalizing process of improvement has been occurring which is immediately important. I would say that there is as much depth to probe as there is distance to traverse horizontally. For instance, the work that Heinz Eulau and others have been doing in the legislative process, which is one of the time-honored subject matters of political science, is as revolutionary as, let us say, the studies of the universe of the political system. The work that should be done and which has not been done on the subject of apportionment, which, again, is a 300-year-old subject of political science, constitutes another area almost bereft of empirical study. Whole legislatures are being turned over or, I should say, legislatures are being turned over wholesale in America on presuppositions about the cause and effects of districting systems, without any but the most unreliable kinds of knowledge.

It seems to me that, on the other hand, I would agree with your written comment on Van Dyke's paper, that there has to be a kind of single directing thrust in an area, that one does not have a progressive science unless a number of people are routinized and concentrated in a certain direction for a certain length of time, enough time to produce results. Ultimately, I think, that is the sociology of scientific development. Now, if a man were a maverick and proposed solutions to problems or subject matter that cannot gather a crowd, he would be out of luck for a long time and, perhaps, would be rediscovered in some future age.

I think that you have indicated in your comment on Van Dyke's paper that science is essentially or fundamentally a kind of routinized administrative activity. Once it decidedly wants to make hypotheses about a given area—and this is done by a combination of political and crowd behaviors—it moves into that area; all of its hypotheses and its methods of proof and rules of proof and the like are formulated as it goes along, and only those that follow that kind of sequence are rewarded.

Now, it seems to me that Fred Watkins is saying that we do not know how people are going to spend their lives; therefore, we do not know precisely what to tell them, and this is, I think, typically a product of our own century. Therefore, we should prepare to be ready to attack any of a wide range of problems. It is almost like modern warfare. We say that we do not know just what we are going to face in the way of a war, so we have to prepare our soldiers with flexible minds and all of that. A couple of centuries ago one knew what soldiers would come up against. They would come up against an even line of other soldiers with rifles, hopefully a little less well drilled than one's own, and one would beat them. Well, we no longer know that; therefore, we broaden everything, and the central focus of political science, as defined by Merriam and Lasswell and Dewey, becomes a very broad system of generalities on how to tackle a problem and comes back to a kind of liberal education, to training in logic, to the formulation of problems, and to broad questions of epistemology.

HARTZ: I agree with much of what you say, but one thing that I would like to stress is that, in my judgment, again looking at the thing perhaps excessively from a historical point of view, main shifts in fields, main shifts in actual work, and main shifts in that consensus which you described have taken place as a result of the conquest of given problems. They have not taken place by virtue of a more consistent, more persuasive charting of the field itself. I know of no field myself—political science or any other field, economics as well—in which this has not been true. In short, the point I am raising, one which may seem a bit heretical at this conference, is this: The type of activity in which we might engage in this conference is precisely the kind of activity which has never made a significant dent in the development of any field. The discovery of evolution produced a new field of biology. The discovery of the unconscious produced a new field of psychology. But it was the discovery of these two things, and not the development of better, so to speak, structural definitions of biology and psychology which produced these changes.

In the context of one of the points that de Grazia has made, I would say this: that where it seems as if a significant impact (as with some of Merriam's generalizations) was made on a purely methodological plane, it is usually because the generalizations of the methodological sort did involve or did reflect some substantive question which people wanted to investigate. The statement, for example, that politics exists in labor unions as well as in what we formally consider a state becomes an interesting point for a number of people when the labor unions begin to press. The same logic would have extended that statement to the church and to the family, but it did not because, at that point, those groups were not relevant. In short, I am pleading, so to speak, for an admission that the question of scope in political science is determined by the nature of the empirical problem, and not by the nature of the scope.

SPITZ: I am troubled by one aspect of Louis' comments. Because I largely agree with what he said, I am concerned about what he did not say. There is a tendency to concentrate on the dramatic, and hence focus on the ephemeral. If I may draw an analogy with academic-freedom issues, a lot of attention and excitement was generated by what happened at Berkeley. We tend to forget that the more pressing problems of academic freedom are the day-to-day interferences and frictions. In the same way, there are questions of political life which continue from generation to generation. They are perennial questions, but they emerge in new situations. One of the papers—I forget which one, perhaps it was Vernon's—accused political science of neglecting international relations as political theory.

VAN DYKE: It was mine, but you do not have it quite right.

SPITZ: My point would be, essentially, that although it is said that we have not paid sufficient attention to revolutions, the fact is that Aristotle paid attention to revolutions, that Machiavelli paid attention to revolutions, that a great many people have paid attention to revolutions. Now, Louis' principle would be that we are in a revolutionary age, so let us focus on revolutions.

HARTZ: Could I interrupt at this point because that is not a view that I subscribe to?

SPITZ: Very well. Let me plead independently, then, that we should concentrate on perennial questions even though they are not dramatic questions, and that much of the substance of politics consists in these ordinary issues. Men like Mill wrote on liberty; people today are writing on liberty; people long before Mill wrote on the problem of liberty. This is a question of where you draw the line concerning the relationship between the individual (or group) and the state. This is a question that always persists and which requires attention just as much as do dramatic events.

HARTZ: Now, I want to say quickly that I do not subscribe to the dramatic-event scheme at all. As a matter of fact, if one looks at intellectual history, one can see very frequently that some of the seminal shifts have taken place as a result of a resolution of difficulties in problems which have seemed quite outside the scope of dramatic events, even though retrospective investigation can often establish a correlation between the dramatic event and the current problems which have been solved. What I am basically concerned with is the problem, and not the dramatic event. What I am really troubled by is scope, so to speak, for the sake of scope. What I am troubled by in your remarks, Dave, is that you seem to drain away from the issue the very experience of an interesting problem which is the impulse behind all of our endeavor. You talk about the persistent routine questions of liberty which we must keep investigating. In those terms, who will have the inspiration to work? Persistent and routine problems really do not get people excited enough to do the work. Exciting problems do, and I am willing to consider those. I am willing to consider those wherever they appear and whoever presents them.

YOUNG: In thinking about the topics which have been discussed, I have in mind an area of interest which is one of the important problems in the world today. Consider the need to grow enough food for everybody. This raises the question of the use of land and the question of how land is allocated. All over the world, except in the Western countries, land is, to a degree, allocated by the family structure, and if we confine our interest to the state, we shall miss, it seems to me, one of the important elements by which the world's supply of food is controlled. So, if one is interested in food production, it is necessary to look at the family structure in many areas of the world to see exactly how land is used and how it is allocated. This is a problem in Harold Guetzkow's sense. It seems to me that it involves method also. It is procedural in Fred Watkins' sense; it is substantive in Van Dyke's sense; and yet it calls for an approach somewhat different from the political-process approach, which is confined to modern systems in the modern state.

GUETZKOW: Roland, is this a particularly good time to tackle this problem as political scientists *qua* political scientists, given the importance of variables exogenous to the political core of the food production problem?

YOUNG: Well, we have a concept of land ownership which is not universally applicable. More people are living in the world today; food is important, and it is impossible for the underdeveloped countries to industrialize quickly. One can increase the productivity of land, but the real difficulty is how land is controlled, how it is allocated and used, and this relates to the whole political and social structure. I do not know whether that answers your question.

PALMER: The problem seems to be broader than that. I would say in answer to your question of how you decide whether these questions are forced on people who are concerned with the public aspects of land reform, that they have to be recognized as much more than economic problems. If you read the article by Charles Lindblom "Has India an Economic Future?" you will find that the Indian economists inevitably find themselves discussing questions which both of you regard very properly as questions with which we should be concerned too—the whole matter of social stratification; the types of opposition to the development process that exist, which are more than just economic; and yet also, at the same time, certain opportunities for a breakthrough in the old patterns of political, social, and economic behavior. This, I would assume, is one of the reasons why a lot of people are talking about political development, whatever that is.

GUETZKOW: These people emphasize exogenous factors; we should want to focus on the endogenous ones. Why is it that role theory and our interviewing skills, for example, could not be brought to bear critically on the study of the political decision-making involved in this kind of problem now? Should we spread ourselves thinly over the economic problems of land utilization and the sociological problems of family structure, for which most of us have neither resources nor competence?

EULAU: This relates to the problem of knowledge, that is, how knowledge can be maximized at any particular time. I believe that it is the new problems that probably define scope, but it is also old problems which define scope. Such traditional problems as liberty or justice acquire a new meaning in new contexts. If I may be allowed to make a critical remark, I think that those who have concerned themselves with the traditional problems have not sufficiently concerned themselves with these problems in new contexts.

SPITZ: I am not pleading here for limiting the field to the history of political thought. What I am saying is that problems of liberty and justice exist in every society. The conditions are different, and therefore we have to attend to these problems in the new situation. But these are old problems. What worried me about Louis Hartz's formulation is, first, the identification of the interesting with the dramatic. I think that there are many interesting problems of liberty, of party systems, within new contexts. One does not have to wait for a riot to discover suddenly that riots are interesting. There are interesting problems in all societies, and one of the things we have to do is to discover the types of situations, the conditions, and the ways of treating them. Interesting does not mean unique or dramatic. What worried me about Louis' formulation is that he almost would have us governed by history, and I want to plead for government by reason. I think that there is a role for human reason—to anticipate the course of history. To wait for history to push us into something seems to me to abdicate the sovereign power of human reason. I am pleading, in a sense, for the autonomy of the human mind to address itself to problems and to guide history. I do not want to be simply a prisoner of history; I want to make history.

HARTZ: I do not identify interesting with dramatic at all. It would be to cheapen the whole conception which I believe in to associate it simply with dramatic events such as riots, floods, and revolutions. I just want to say, secondly, that the surrender to history which you attribute to me—I take it on the basis of my concluding remark of the paper—is also, in my judgment, a bit misplaced. Historical experience does come to the help of people who challenge the intellectual status quo. I am not in favor of a sort of blind subordination to history.

YOUNG: Could I make a remark on Louis' remark and on the nature of the discipline? It seems to me that we ought to distinguish the nature of the discipline, say, from this constant process which goes on in resolving conflicts. In considering other disciplines, the economists seem to have been more successful than the political scientists in finding basic units, such as the price structure, which can be quantified, and some of the men who helped to establish the discipline, such as Alfred Marshall, were extremely perceptive. The economists, moreover, seem to have developed their discipline independently, and are not, on the whole, interested in interdisciplinary endeavors.

Our discipline is primarily the result of the development of the American Political Science Association, and the founders had no very clear idea of its purpose, other than to make representative government effective. Political development in other areas of the world went under the heading of comparative government, but normally it did not include the nonstate systems. The structure of the discipline has reflected the period in which it developed. We have not developed a limited set of categories, such as the economists have developed, and our discipline has been eclectic and often without focus.

PALMER: I have not been overly impressed with these comments, in general, because most members of the discipline seem just as confused as we are. I do not see why one expects organizations, as such, to make any major theoretical breakthrough in the various disciplines, generally speaking. When the American Political Science Association (APSA) was organized, and much later the International Political Science Association, this was done largely as a vehicle for the exchange of ideas, without necessarily any particular basic assumption as to exactly what the nature of the discipline was. It simply provided a forum for the exchange of ideas rather than anything else.

After all, this subject of the scope of political science has come up for a great many years, in this country for fifty or seventy-five years. At least seventeen years ago the United Nations Educational, Scientific, and Cultural Organization (UNESCO) sponsored a major effort to discuss it on an international level. It was considered in the Report of the Committee for the Advancement of Teaching of the American Political Science Association, published in 1951 under the title, *Goals for Political Science*.

I wonder if we could, just in terms perhaps of possible interest of others who will be looking at some of our deliberations, have a look at the problem of scope within the fields, as well as on the periphery or boundaries of the discipline. As you say, problems exist on the boundaries, but is it not true that with the so-called discipline of political science, you have a variety of divisions, various ways of cutting up the thing? Certainly, there are wide varieties of emphases, approaches, and methods.

EULAU: Norman, should one not distinguish between political science as a discipline, a kind of holding corporation for many subsidiaries that define its scope, and political science as a theoretical focus of inquiry? In the last ten years we have been able to take a long look at some formal models. David Easton's work is a case in point. In reducing a great many variables to a few—inputs, conversion process, outputs, and the like—he seems to present a fairly elegant model. It seems to me that we shall have, in the next twenty-five years, a series of other models that may help us to determine what politics is all about. What will come out of this theoretical endeavor depends largely on the intelligent use of these models in empirical research, so that knowledge can be both expanded and intensified. On the other hand, the "economic" models, such as Buchanan and Tullock's or Downs', which use such concepts as "utility," are very difficult to operationalize for empirical research.

I think that the dilemma in which we find ourselves is this. On the one hand, we are developing models on the microlevel of the individual that have great theoretical power, but, on the other hand, it is very difficult to derive from these models viable propositions for macrosystem analysis. Let me give an example. David Truman wrote a very good book in 1952 on interest-group politics. But the amount of careful empirical research that could have been inspired by the book has been minimal. I am not aware of much research on interest-group politics that really used the categories about which Truman talked in his book. This is why most people who are doing empirical research are settling for partial theories, or rather low-level propositions. It seems to me that the scope of political science will expand at the boundaries of research and will be determined only in part by the development of additional theories. Therefore, what political science will be, in terms of its scope, will be determined by what people are doing by way of research in the next ten or twenty years.

DE GRAZIA: It is my feeling, if I may comment on that in terms of a triad, that there should be more basic models in political science than the Platonic, the Machiavellian, and the Merriam-Lasswell. The first is society in search of justice— how you structure it. With the second, one does not assume very many virtuous activities in Machiavelli and Hobbes; the problem is how to get hold of power. Then there is the very modern model which sees politics everywhere and more or less explodes the total field of political science into all these associational, parapolitical areas which are found in the Chicago school.

Then there are other attempts at models. I must say that the physical task of trying to keep up with them is already enormous—the economic models, the attempts to set up models made in comparative fields, not to mention those in international relations where at least a dozen works—major works—purport to establish models that are to direct the profession. There are bound to be only one or two or three successful middle-level models coming out of it.

I do think that the work on legislatures is extraordinarily successful, partly because it deals with matters concerning real people that can be recognized by others who have to do with legislatures. That is something which cannot be said for some of the models of values, of input-output systems, and foreign-affairs policy.

And it is going to take a lot of work before some of the model-builders, who are perhaps most sophisticated in handling the tools of mathematics and the like, can get around to making their work meaningful. Meanwhile, we are in a kind of a confused state where some of us do not pay any attention to models at all because they can only serve to keep people from solving problems of fact and method.

VAN DYKE: If I may, I would like to revert to a statement that David Spitz made a while ago to the effect that he thought that the thing to do was to focus on problems, whether dramatic or perennial.

SPITZ: My interests are in problems. I am not denying the importance of focusing on structure.

VAN DYKE: The question would be, then, what kinds of guidelines you follow, what kinds of criteria are useful in the selection of the problems. The problems are really very numerous, if not infinite; to say that you are concerned with problems is helpful as far as it goes, but then how do you decide that one problem is worth tackling and another problem can be postponed or ignored?

SPITZ: I do not think that there is any one answer that will satisfy you, Vernon. I suppose, first, I would distinguish the problems that I think important enough to raise in the classroom as a teacher and problems that I am interested in resolving as a scholar. I happened at one particular time to be interested in the problem of abuses in power in democratic states, and wrote a book about it. At the moment I am interested in the problem of liberty, so I am doing a book on the theory of liberty. When I finish this I hope to do a study of elites. Now why do I pick those? There are dozens of possible topics. I happen to be excited by this particular problem at this particular time, and so I address myself to it. I do not argue that these are the most important problems in the world, and I certainly do not mean to say that everyone should write on the things that I write about. I am very happy if Louis Hartz is worrying about the problem of new societies and working on them. I do not say that my problem is more important than his or his more important than mine. There are a wide variety of problems that confront us, and each man addresses himself to the problems that he finds intrinsically interesting.

WATKINS: But, Dave, where then is the rational test that you and Louis sometimes argue about?

SPITZ: No, I am doing something other than that. I am saying that within the tradition of political science I have been attracted to a wide range of problems; to use traditional terms, the problem of liberty and authority and the problem of the control of power and misuse of power. Now, these are themes that have been dealt with by any number of political theorists or political scientists in the course of the history of our discipline; certainly in reading people like Tocqueville and Mill you come again and again upon these problems.

One of the things that happened to strike me at a particular time in my intellectual development was the easy assumption that one controls power by setting up an appropriate structure. I did not believe it, and so I wrote a book about it. One of the things that interests me now is the considerable discussion about the meaning of liberty and the criticisms that have been generated by Mill's essay on liberty. People are still writing about Mill, but when I began to review the literature on him, I discovered that a great many people were simply repeating what had been said without ever reading Mill, and so I find myself doing a book on the theory of liberty. On the question of elites—why pick this? Well, this is an old theme, certainly not new. The word *elite* may be relatively new, but the notion of a small few who operate a political system is an old one. Now, I was asked to write a paper a couple of APSA meetings ago on the problem of elites. I reread Hunter, and I read Dahl's *Who Governs?* I thought Dahl was wrong; so I wrote a rather long paper on elites and democratic theory, but since I had only a summer in which to do it, it is an incomplete paper. I want to finish the book on the theory of liberty, and then return, I hope, to the study of elites, write it up, and make a book out of it on elites and democratic theory.

Now, all of these, I take it, are staple problems of political science. I think these are problems that all of you deal with in one sense or another. You all talk about elites, you all talk about democratic theory, you all talk about liberty, you all talk about power, you all talk about authority. Now, all I am doing is taking a particular slice out of this huge pie. But these are the concerns of political science. It may be that if I live long enough, and if suddenly I should be blessed with the encyclopedic vision of an Aristotle, I may undertake a general work. At the moment, I am not ready for a general work, so I take pot shots.

Hartz: As a relativist in this matter and the person who is defending a relativistic position, I myself would want to intrude certain other observations. I do not think that every theory is as good as every other theory or every concern, so to speak, as good as every other concern. But despite my objection, when I hear David enunciate his intellectual development, it strikes me that the only principle implicit there is the absence of any criterion other than pure biography for distinguishing interests or enterprises. Without establishing a single scope of political science, we certainly would agree that certain achievements are of greater significance than others, and there are one or two pretty obvious criteria by which one can judge these achievements. One is that of relevance. Some enterprises are simply not as relevant as others to problems with which we are concerned. For example, I do not think that you can contend that a study of Douglas County in the state of Nebraska, let us say of the obsolete legal machinery, is as significant as the study of a larger phenomenon. I grant that you may generalize Douglas County, and if you extract from the study of the obsolete legal machinery of Douglas County some principle of larger application, then you will clearly have elevated that concern to a major concern. Still, I can see a clear distinction between the study of Douglas County and a study which has a relevance to a much larger field of inquiry.

In addition to the criterion of relevance there does seem to me a purely intellectual criterion by which one could differentiate enterprises. The degree to which an analysis assembles relationships is a very important matter. For example, we distinguish certain theories as great theories precisely because they bring a large number of unrelated things into relationship. Now, I believe that that is a purely intellectual criterion which we also apply. I would differentiate the application of and concern with those criteria which are fundamental to the evaluation of any intellectual pursuit from the creation of a single idea of scope.

CHARLESWORTH: Yes, but when a political scientist turns to the really great theories, to the integration of a large number of previously apparently unrelated data, he is often not able to remain strictly within the scope of his field. He must either develop expertise in the other social sciences, the natural sciences, perhaps even the humanities, or he must invite professionals in these areas to participate in his endeavor. Norman Palmer is chairman of an interdisciplinary program of international relations. He has historians, economists, linguists, demographers. Now, this crossing of the disciplines is not confined to international relations. For example, city and regional planning call on different talents. Labor relations cannot be lodged in any one academic department. Look at the whole subject of public welfare. Where does that belong? I was wondering if you would like to put on record some of your views as to whether this development which we see in international relations should be extended to these other areas that are multidepartmental.

Van Dyke: I shall comment on that, partly because it permits me to try to clarify apparent misunderstandings of my own references to international politics in my manuscript. I think two of the three who commented on my paper were surprised that I thought international relations was neglected. Actually, I kept talking about international politics. I used the term "international relations" only to deprecate it and to indicate that it is so broad and so diffuse that it does not give any particular guidance. My point was that the people who tend to think of political science in terms of the study of government or in terms of the study of constitutions and constitutional systems are inclined to forget about international politics because there is no international government or constitution. Further, I indicated that, however much I admire Easton, I think that his framework for political analysis is much more clearly suited for the study of domestic politics than it is for the study of international politics. I am not saying that it is inapplicable to international politics, but I would say that if he had approached the whole subject from the point of view of international politics, it is very unlikely that he would have arrived at the scheme at which he did arrive. Now, the references in our discussion have been to international relations. When you use this term "relations," you open up the subject wide.

Young: And what is the difference?

Van Dyke: Well, for example, I was on an international relations committee at Iowa once, including people from a good many different disciplines. One of the members of the committee in all solemnity indicated that whenever the music of Beethoven is played in the United States, this is an aspect of international relations. And in a sense it is.

Young: Without politics?

Van Dyke: It is not an aspect of international politics except in extreme and unusual circumstances.

PALMER: I see that it always seems to come around to the question of focus.

VAN DYKE: Well, music may have political significance, just as the Olympic Games sometimes have political significance. I am not saying that they are ruled out of the realm of politics, but I think that it would be an unusual circumstance in which you would consider the playing of a symphony to be a political act. I would argue, on the one hand, that there is a perfectly appropriate set of things for political scientists to do in the realm of international politics, and I say that international politics is a subarea of international relations. International relations can be musical or cultural. Art is by nature international, and when tourists travel abroad one has international relations of a sort. When Shakespeare is studied, an international relationship is involved.

EULAU: Let me make a very outrageous statement, one which I have always made in my "Scope and Methods" class. Even if we were to drop the whole profession—I think 8,000—of political scientists into the ocean, I think that the study of politics would go on. I think that political science is certainly not autonomous. It happens to be an organization which focuses on a subject matter. I think that political science has to be interdisciplinary in its own right. I think that it would be impossible to be a good political scientist without having had a good dose of what is called psychology, what is called sociology, what is called economics, and even, today, what is called mathematics.

DE GRAZIA: All this was a part of political science at one time.

EULAU: Yes, that is the point that I want to make, you see. It seems to me that if political science were abolished as an establishment, we could all find a comfortable role in the American Psychological Association or in the American Sociological Association. There are many other social scientists today who are concerned about politics.

GUETZKOW: But is that not true of every field, though, Heinz? Do you know of any field that has this kind of integrity that we eulogize here?

DE GRAZIA: I know of no field that has the theoretical integrity you are speaking of.

SPITZ: I want to ask whether anyone here is familiar with the experience of Chicago. Shortly after the war they set up a number of interdepartmental committees. These were not research but teaching institutes. I am thinking of the committee on social thought and that on labor, where, instead of giving a degree, say, in political science or in philosophy, they gave a degree in social thought, and the student cut across several fields— economic theory, political theory, sociological thought, philosophy. They had a similar arrangement on labor.

VAN DYKE: One on international relations, too.

SPITZ: I do not know who or what came out of that program at Chicago, but unlike most schools where labor is in the economics department, the Chicago position was that if you wanted to study labor relations you had to know a variety of disciplines, so they integrated the relevant fields. Now they have a committee on economic development. Is anyone familiar with what success they have had with these programs?

CHARLESWORTH: I want to observe our time limits strictly. Before closing this discussion, however, the author of our basic paper for this session ought to have an opportunity to comment on the discussions this morning. Would you be willing to do that, Vernon?

VAN DYKE: Well, I am willing, yes, although as Charlesworth knows, he asked me to do this only fifteen minutes ago, so I have no particular scheme to follow. Furthermore, I think that any effort to crystallize this discussion is doomed to failure from the outset. I think we have probably agreed that we are not ready to fix any outer limits for political science. In fact, I think that we have probably put it more strongly than that. The prevailing view here, as I sense it, seems to be that it would be a mistake even to attempt to fix any outer limits for political science. There was a possibility that at least we might set limits in terms of focus on "process" rather than on the "content" of decisions made, but then, I think, the discussion indicates that the differentiation here is not really very sharp, and so we do not have clear outer limits indicated by those words.

We have had a good deal of discussion about the question of trying to decide on scope and then selecting problems accordingly, but I think that the implication is, really, that we ought to look at the problems first, and then if the question of scope ever arises, that is a secondary matter. It is the problems that we are after, the problems that interest us. In fact, I think that there is a fair prospect that major contributions are going to be made by the individual mavericks rather than by the people who all team up in connection with some one approach or method. So I end, I guess, with the notion that all of us are in a very permissive mood. We are political scientists. We are inclined to give the benefit of the doubt to any political scientist in connection with whatever he does. If he can produce something good in political science, we applaud and reward him. If, in taking advantage of the permissiveness, he does something that goes sour, well that is tough luck, too bad. It is the results that count, not the fact that the project falls inside or outside what might be thought of as the foreordained limits of the field.

The Purpose of Political Science

By Hans J. Morgenthau

THE purpose of political science is obviously to understand politics in a theoretical manner. However, what appears to be obvious on the face of it presents on closer examination a number of formidable problems. I shall not enter here into a discussion of what is meant by politics, that is, of the scope of political science, beyond stating dogmatically that political science deals with the nature, the accumulation, the distribution, the exercise, and the control of power on all levels of social interaction, with special emphasis upon the power of the state. Concentrating upon the purpose of political science, I shall try to answer four questions: How can we understand politics in a theoretical manner in view of the nature of the subject matter? How can we understand politics in a theoretical manner in view of the nature of the observer? How do we distinguish between political phenomena which are worthy of theoretical understanding, and those which are not? What is the purpose of the theoretical understanding of politics?

I

A scientific theory has the purpose of bringing order and meaning to a mass of phenomena which without it would remain disconnected and unintelligible. Thus, a scientific theory must meet the dual test of experience and reason. Do the facts as they actually are lend themselves to the interpretation that the theory has put upon them, and do the conclusions at which the theory arrives follow with logical necessity from its premises? In short, is the theory consistent with the facts and within itself?

What makes a scientific theory of politics a perennially problematic undertaking is the nature of the empirical data to be understood. This is a problem with which all the social sciences have had to wrestle and are likely to continue wrestling until the end of time. It is the result of the intrinsic ambiguity of the social facts. These facts are, on the one hand, unique historic occurrences. They happened in this way only once and never before or since. On the other hand, they can be distinguished by their similarities; for they are manifestations of social forces. Social forces are the product of human nature in action. Therefore, under similar circumstances, they will manifest themselves in a similar manner. "As no event and no shape," observes Montaigne,

is entirely like another, so also is there none entirely different from another: *an ingenious mixture on the part of Nature. If there were no similarity in our faces, we could not distinguish man from beast; if there were no dissimilarity, we could not distinguish one man from another.* All things hold together by some similarity; every example is halting, and the comparison that is derived from experience is always defective and imperfect. And yet one links up the comparisons at some corner. And so do laws become serviceable and adapt themselves to every one of our affairs by some wrested, forced and biased interpretation.[1]

But where is the line to be drawn between the similar, which is susceptible to theoretical understanding, and the unique, which is the proper province of history?

What makes social science possible is the existence of these similarities, imbedded in, and interwoven with, the contingencies of the social world. The contingencies of the social world are, as it were, orderly contingencies. They appear to the observer in the form of typical patterns, opening up a limited number of possibilities. A historical situation always contains only a limited number of potentialities into which it might develop. The German situation in 1932, for instance, contained essentially three such germinal developments: parliamentary democracy, military dictatorship, and naziism. Which one of these three possibilities would finally materialize depended upon the contingent elements of the situation and therefore could not be foreseen. It was, however, inevitable that one of those three possibilities should occur. Within each of those general trends,

---

[1] *The Essays of Michel de Montaigne,* edited and translated by Jacob Zeitlin (New York: Alfred A. Knopf, 1936), Vol. III, p. 270 (Montaigne's italics).

a limited number of possible patterns of a more specific nature were again discernible. Under the assumption, for instance, that the potentiality of naziism would materialize, one of three possible developments could be anticipated: conservative militarism, social revolution, totalitarian party dictatorship. On lower levels of specialization, similarly limited patterns of future developments present themselves. Thus, one would, for instance, find a limited number of possible trends in Nationalist Socialist foreign, economic, labor, or religious policies at any state of the historic development. The same method of analysis, which perceives history from the point of view of a limited number of potential trends, applies to any other political or social problem at any period of history, be it Napoleon's military policy of 1812, the political and military problems of India in 1966, the outcome of a lawsuit, or the political, military, and economic problems of world peace in an indefinite future.

Ultimately, the whole future of the social world appears to the analytic mind as a highly complicated combination of numerous systems of multiple choices which, in turn, are strictly limited in number. The element of irrationality, insecurity, and chance lies in the necessity of choice among several possibilities multiplied by a great number of systems of multiple choice. Viewed with the guidance of a rationalistic, blueprinted map, the social world is, indeed, a chaos of contingencies. Yet it is not devoid of a measure of rationality if approached with the modest expectations of a circumspect theory.

The empirical political world, then, presents theory as well as practice with a limited number of rational choices. For some strange reason these choices generally number three. What a theory of politics can hope to achieve is to state the likely consequences of choosing one alternative as over against another and the conditions under which one alternative is more likely to occur and be successful than the other. Theory can also say that under certain conditions one alternative is to be preferred over another. But all these theoretical analyses are contingent upon factors of whose occurrences we either know nothing or whose consequences we cannot foresee.

Take for instance so crucial a problem of international relations as the problem of nuclear war. It is possible to develop a theory of nuclear war, as Herman Kahn has done in his book *On Thermonuclear War,* which assumes nuclear war to be just another kind of violence, greater in magnitude but not different in kind from the types of violence with which history has acquainted us. It follows from this assumption that nuclear war is going to be much more terrible than prenuclear war, but not necessarily intolerable, provided we take the measures which will enable at least some of us to survive it. In other words, once one starts with this theoretical assumption of the nature and the consequences of a nuclear war, one can logically arrive at Mr. Kahn's conclusion that the foreign policy of the United States does not need to limit itself to trying to avoid nuclear war, but that the United States must also prepare to survive it. And then it becomes perfectly legitimate to raise the question, provided fifty million Americans were to be killed in a nuclear war and nine-tenths of the economic capacity of the United States were to be destroyed, of how we enable the surviving 130 million Americans to rebuild the United States with the remaining one-tenth of economic capacity.

The contingent element in this theory of nuclear war is its utter uncertainty, and this uncertainty is typical of all levels of theoretical analysis and prediction in the field of politics, domestic and international. Even if one were to accept all its estimates of deaths and material destruction and of the rate of material recovery, this theory would have to be uncertain about the human reactions to the kind of human and material devastation which nuclear war is likely to bring about. Obviously, if a highly complex human society could be visualized to operate like a primitive ant society, its recuperative ability could be taken for granted. If one-third of the ants of one ant hill have been destroyed together with nine-tenths of the material of the ant hill, it is safe to conclude that the remaining ants will start all over again, building up the ant hill and reproducing until the next catastrophe will force them to start all over again.

But it is a moot question whether a human society has this type of mechanical recuperative ability. Societies have a breaking point as do individuals, and there is a point beyond which human endurance does not carry human initiative in the face of such unprecedented massive devastation. Under the impact of such devastation, civilization itself will collapse.

It is at this point that theoretical understanding of international relations reaches its limits. It can develop different alternatives and clarify their necessary preconditions and likely consequences. It can point to the conditions which render one alternative more likely to materialize than the other. But it cannot say with any degree of certainty which of the alternatives is the correct one and will actually occur.

This is but an extreme example of the utter uncertainty of theorizing about foreign policy beyond the clarification of alternative policies, their likely occurrence, and possible consequences. The Munich settlement of 1938 is another case in point. In retrospect, of course, we all know from practical experience that it was a great failure, and from that experience we have developed the theoretical categories which demonstrate that it was bound to be such a failure. But I remember very well the near-unanimity with which the Munich settlement was approved by theoreticians and practitioners of foreign policy and by the man in the street as well. The Munich settlement was generally regarded at the time of its conclusion as a great act of statesmanship, a concession made to a would-be conqueror for the sake of peace. E. H. Carr so regarded it then, and A. J. P. Taylor so regards it now. The flaw in that reasoning, which few people were—and perhaps could be—aware of at the time, was, again, the neglect of the contingencies inherent in political prediction. That which reveals itself as a simple truth in retrospect was either completely unknown in prospect or else could not be determined by anything but an uncertain hunch.

II

It is a great paradox that nature is much more unambiguously susceptible to human understanding than is society past and present. That which man has not created and which it is beyond his power to create—the macrocosm of the stars and the microcosm of the cells and atoms—man can understand with an adequacy that points to the common source of both. How else explain the affinity between the cognitive qualities of the human

mind and the laws by which the universe moves?   Not only is
man able to retrace and project into the future the movements
of the natural bodies, but by virtue of that ability he is capable
of re-creating the forces of nature and harnessing them to his
will.   Nowhere is man more triumphantly aware of his kinship
with the universe than in his cognitive and manipulative relations with nature.

In the world of nature, which he faces ready-made and which
he leaves as he finds it, man proves himself a master of understanding, imitation, and control.   How different, how frustrating
and humiliating is the role he plays in understanding and controlling the social world, a world that is properly his own, which
would not exist if he had not created it, and which exists the
way it does only because he has given it the imprint of his nature.   Of this social world man can at best have but a partial
and corrupted understanding and but a partial and ultimately
illusory control.   For the social world being but a projection
of human nature onto the collective plane, being but man writ
large, man can understand and maintain control of society no
more than he can of himself.   Thus, the very intimacy of his
involvement impedes both understanding and control.

The political scientist is a product of the society which it is
his mission to understand.   He is also an active part, and frequently he seeks to be a leading part, of that society.   To be
faithful to his mission he would, then, have to overcome two
limitations, the limitation of origin and the limitation of purpose, which make him wish to remain a member in good standing of that society or even to play a leading role in it.

The mind of the political scientist is molded by the society
which he observes.   His outlook, his intellectual interests, and
his mode of thinking are determined by the civilization, the national community, and all the particular religious, political, economic, and social groups of which he is a member.   The "personal equation" of the political scientist both limits and directs
his scholarly pursuits.   The truth which a mind thus socially
conditioned is able to grasp is likewise socially conditioned.   The
perspective of the observer determines what can be known and
how it is to be understood.   In consequence, the truth of political science is of necessity a partial truth.

Upon a mind which by its very nature is unable to see more than part of the truth, society exerts its pressures, which confront the scholar with a choice between social advantage and the truth. The stronger the trend toward conformity within the society and the stronger the social ambitions within the individual scholar, the greater will be the temptation to sacrifice the moral commitment to the truth for social advantage. It follows that political science can remain respectable, in terms of the society to be investigated, only as long as its interests do not conflict with those of that society. But such conflict is inevitable since the interests of political science are incompatible with those of society. On the one hand, a political science which is faithful to its moral commitment of telling the truth about the political world cannot help telling society things it does not want to hear. The truth of political science is the truth about power, its manifestations, its configurations, its limitations, its implications, its laws. Yet, on the other hand, one of the main purposes of society is to conceal these truths from its members. That concealment, that elaborate and subtle and purposeful misunderstanding of the nature of political man and of political society, is one of the cornerstones upon which all societies are founded.

In his search for truth, the political scientist is hemmed in by society in three different ways: with regard to the objects, the results, and the methods of his inquiry.

In all societies certain social problems cannot be investigated at all, or only at grave risk to the investigator. The basic philosophic assumptions by which society lives are beyond scientific investigation, for to question them is tantamount to questioning the worth of society itself, its justice, its rationality, its very right to exist. Thus, a theoretic society cannot permit the scientific investigation of its religious beliefs. A Marxist society cannot tolerate scientific inquiry into dialectic materialism. In a society based upon racial discrimination, race problems are beyond the ken of social science. The profit motive and free enterprise are taboo in capitalistic societies, and the popular control of government will be taken for granted rather than questioned in democracies.

Similarly, in all societies certain results are beyond the reach of scientific inquiry, or they can be reached only at great personal risks.   No Russian economist is likely to conclude publicly that capitalism is superior to communism, nor is an American professor of economics likely to maintain the reverse position. Social scientists in monogamic societies are not likely to see virtue in polygamy, and in a scientific civilization they will emphasize the advantages of science rather than its liabilities.

What is true of the objects and results of scientific investigation is true likewise of its methods.   In a humanistically or religiously oriented society, quantitative methods and experimental methods in general will be at a disadvantage.   The same fate will befall the methods of philosophic inquiry and rational deduction in a scientifically oriented society.   Thus, different societies put the stamp of social approval or disapproval upon different methods of inquiry, and the political scientist is again confronted with a dilemma between his commitment to the truth and his concern with social convenience and advancement.

No lengthy explanation is needed to show that those different pressures against which the political scientist must maintain his moral commitment are multiplied in the actual situation in which he must make his decisions.   For the political scientist to be a member of a pluralistic society, such as America, means actually to be a member of a multiplicity of sectional societies of a religious, political, social, and economic character, all exerting parallel or contradictory pressures upon him.   All these groups are committed to a particular social "truth," and the political scientist cannot help deviating from one or the other of these "truths," if he does not want to forego his moral commitment to discovering *the* truth about society altogether.

These pressures account for the enormous positive and negative influence which foundations exert upon the objects, results, and methods of research.   They reward certain types of research by supporting them and stimulate more research of the same type by promising to support it.   On the other hand, they thwart or make impossible other types of research by not supporting them. The political scientist who wants to share in these rewards and, by doing so, gain prestige and power within the profession cannot help being influenced by these positive and negative expectations in his concept of the social truth, of the methods by which to seek it, and of the relevant results to be expected from it.

The influence which the government exerts upon political science is as pervasive as that of the foundations and more varied, subtle, and insidious. The intimate connection which research contracts have established between the government and the universities has recently been brought to public attention; it has even been made the subject of congressional hearings. It stands to reason that a political scientist who is working on such a contract or who expects to work on one cannot feel as free to raise fundamental political issues, either within his contractual research or outside it, as a political scientist who is not, either in fact or expectation, under obligation to the government. Thus, the interests and expectations of the government not only determine the subject matter of contractual research but also influence ever so subtly its scope and in a certain measure its results. Beyond these specific limitations, the connection with the government cannot help but narrow the scope and direction of the scholar's general interests.

However, the influence which the government is able to exert upon the academic community in general and political science in particular by far transcends these formal contractual relations. The government disposes of a whole gamut of professional and social rewards from appointments and consultantships to foreign travel and to invitations to social functions at the White House. By adroitly promising, dispensing, and withholding them, it keeps a large segment of the academic community at bay. The political scientist, by accepting one or the other of these rewards, enters into a subtle and insidious relationship with the government, which imperceptibly transforms his position of independent observer to that of client and partisan. In consequence, his intellectual function is also transformed. In the measure that he values these social rewards and professional advantages more highly than his commitment to the truth, he becomes a political ideologue, justifying morally and rationalizing intellectually what the government is doing. Yet he performs this ideological function while drawing upon his prestige as a scholar. Thus, his reputation as an independent searcher after the truth is put at the service of the government, and what is nothing more than the ideological defense of a partisan position is made to appear as the objective truth.

This corruption of political science through affiliation with the government is much more widespread than one would think likely at first glance. Its pervasiveness and thoroughness are the greater for its victims being generally unaware of it. To give only two recent examples: the public silence of most political scientists competent to judge with regard to the MLF (the multilateral sea-borne nuclear force) and the Vietnam war or the half-hearted and frequently tortured defense of these policies contrast sharply with the private criticisms and doubts of these policies by these same political scientists. Perhaps not surprisingly, but still regrettably, political science here partakes of the general mood of conformity: it sacrifices its commitment to the truth, whatever it may be, to ephemeral social advantage.

A political science that is true to its moral commitment ought at the very least to face the risk of unpopularity. At its very best, it cannot help being a subversive and revolutionary force with regard to certain vested interests—intellectual, political, economic, and social in general; for it must sit in continuous judgment upon political man and political society, measuring their truth, which is in good part a social convention, by its own. By doing so, it is not only an embarrassment to society intellectually, but it becomes also a political threat to the defenders or the opponents of the status quo or to both; for the social conventions about power, which political science cannot help subjecting to a critical—and often destructive—examination, are one of the main sources from which the claims to power, and hence power itself, derive.

It stands to reason that political science as a social institution could never hope even to approach this ideal of a completely disinterested commitment to the truth, for no social institution can completely transcend the limitations of its origin; nor can it endeavor to free itself completely from its commitments to the society of which it forms a part, without destroying itself in the attempt. Only rare individuals have achieved the Socratic distinction of unpopularity, social ostracism, and criminal penalties, which are the reward of constant dedication to the relevant truth in matters political. Yet, while political science as a social institution cannot hope to approach the ideal, it must be aware of its existence; and the awareness of its moral commitment to the truth must mitigate the limitations of origin as well as the compromises between the moral commitment and social convenience and ambition, both of which no political scientist can fully escape. It is the measure of the degree to which political science in America meets the needs of society rather than its moral commitment to the truth that it is not only eminently respectable and popular, but—what is worse—that it is also widely regarded with indifference.

A political science that is mistreated and persecuted is likely to have earned that enmity because it has put its moral commitment to the truth above social convenience and ambition. It has penetrated beneath the ideological veil with which society conceals the true nature of political relations, disturbing the complacency of the powers-that-be and stirring up the conscience of society. A political science that is respected is likely to have earned that respect because it performs useful functions for society. It helps to cover political relations with the veil of ideologies which mollify the conscience of society; by justifying the existing power relations, it reassures the powers-that-be in their possession of power; it illuminates certain aspects of the existing power relations; and it contributes to the improvement of the technical operations of government. The relevance of this political science does not lie primarily in the discovery of the truth about politics, but in its contribution to the stability of society.

A political science that is neither hated nor respected, but treated with indifference as an innocuous pastime, is likely to have retreated into a sphere that lies beyond the positive or negative interests of society. The retreat into the trivial, the formal, the methodological, the purely theoretical, the remotely historical—in short, the politically irrelevant—is the unmistakable sign of a "noncontroversial" political science which has neither friends nor enemies because it has no relevance for the great political issues in which society has a stake. History and methodology, in particular, become the protective armor which shields political science from contact with the political reality of the contemporary world. Political science, then, resembles what Tolstoi said modern history has become: "a deaf man answering questions which no one has asked him."

By being committed to a truth which is in this sense irrelevant, political science distorts the perspective under which the political world is seen. Certain eminent exceptions notwithstanding, it tends to pass in silence over such burning problems as the nature of power and the truth about it; political ideologies; the political power of economic organizations; alternative foreign policies; and the relations between government and public opinion, between tyranny and democracy, and between objective truth and majority rule; as well as most of the other fundamental problems of contemporary democracy. By doing so, it makes it appear as though these problems either did not exist or were not important or were not susceptible to theoretical understanding. By its predominant concern with the irrelevant, it devaluates by implication the really important problems of politics.

Thus, the political scientist, oblivious of his moral commitment, has completed his descent. The custodian of the truth and disturber of society's complacent conscience first descends to the role of the ideologue of society and mollifier of its conscience. This role still requiring a social commitment, not to the truth but to society as it is, and, hence, implying a long-term risk, the political scientist who wants to play absolutely safe must take another downward step. In this final role, concerning himself with issues in which nobody has a stake, he avoids the risk of social disapproval by foregoing the chance of social approbation. In the end, then, the concern with social convenience triumphs over social ambition. The commitment to the truth in matters political is dangerous all the time, while carrying within it the promise of ultimate triumph and spiritual perfection. The commitment to society as it is may be dangerous in the long run, carrying within it the promise of social rewards. Retreat from any commitment, to relevant truth or to society, is free from danger, carrying within it no other reward but that freedom from danger itself.

III

With these considerations, we have already opened the discussion of the third issue before us: how to distinguish between political phenomena worthy of theoretical concern and those that are not. In order to answer this question we must distinguish between problems which ought at all times to be of theoretical concern because they touch the very nature of political life, and those, comprising the main body of political science, which have been brought to the fore by a concrete historic situation, to be replaced by others emerging from a different historic situation. To the former belong questions such as: Why is it that all men lust for power? Why is it that even their noblest aspirations are tainted by that lust? Why is it that the political act, in its concern with man's power over man and the concomitant denial of the other man's freedom, carries within itself an element of immorality and puts upon the actor the stigma of guilt? Why is it, finally, that in politics good intentions do not necessarily produce good results and well-conceived plans frequently lead to failure in action, and why is it, conversely, that evil men have sometimes done great good in politics and improvident ones have frequently been successful?

Aside from fundamental philosophic questions such as these, the content of political science cannot be determined *a priori* and in the abstract. There is a strong tendency in contemporary political science to force theory into a Procrustean bed by judging it by its conformity with certain pre-established methodological criteria rather than by its intrinsic contribution to knowledge and understanding. The result is an academic formalism which in its concern with methodological requirements tends to lose sight of the goal of knowledge and understanding which method must serve. One is reminded of the answer which Galileo is reported to have received when he invited some of his critics to look through a telescope at an astronomical phenomenon the existence of which they had denied; they said that there was no need for them to use this empirical instrument, since, according to Aristotle, such a phenomenon could not exist. One is also reminded of Henri Poincaré's reference to the sciences "with the most methods and the fewest results."

The content of theory must be determined by the intellectual

interest of the observer.   What is it that we want to know about
politics?   What concerns us most about it?   What questions
do we want a theory of politics to answer?   The replies to
these three questions determine the content of political science,
and the replies may well differ, not only from one period of history to another, but from one contemporaneous group of observers to another.

Hypothetically, one can imagine as many theories of politics
as there are legitimate intellectual perspectives from which to
approach the political scene.   But in a particular culture and a
particular period of history, there is likely to be one perspective
which for theoretical and practical reasons takes precedence over
the others.   At one time, theoretical interest was focused upon
the constitutional arrangements within which political relations
take place; in view of the theoretical and practical problems to
be solved, this was then a legitimate interest.   At another time
in the history of political science, theoretical interest was cen-
tered upon political institutions and their operations; in view of
what was worth knowing and doing at that time, this theoretical
interest was, again, legitimate.   Thus, political science is like a
spotlight which, while trying to illuminate the whole political
world, focuses in one period of history upon one aspect of politics and changes its focus in accordance with new theoretical and
practical concerns.

In our period of history, the justice and stability of political
life are threatened, and our understanding of the political world
is challenged, by the rise of totalitarianism on the domestic and
international scene.   The novel political phenomenon of totalitarianism puts in doubt certain assumptions about the nature
of man and of society which we took for granted.   It raises issues about institutions which we thought had been settled once
and for all.   It disrupts and overwhelms legal processes which
we had come to look upon as self-sufficient instruments of control.   In one word, what has emerged from under the surface
of legal and institutional arrangements as the distinctive, uni-
fying element of politics is the struggle for power, elemental,
undisguised, and all-pervading.   As recently as at the end of
the Second World War, it was still held by conservatives, lib-
erals, and Marxists alike either that the struggle for power was

at worst a raucous pastime, safely regulated by law and channeled by institutions, or that it had been replaced in its dominant influence by economic competition, or that the ultimate triumph of liberal democracy or the classless society, which were expected to be close at hand, would make an end to it altogether. These assumptions and expectations have been refuted by the experience of our age. It is to the challenge of this refutation that political science must respond, as political practice must meet the challenge of that experience.

Yet, while political science must thus come to terms with the problems of power, it must adapt its emphasis to the ever changing circumstances of the times. When the times tend to depreciate the elements of power, it must stress its importance. When the times incline toward a monistic conception of power in the general scheme of things, it must show its limitations. When the times conceive of power primarily in military terms, it must call attention to the variety of factors which go into the power equation and, more particularly, to the subtle psychological relation of which the web of power is fashioned. When the reality of power is being lost sight of over its moral and legal limitations, it must point to that reality. When law and morality are judged as nothing, it must assign them their rightful place.

IV

All lasting contributions to political science, from Plato, Aristotle, and Augustine to *The Federalist*, Marx, and Calhoun, have been responses to such challenges arising from political reality. They have not been self-sufficient theoretical developments pursuing theoretical concerns for their own sake. Rather, they were confronted with a set of political experiences and problems which defied understanding with the theoretical tools at hand. Thus, they had to face a new political experience, unencumbered by an intellectual tradition which might have been adequate to preceding experiences but which failed to illuminate the experience of the contemporary world. Thus, they were compelled to separate in the intellectual tradition at their disposal that which is historically conditioned from that which is true regardless of time and place, and to pose again the perennial truths of politics in the light of contemporary experience. This has been the purpose of political science throughout its history and this is the purpose of political science today. There is, then, in political science what might be called a "higher practicality," which responds to practical needs not by devising practical remedies, but by broadening and deepening the understanding of the problems from which the practical needs arose.

Political ideas have political consequences. Like military force, economic influence, constitutional authority, legislative votes, and court decisions, they are a factor in the political equation. In the spectrum of these factors, ideas stand at the opposite extreme of force. At first glance and in the short run, it appears that political issues are decisively settled by force rather than by ideas. War, revolution, and the government's monopoly of organized violence, so it seems, decide political issues with finality. Compared with that final effectiveness, ideas appear at worst as nothing more than idle speculation and at best as ideological justifications and rationalizations of what material power has achieved. The modern schools of social and, more particularly, economic determinism partake of this disparagement of the effectiveness of political ideas suggested by the apparent effectiveness of force. They deny the ability of political theory to discover objective truth and reduce it to a mere reflection of material social forces.

However, if one considers the history of Western political thought from the ancient Hebrews and Greeks to the present and the relation of that thought to political events, one notices two fundamental facts. On the one hand, Western political thought has drawn upon a limited number of propositions whose core has remained unchanged throughout history. That core has proven to be impervious to the radical changes that have occurred in political interests and social configurations. It constitutes the truth about matters political which Western civilization has discovered.

On the other hand, the political history of the West, at least in its secular moves, is the story of the attempts to realize these propositions in political practice. In the long run, men have fought and died not for naked material power but for political power at the service of these propositions. These propositions have indeed performed the ideological function of moral justification and intellectual rationalization. But they have been able to perform that function persistently only because they have contained an immutable core of objective truth through which the rational nature of political man meets the rational nature of the political universe.

American political science started out from practical concerns with hardly any regard for theoretical ones. It then moved into a period of theorizing for its own sake without any practical concerns. Its future lies in the combination of the two approaches: practical concerns based upon a firm theoretical foundation. Conceived in such terms, the purpose of the American political scientist in the political world is a special instance of the function which the intellectual must perform for politics. That function is problematical, and it has recently come under especially virulent attack and been exposed to particularly heavy social pressures.

On the one hand, the intellectual is being reduced to a mere servant of the government, improving, justifying, rationalizing what the government is doing. On the other hand, the intellectual who refuses to perform this political function is being relegated to the ivory tower where he is left to his own theoretical devices divorced from the political concerns of the day. The intellectual in general and the political scientist in particular, to be true to their mission, must be committed in a dual way. They must be committed to the objective truth, and they must be committed to the great political issues of the contemporary world. They must descend into the political arena not on behalf of the government or any other political interest but on behalf of the objective truth as they see it. It is inevitable that what they have to say will be used by these political interests for their own ideological purposes and that they will not be able to transcend completely the limitations of historic time and social place. But by searching for the timeless truth in the political configurations of the day, they will, if they are successful, at least catch a glimpse of that truth, however dimly seen, thereby contributing to the rational solution of the political issues of the contemporary world. This is the best that political science has been able to achieve in the past, and this is what American political science ought to aspire to.

Comments on Professor Morgenthau's Paper

By Alfred de Grazia

IT is nice to think of difficult problems being mastered by cool minds. But the history of science, like the history of man in all other fields, is an account of intense emotions cracking against the stone of existence. Isaac Newton's equations, in their impersonality, have misrepresented for centuries the frantic mind of that genius wrestling with nature. Machiavelli's cool *Prince* came from an impassioned mind, which, if it had been less emotional, would have written just another humdrum manual of statecraft.

We should not, therefore, be put off by Professor Morgenthau's indignant assault on the stone of existence. His paper contains an anguished cry against the eternal failure of a society to love people who say what they think about politics. This wholly understandable sentiment neither proves nor disproves any statement about political science. Let us take it, then, sympathetically, and go on to examine the validity of some of Professor Morgenthau's theses.

One major proposition is that the science of international relations treats a large area of uncertainty where what it says about behavior is likely to be as nearly incorrect as correct. Scientific study can expose more and more of the elements at work, however, and this exposure has some uses in orienting thought.

We would agree, but would say that the science of international relations is, in these regards, only like every other science. Every science has more failures to know than successes; every science, where it cannot be complete in predicting and controlling, has at least an orienting value. It positions its people to say more intelligent things than other people can about what matters within their ken. Any science can be made into a "failure" by giving it impossible tasks. If we asked for the earth to be moved into a new orbit, the applied physicists would

80

COMMENTS ON PROFESSOR MORGENTHAU'S PAPER

be in trouble. If we asked the physicians to resurrect the dead, they would be aghast. The limits of science do not remain the same nor do the questions that science is asked by society to answer.[1]

Professor Morgenthau then also pauses, as so many natural and social scientists do, to marvel at the ability of the human mind to comprehend and make correct propositions about non-human nature, as contrasted with human behavior. I do not believe this to be demonstrable, even while so many will agree to it. One has to judge this question by criteria of some kind; few are ever advanced. In one of my own studies, I cast doubt upon the easy acceptance of the "innate superiority" of the natural sciences over the social sciences.[2] The pyramids were built upon *administrative inventions;* so was the Roman Empire; so is the manned space craft orbiting as I write these lines.

This common error is related to yet another misconception, that fails to distinguish between applied and pure science. Pure science states relations only; applied science postulates a goal (a moral preference) and states how to manipulate relations in order to achieve that goal. The more a political scientist works in the format of applied science and the more he works on problems close to strife and conflict, the more likely is he to be hated and loved. So it goes in any field of science.

All science is "social science" in the sense that it is ruled by laws of sociology to some considerable degree.[3] Instead of saying that "the truth of political science is of necessity a partial truth," Professor Morgenthau might say that "all truth is of necessity a partial truth." This point is critical to the next, wherein Professor Morgenthau indicates that, in political science,

---

[1] I do think, however, that the example chosen, the Munich Pact of 1938, was unfortunate. Most American social scientists, to my recollection, were deeply disturbed by the short-range thinking that supported it. Several other factual assertions of the paper about history strike me as questionable, but I am not dealing with them here.

[2] Cf. "The Science and Values of Administration," 5 *Administrative Science Quarterly* (1960), pp. 362–397, 556–582. I cite here and elsewhere in the notes several works that detail my views on points to which I can only allude here.

[3] Cf. my "Social Invention in the Age of Controls," 4 *American Behavioral Scientist* (1960), pp. 36–38.

the pressures for conformity will tempt the distortion of truth for social advantage.

The same pressures are present in every science. The publics may be different—they may consist of one's colleagues alone instead of one's colleagues plus the front pages of newspapers plus the bureaucracy—but they are present, nevertheless. I have demonstrated elsewhere in some depth the kinship that such pressures in natural science have with the pressures in the political sphere.[4] I believe the milieu with which heretical thought must contend is basically the same in every field of knowledge.

Furthermore, there is a problem of the social utility of myths. Now, here Professor Morgenthau is correct in saying that "a political science which is faithful to its moral commitment of telling one truth cannot help telling society things it does not want to hear." But he tends to cover up the fact that lots of truth can be told that society *does* want to hear. Still he is correct in part. Some truths cannot be suffered. Physicians have experiences of the same kind, and have a number of ways of concealing their diagnoses of illness.

Now, the aspect of this matter that Professor Morgenthau does not touch is *the need of every society to tell itself some untruths*. Social morale, on which a great many things hang, apart from a position on any given issue, requires that certain truths be taken hard indeed. For example, a man had better have a full sense of alternatives and a well-developed sense of social responsibility before he takes it upon himself to tell a society it is morally rotten. If he were a physician, he would think twice before putting out flags and declaiming before a patient's family and creditors that the patient is about to die a horrible death. A great deal of emotion is, must be, and should be locked into the fundamental myths of a society and its component institutions. If a society pays no attention to prophets of its doom, it is already dead. If it smiles at them, it is either very healthy or very sick.[5]

[4] Cf. "The Scientific Reception System and Dr. Velikovsky," 7 *American Behavioral Scientist* (1963), pp. 556–582.

[5] Cf. my article, "The Hatred of New Social Science," 5 *American Behavioral Scientist* (1961), pp. 5–13.

Professor Morgenthau next analyzes the present society and finds it to be pluralistic, composed, that is, of religious, political, social, and economic groups, all "committed to a particular social 'truth.'" The political scientist, he says, has to deviate from one or more of these in search of "*the* truth of society altogether."

He evidently assumes that there is an entity called "*political science*" and an entity called "*the* truth of society." Actually, political science is pluralistic, and so is the nature of this "truth."

Political science contains many men, many schools, many traditions, many methods, many issues. At any given moment of time, some are in trouble for their version of the truth and some are in clover. For example, just to take several areas of political science, at present those political scientists who believe that to continue the war in Vietnam will have generally favorable consequences given a set of standards are content with the social recognition of their truths; those who disagree are not. Political scientists who think that they know that reapportionment will bring certain beneficial results to state and national government find the going easy; those who disagree do not. Those who dedicate themselves to expressing the Brownlow theories of administration in government find an appreciative audience; those who pursue a Dewey-Follett line of criticism find incomprehension and irritation.[6]

Now it would be an intellectual sin (which, I fear, Professor Morgenthau may be encouraging) to believe that the only test of whether you are talking truth in political science is whether you are hated for what you are saying. He does say: "A political science that is mistreated and persecuted is likely to have earned that enmity because it has put its moral commitment to the truth above social convenience and ambition." I would say: sometimes yes, and sometimes no. And, conversely, scientists who receive social adulation are sometimes speaking truth and sometimes not. Is it not better to assert that truth-finding and truth-saying are irrelevant to social applause? Heretics are burned, not for telling the truth, but for annoying people.

[6] Cf. my paper on "Research in Voters and Elections," pages 104–134 in *Research Frontiers in Politics and Government* (Washington, D.C.: Brookings Institution, 1955), on the roles of practitioner and scientist as they interact.

Why is this so?   Why is the connection between truth and acceptance so tenuous?   There are at least several reasons.

1. People may be ready to receive truth (ideas) and be longing for it.
2. Some people are ready for any truth: every assertion will find some friends; and for many scientists, a "discerning few" is better than the "fawning crowd."
3. Some truths have such indirect consequences that their potential threats to pomp and power go unnoticed.
4. Truths can often be put as seductively as untruth.
5. Truth-sayers may be associated with power-holders.
6. A great many truths have to do with areas of activities on which the goals of people are nearly unanimous.
7. The truths may be stated in scientific jargon that few understand.
8. The truths may be put contemplatively rather than manipulatively—that is, they are pure propositions, rather than applied ones, and since people are not being urged to act a certain way, they do not mind hearing dissident thoughts.

There is, in brief, a complex field, scarcely developed, called "The Sociology of Political Science," and Professor Morgenthau's eloquent paper is a quick and intriguing lift of the flap to induce us to enter its carnival tent.

Why is Professor Morgenthau so partial and exaggerated in dealing with so large and diverse a set of problems?   One might essay biography, but I would like to avoid the responsibility of making *ad hominem* statements about a friend whose character, for all I know, may be too much like my own.   Let me instead argue on a phenomenological level.

Professor Morgenthau, in his worthy rage, has, like the painter Gauguin and the philosopher Rousseau, given us a "Noble Savage," the political scientist uncorrupted by society who pursues the simple Truth single-mindedly and is misunderstood and condemned by society.   I say that this model—and it is a model— is simplistic.   It violates reality in so many ways as to introduce more problems than it solves.

Professor Morgenthau, as we follow him through the jungles of politics, uncovers two enemies of the Noble Savage. These are the "Apologists" and the "Formalists." The Apologists are those who earn the praises of the elites by flattery, servility, and turning their backs to the truth. The Formalists avoid political commitments, study trivia, and in many cases turn their formalism and triviality into practical virtues by proclaiming a new, objective, and morally indifferent behaviorialism.[7]

By contrast, Professor Morgenthau would have political scientists act as counterpoises to cant: whenever a new theory becomes old and is accepted, they would show what is wrong with it. (This does seem to contradict his earlier model of the single Truth.) He believes especially in a *practical* political science: "It ought to be the conscious purpose of the political scientist to influence the solution of political problems in the light of his theoretical insights." [8]

I would guess that the Noble Savage, by his very nature, is going to have a tough time proposing *practical* solutions. And he will be especially baffled because his theoretical insights are based upon an idealistic, nonpluralistic obsession that there is a Truth of politics. I do admire, however, the way in which Professor Morgenthau casts himself against the stone of existence.

[7] Cf. my remarks on "First Things First in Methodology," in II *American Behavioral Scientist* (1959), p. 35 and on "What Is Political Behavior?," in I *American Behavioral Scientist* (1958), pp. 42–43.

[8] Cf. my "Fact and Value in Teaching," 3 *American Behavioral Scientist* (1960), pp. 14–18.

Comments on Professor Morgenthau's Paper

By Norman D. Palmer

PROFESSOR Morgenthau's paper, drawn largely from previous writings over a period of many years, raises some of the basic questions of purpose which are of continuing concern to political scientists. He provides an opportunity to subject some of his favorite theses to collective examination, an exercise which is bound to be both stimulating and frustrating.

In his first paragraph Professor Morgenthau suggests enough avenues of exploration for a lengthy symposium. These include the perennial questions of the nature of political theory and political science and the relations between political theory and political practice; the validity of the concept of power as a—or indeed *the*—central concept in political science; and the problem of determining which political phenomena "are worthy of theoretical understanding."

The importance of developing a theoretical and conceptual framework for the study of politics has seldom been challenged, even by American political scientists who have been primarily concerned with "practical" problems, the accumulation of empirical data, and methodology, behavioral or otherwise. Professor Morgenthau's approach to theory is obviously conditioned by his own background, training, and interests. He recognizes the difficulties in the way of developing a "scientific theory of politics," but he sees real value in trying to use theoretical yardsticks in the study of political problems. For example, he believes that a contingent and circumspect theory can help to clarify alternative choices of policy, which he finds "for some strange reason" generally "to number three."

Professor Morgenthau's emphasis on power—or on interest defined in terms of power—is well known. It runs like a scarlet thread through most of his writings, and it provides a central theme for the study of political science generally, as well as for the study of international politics, to which Professor Morgenthau has made so many valuable contributions. His concept of power is a broad one, and his reminder that political science "must adapt its emphasis" on the problems of power "to the ever changing conditions of the times" is a useful one indeed. As an exponent of the concept of power in political science and international relations and as a "political realist," Professor Morgenthau has many admirers and many critics. For the present discussion of the purpose of political science, however, it is not necessary to attempt to evaluate the utility or validity of the concept of power as the central concept of political science, or the desirability of adopting any central concept whatever in such a complex and varied field as political science.

Professor Morgenthau seems to be obsessed with what he has called elsewhere "the mystery, the sin, and the tragedy of politics." He seems to be a proponent of the "hair shirt" school of political science. At times he even seems to call for, and to glory in, political martyrdom. A political scientist, above all, has a "moral commitment to discovering *the* truth of society altogether." Yet society hems him in, and keeps him captive. He first "descends to the role of the ideologue of society and mollifier of its conscience," and then he retreats from any commitment whatever. He becomes predominantly concerned with the irrelevant. His real mission, however, is to be "the custodian of the truth and disturber of society's complacent conscience." Hence:

it follows that a respectable political science—respectable, that is, in terms of the society to be investigated—is in a sense a contradiction in terms . . . [for] a political science that is true to its moral commitment ought at the very least to be an unpopular undertaking.

Since there are many critics but few martyrs in our profession, I assume that most of us have sold our birthright for the pottage of "social convenience and ambition." We are either engaged, consciously or unconsciously, in propping up the social order of which we are a part, or we have retreated into the wilderness of noncommitment and political irrelevance. If we do not find refuge in empiricism and methodology, we become organization men, allowing our work to be shaped by the dictates of foundation- or government-sponsored research. In the process, presumably, we have not only failed to live up to our moral commitment or to our responsibility for developing a systematic theory or theories of politics, but we have become servants of the market place and in the process have lost our souls. What is needed for such sycophants, it seems, is not a political symposium but rather a wake or a Moral Rearmament house party.

Political scientists certainly should endeavor to give structure and meaning to the great political issues of their time as well as to the great political issues of all time. They will inevitably be critics of many aspects of the political systems and ideas with which they are concerned. In consequence, they may incur social or governmental disapproval, or much worse. But surely they need not be unduly concerned if they enjoy a certain degree of respectability, or even of influence and position. Possibly they can remain true to their basic commitment and their essential functions within the framework of the society in which they live. They can help to improve that society, not only by challenging it, in specific and fundamental ways, but also by contributing whatever insights and expertise they possess to an understanding of the fundamental problems of the day and to the development of improved ways and means of dealing with these problems.

The extent to which political science should serve public policy is a question which admits of many answers and many points of view. As William Graham Sumner observed: "No man can get far from the folkways and mores of his own time." Obviously political scientists, like all human beings, are conditioned by the folkways and mores of their own societies. Yet Professor Morgenthau's statement that "the mind of the political scientist is molded by the society which he observes" is only partially true. Even in his own society he may be able, if the quality of his mind is superior and if his horizons are broad, to achieve a certain degree of objectivity and perspective; and in observing other societies—one of the chief preoccupations of many in the political science profession who are concerned with comparative politics and cross-cultural surveys—he has the advantages, and disadvantages, of relative detachment. But few political scientists can divorce themselves from the problems of their time, even if they would. Perhaps this is all to the good, for, as Oliver Wendell Holmes once said, no man has really lived who has not participated in the battles of his own age. In the cockpit of contemporary politics the political scientist can perhaps gain wisdom and experience, and also find the data which he needs for his theoretical and applied research. As Professor Morgenthau wrote, in an excellent essay on Walter Lippmann:

All great contributions to political theory . . . have reflected not upon the theories of others, let alone upon theories about theories . . . but upon the concrete, burning, "controversial" political problems of their times.

Some of these reflections have little value as solutions to the specific problems to which they are addressed, and even less as solutions to the problems of later times, but some nevertheless have enduring value as fundamental principles of political theory and political science. (I would avoid such terms as "perennial truths," which Professor Morgenthau likes to use.) Even that part of political science—by far the larger part—which is mainly concerned with "practical" issues which Professor Morgenthau might regard as "irrelevant," and which makes little direct contribution to the "scientific" study of politics or to the development of systematic theory, has its place in the universe of political science—although it may be branded with the scarlet letter of respectability.

For "the theoretical understanding of politics" there is obvious need for both empirical and theoretical research, for both macrocosmic and microcosmic studies, for the development of both "traditional" and "modern" approaches, for both the synthesizing and the clinical mind.

New challenges to excellence in his field confront the political scientist as a result of the changing values and gigantic new problems and demands of the nuclear age, the widening dimensions of his field, and new techniques for the study of politics, on both theoretical and practical levels. Many of the most exciting developments in political science are occurring on the periphery of the discipline, or even beyond. As Charles A. Beard noted thirty-five years ago, in a report of the Committee on Policy of the American Political Science Association: "Great discoveries are made sometimes at the center of a theme; more often they are made at its periphery—in combinations not dissections." Twenty years later, in the first major international survey of *Contemporary Political Science* (Paris: UNESCO, 1950), Charles E. Merriam wrote:

The periphery of political science as in other intellectual expansion is the thing to watch. . . . Above all there is a deep and restless concern with the traditional boundaries of political science, driving toward the revision of the old and formulation of new hypotheses and conclusions regarding political phenomena, and toward new contributions to intelligent policy making.

"To understand politics in a theoretical manner" is perhaps the purpose of political science, but this is by no means as obvious as Professor Morgenthau assumes. Much depends on the meaning which is assigned to "politics" and to "theory" in this connection. Fortunately, this is not the place to discuss the scope or nature of either politics or political science, the relation of politics to political science, or of political philosophy to political theory, or of both to political science. A further limitation is imposed by the different interpretations of most, if not all, of these concepts and terms in different countries, and at different times. In his essay Professor Morgenthau approaches the question from the point of view of a highly trained and sophisticated intellectual who is a product of a European background and an American exposure. A scholar from a different cultural and societal background would undoubtedly have presented a rather different kind of analysis. In many societies, even today, an emphasis on theory might be expected because of the narrow theoretical training of most political scientists (if indeed they exist at all), the relatively underdeveloped state of the study of political science in their area, or the restrictions imposed by the political and cultural climate or the political system.

In the United States the study of political science is clearly in a transitional stage. Attempts are being made to expand its horizons, to give it a sounder theoretical underpinning, and to make it more relevant to the burning problems of the modern world. The subjects which were formerly regarded as constituting its core, including traditional approaches to political theory, are losing their relative pre-eminence. Exciting developments are occurring on the periphery of the discipline, and beyond, and significant work is being made possible by new methods of research and new approaches to theoretical and conceptual analysis. To some extent, political science has reached a new stage of development, in both theory and practice. There is even hope that the new emphasis on theory, including systems and behavioral theory but not neglecting "the great issues of politics," may provide some balance to "the commitment of modern political science to practical ends," which, according to Professor Morgenthau, "has profoundly contributed to its decline as theory." Even while remaining suspiciously respectable, political science may still be true to its "moral commitment" and to its higher obligations and purposes.

The purpose of political science is to give purpose to political science. This involves due attention to theory and to practice, to old approaches and to new, to the political problems of mankind today and tomorrow as well as to "the great issues of politics" that seem to be timeless. Thus stated, the purpose of political science is grander in concept than "the theoretical understanding of politics." It provides ample scope for both painstaking research and creative thinking, without aspiring to be a "master science" or to "discovering *the* truth of society altogether."

Comments on Professor Morgenthau's Paper

By Paul N. Ylvisaker

I SHARE Professor Morgenthau's penchant for political science in action, his sense of commitment to the problems and predicaments of his times, his instinct for the jugular vein of power, and his (sometimes) resignation to the fact that even the wisest among us will never know truth absolutely.

Being a preacher's kid, who grew up with the Old Testament prophets, I also come alive to his call for social criticism, notwithstanding a decade among the fleshpots of philanthropy and the comforts of the Establishment. But there were several things in his sermon that made me restive. One was his quick switch from uncertainty to absolutism. His early admissions of fallibility are immediately followed by pontifical statements about "the truth"—and indeed *the* truth becomes so apparent to Professor Morgenthau that he underlines it.

This sudden dogmatism roused me to listen for the other sure signs of orthodox theology for which I have developed perhaps too much of an ear and an allergy. Among them is the doctrine of original sin ("Why is it that all men lust for power, why is it that even their noblest aspirations are tainted by that lust?"). I thought we were farther along in our conception of power than that; and I could see Ingmar Bergman's gaunt horse of guilt riding across this bleak medieval horizon. We all know what hurt men have caused when they had a chance to do it and what fools we become when elevated above the view of a faithful mirror. But power ennobles as well as it corrupts; it can heal as well as hurt; it can be reciprocal as well as unilateral; and it is about as factual and inevitable as heat, electricity, and every other form of energy by which the world's work gets done.

There was also the doctrine of "unam sanctam"—only through unpopular analysis will the political scientist make it to heaven. By that test Hubert Humphrey—and a lot of other men I respect—would lose their membership in the Association.

And I cannot see where social criticism is producing many martyrs among us.

This society does not exile or crucify its critics. It publishes them, televises them, and pays them consulting fees. The surest way to literary lionhood is to sharpen one's intellectual claws on the foibles of our society—and especially on the way it does its political business.

In this age of popular protest, I guess, a political scientist could be corrupted more quickly by playing prophet than by acting as king's consort. The agonies of carrying responsibility, of making decisions out of uncertainties, of melding egos into programs, and of sifting grains of hope out of ashes of trial and error—these are harder to bear, and no less edifying, than speaking loudly and critically of the mess we are in and the mice we are.

And I believe they are equally as central to the purpose of political science.

Political science is, after all, an instrument of man to improve his human condition. Like all our mortal sciences, it builds on man's capacity to see beyond himself and to find ordering principles that transcend his own circumstance and self-interest. But this does not mean that political science need be the jealous domain or exclusive preserve of those who have the time to think apart from shaving or who prefer analysis to engineering.

There is room and need for both.

Yet political science, as students come to know it, has been cast in the mold of those who, without political responsibility, act as critic and psychiatrist of those who have it. In their hands the purpose of political science becomes theory, analysis, and publishable manuscript more as ends in themselves than as instruments for the advancement of human welfare. Treatises on the methods of political science either exclude participation, or add it only as a condescending afterthought. And the scope of political science is shaped more by what pedagogical empires in the university one has to live with or can get away with, than by the nature of the subject itself.

But I sense in our students these days a rebellion that professors as well as university presidents will have to conjure with.

It combines a commitment to the ultimate social goals of political science with a sixth sense that involvement may be essential to a full understanding of the political process. And I would guess that our Schlesingers, Hellers, Gordons, Humphreys, Keynes, *et al*. might agree.

Conference Discussion on Objectives

PALMER: It is rather hard to discuss Morgenthau's paper in his absence. I must confess that I was a little disappointed with the gist of the thinking which is embraced in this paper on the purpose of political science, which, as I noted earlier, was presented by him many years ago. Does this mean that great political thinkers reach their peak at a certain stage and do not go beyond that, or have they already developed such soundly based ideas that they can stand on those and repeat variations of them? It seems to me that we need to look at the purpose of political science in the light of all the major developments that are affecting our field, and that there needs to be some new thinking on the purpose of political science and on the extent to which new approaches to political science are effective these days. I must say, I did not detect too much of this in the paper.

It is very hard, of course, to know whether you are talking about scope or purpose. The problem of methods is a little bit easier to detect, especially in the Deutschian sense, but some of the things that we talk about concerning purpose, I suppose, do deal with scope, and vice versa.

There are a number of hardy perennials here with which all of us are concerned, and a number of Morgenthauisms with which we are all very familiar. Certainly, he has made some of the most significant contributions to our thinking, and I assume that this applies not only to the field of international relations, but to political science generally.

Take, for example, this whole matter of power. I do not know to what extent one needs to kick this around anymore, but I have been impressed with the antiquity of most of the "new" ideas about power which have developed in our profession. It can easily be shown that people were talking about the power concept twenty-five or thirty or more years ago. This fact is pointed out by various people. I recall seeing an article in which the author pointed out that he and Harold Lasswell were ringing the changes on this theme a very long while ago. It is, however, true, at least in the international field, that in the pre-World War II era perhaps not as much attention was given to the concept of power.   E. H. Carr's book *The Twenty Years' Crisis* was a significant contribution.   Almost every discussion in the international field, at least—and to some extent, I think, in the political science field generally—that has come out since then, it seems to me, has dealt with the power theme in one way or another. In some cases it may be disguised, but even if one is dealing with problems of consensus, for example, one might easily be concerned with problems of power.   The question of conflict situations, how one deals with them, the types of sanctions that may be applied, the pressures, and the like would come under this heading.

I notice that Professor Morgenthau started his paper in one way and ended in another.   I am sure that he would deny that and would prove that this is a completely false interpretation, but I got the impression that he started out on a rather highly generalized theoretical plane and ended on a fairly pragmatic level.   For example, his concept of what can be expected of political science with relation to such things as moral commitment, the "perennial truths" of politics, to use another one of his terms, or "*the* truth" in an absolute sense seems to be fairly realistic by the time one gets to the end of the paper, especially in the light of the rather perceptive comments which I find on the very last page.   It seems to me that if some of his concluding observations had been presented at the beginning of his paper, we could have gone through his preachments about moral commitment and the truth and the like with a bit more understanding of the different levels at which I judge he is considering these matters.

I notice that Professor Morgenthau does not really talk about the whole matter of philosophy versus theory.   It seems to me that this is still worth discussing.   I assume that there is considerable difference between philosophy and theory.   At least the word *theory* seems to admit of lots of permutations and combinations, all of which I would not include under the heading of philosophy.   It does seem, in the light of the circumstances of our age—all the problems and all the worries and concerns and all the different dimensions of problems in politics—that one needs to be broadly philosophical, or at least to seek some kind of philosophical approach to political problems, as well as to talk in terms of theory, whether one is talking about a general theory of politics or theories of politics or even theories of methodology.

The question of theory and practice is another hardy perennial. Sometimes, perhaps, the political scientist is likely to avoid the realm of practice simply because he does not feel very much at home there, does not think that he has very much to offer. On the other hand, it seems to me that one of the major functions of a political scientist should be to call attention to basic theoretical aspects, to help to lift consideration of issues above the level of the immediate, which preoccupies busy policymakers most of the time.

I must confess that I am simply lost in some of the aspects of Professor Morgenthau's approach. For example, I have no idea of the significance of the "fact" that the rational choices usually seem to be three. If one reads some of the ancient literature of our profession one will often find that there are varying numbers of points, but now, it seems, there are usually always three. I am not sure how the Holy Trinity came into the picture. When one is dealing with the matter of rational choices, is it possible to say as a general principle that the number of rational choices is always quite limited, not only limited but limited to a relatively few categories which presumably can be isolated and stated, if not easily identified in a way which would receive general agreement?

I am also concerned with the limitations which Morgenthau seems to put on theoretical analysis. He refers to the uncertainty which is typical of all levels of theoretical analysis and prediction in the field of politics. I suggest that we limit theoretical analysis much more rigidly than I think he would. Surely, there are lots of other ways of dealing with theoretical analysis in our field.

Now, regarding moral commitment and the point that a political scientist if he is any good has to be unpopular, I notice that every one of us tees off on this one. One gets the impression that Morgenthau belongs to that school of thought which seems to emanate quite heavily from European sources, subscribers to which would be unhappy if you are happy and happier when they are unhappy. Perhaps this is a matter of approach to political problems. As an American, I am inclined to be an optimist, even though the evidence is against it—maybe for the same reason once given by Winston Churchill: "I'm an optimist because there doesn't seem to be much point in being anything else." Whereas so many of the scholars from other lands (Not just Europe; I apply this certainly to the Orient and part of Latin America; I am not sure about Africa) are professional pessimists, and if they become optimistic it is in a long-range philosophical way. As the Japanese say about the Irish: "These optimists—they want to do something in two hundred years." I remember once having a pleasant talk with a Japanese political scientist. After he got back to Japan, he wrote a very nice letter to me, saying that he was very pleased to find that we had such a wide area of agreement, but that the basic difference between us was that I am an optimist and he is a pessimist. It seems to me that Professor Morgenthau feels that he is impelled to be a pessimist and that it would be quite a considerable lowering of his professional standards if he took any other approach.

Now, it is a real problem, certainly, the extent to which political scientists test the effectiveness of their criticism by the degree of acceptance or nonacceptance of their views. I suggest that Professor Morgenthau takes too strong a position in suggesting that one cannot have respectable political science; I assume that that means that one cannot have respectable political scientists unless their positions are unpopular and unless they are, in a sense, suffering the consequences. I would certainly feel that one can be a "respectable" political scientist and still be more or less acceptable in the social framework within which one is operating. It is probably true that one of the main purposes of political science is to raise unmentionable, unthinkable problems which, perhaps, are somewhat embarrassing, which possibly challenge the pillars of the social order, which break away from the prevailing patterns.

I am very conscious of the fact that political scientists take different approaches in different social systems. A political scientist in the Soviet Union, for instance, is obviously going to take certain positions which would not be popular in the United States but which are popular in his country. I assume from Professor Morgenthau's criteria that the test of acceptance, the test of respectability, is the test within one's own political system, and in some ways it is a kiss of death if one finds that ideas are accepted too freely outside, unless they are on a very theoretical level. I was reminded of this recently in listening to one of the news correspondents who had just returned from Moscow. He was pointing out, in connection with the Shelepin mission to Vietnam, that one of the worst contributions that we in this country, on either the official or unofficial level, can make to the cause of peace in Vietnam is to talk about this mission as a peace mission. This would make it more embarrassing for the Russians because then they would have to try to convince the Chinese and some others that they are not just playing the revisionist role and departing from their principles.

It does seem to me that Professor Morgenthau takes a somewhat old-fashioned approach to political science. I had anticipated a more revolutionary analysis; this, to me, is rather straight European jurisprudence and morality. It is the kind of theory which will still have considerable validity, but, by and large, I would hope that we can go beyond his concept of the purpose of political science and consider possibly broader dimensions than the concept of power. I suggest that he has put us all on the spot in the wrong sense. The test should not be whether certain ideas of political scientists are accepted or not accepted. We have to seek other criteria, other tests, to determine their validity or invalidity. I would not worry if occasionally we find that in the prevailing market place of ideas in a particular society some of the views of political scientists happen to have a certain measure of acceptance. The basic test should be something different from that, perhaps in terms of comparative and sociological or sociopsychological analysis of political issues. It is on this level that the value of contributions by political scientists should be tested.

Finally, we might consider the validity or lack of validity of ideological approaches to problems. To what extent are the great issues today ideological in nature, whether you consider them in the sense of a fairly well-defined ideological point of view or more from the point of view of a breakdown of the old state patterns and interstate relations?   In international relations, for instance, some people now say that we should be concerned not so much with international relations as with intercultural relations.

So, I just end as I began by suggesting the importance of as deep philosophical insights as one can have.   In this area, obviously, political scientists have a limited but important role, in considering the nature of theory and the relation of theory to practice and to immediate problems.

YLVISAKER: I feel like a genial Scandinavian who has learned the value of the *smörgåsbord*.   He can tolerate a tremendous amount of diversity as long as it all tastes good and he is not compelled to make too limited a choice.   As I shall explain, I thought Professor Morgenthau a stranger to the *smörgåsbord*. He does have a compulsion to the narrow choice: to the right as against the wrong, to the single way to truth.

I should confess, too, that being a philanthropoid, I am probably disqualified as a political scientist.   By the usual ratings, we are social engineers rather than social scientists, concerned with the application rather than the advancement of knowledge. Yet I would retort that it is wrong, or at least unwise, to press the distinction, for the same reason that divorcing engineering from physics or any other of its basic sciences is not wise.   You will find this doubt about distinction embedded in my reaction to Professor Morgenthau's paper, as you will also find a strong reaction to strict doctrine.   I rebel now as I once rebelled against stern theology.   I kidded the good professor a bit, and I hope that he will discern this even if he may resent it.   But I certainly did sense in his essay a feeling of guilt when he dealt with power, as though anyone who exercises it ought to go regularly to confession.

I also found some relics of "unum sanctum"—only one way to salvation, which, by Professor Morgenthau's lights, is to play martyr and critic against the holders of established power.   Critics and rebels we need; but in our day they rarely become martyrs, and they are not the only ones who get to heaven.   Besides, other things than power corrupt, and I find as much evidence of self-serving, self-justification, and blind pretension in the ranks of the critic and academic as I do in the company of established power.

Contrary to what I found Professor Morgenthau saying— that political science is centrally, if not exclusively, concerned with criticism of the use of power—I believe that our discipline's ultimate purpose is the improvement of the human condition. Critical analysis is a healthy instrument—it can and has saved us from a lot of social rubbish. But there are other tools and other modes, and I am impressed with the instincts of many "political scientists," ranging from Lord Keynes to present-day student activists, who have sensed that there is something in the agony of exercising power and carrying responsibility which ennobles rather than corrupts, which may edify and enlighten as often as it blinds.

Professor Morgenthau's paper also left me with an uneasy feeling that he had, by disputation, narrowed the province of political science. In my business, social engineering, we attempt to use every bit of science that we can come across. The lines between the sciences are certainly becoming indistinct; as a matter of fact, I do not see them any more. It is easier to classify types of minds and personal roles than to set the boundary lines and exclusive concerns of the several disciplines. (Sooner or later, I think, the disciplines themselves are going to be forced to meld, and some of the old names and jurisdictions will fade and disappear.)

Let me draw from one case history of the work we do in the Ford Foundation: that mix of social science and engineering which conditions my own thinking about political science and my reaction against the narrowing prescriptions I read in (or into) Professor Morgenthau's essay. For a number of years, we have been trying to help shape and reshape community efforts to deal with the problems of those who are newcomers to the city or for other reasons are low on the urban totem pole. In those few years, by the way, I have seen especially the large city mayors move from a political position and constituency which was essentially conservative to one which is, in every respect but its articulation (they need a political theorist at this moment), essentially radical. The opposition to the war in Vietnam, which so far has been identified with the campus, is far more prevalent and powerful in city hall. Professor Morgenthau has a lot more company than he realizes, and his life would be less lonely if his view of political science let more members into his club. The reason for this political shift is obvious—the increasing assertiveness of low-income urban voters and the financial squeeze on beleaguered mayors which the war in Vietnam has so sharply intensified.

One of the first communities we worked with was New Haven. The mayor of that city had, by 1960, played out the political string of urban renewal; a reaction had set in among the dislocated and the like which had reduced Lee's voting majority to a bare 2,000. Lee was sensitive and astute enough to recognize that he would have to respond to an entirely different schedule of urban needs—the human as against the physical. Before we talked seriously to Lee about Foundation help, we met with Bob Dahl, then fresh from his manuscript *Who Governs?* We asked two questions from his analysis: (1) Was New Haven capable of a second round of civic action, or had the "reformers" shot their wad? (2) If capable of another round, who beyond Lee was in a position to direct it? Bob—in that moment and later in the test of events—won my abiding respect as a political scientist. His answers were: (1) Yes, but New Haven's second round would find its motive force in the schools and neighborhoods rather than in the central business district; and (2) the galvanizing figure beyond (and with) Dick Lee could be Mike Sviridoff. What New Haven and Sviridoff have since become in the annals of the Poverty Program I need not detail for any reader of the *Congressional Record* and the *New York Times*.

After that critical beginning, we did not get much help from the discipline—not even with *ex post facto* analysis and criticism, which would seem the profession's surest skill. With rare exceptions, the political scientists of the inner sanctum (and their counterparts in sociology, economics, and the other social sciences) were working on short tether, hobbled by anxiety over what their peers would think of them if they were found "sciencing" in the world of the uncertain, the here and now, without benefit of approved methodology or the blessing of the patronizing saints.

So we stumbled on and onto an assortment of "political scientists" whom I would gladly honor with the Ph.D. if they would ever stand still long enough to accept it. Thought and action, induction and intuition, the exercise of power and self-restraint, feedback and self-criticism, appraisal and invention—all these are fused in their very being and every action. (And why not declare them professors, with students attached to them where they live and work?) One of them is the Reverend Leon Sullivan, the Negro minister of North Philadelphia who is scoring a theoretical and actual breakthrough in integrating the simplistic force of the civil rights movement with the complexities of a sophisticated, bureaucratized, and refractory society. There are many such others, but still not enough.

Well, I began by admitting my bias as a social engineer, a genial Scandinavian, and a rebel against doctrine—pragmatic, eclectic, one foot out of any batter's box. This was the spirit in which I reacted to Morgenthau's presentation—to what I thought was narrowness, an orthodoxy which freezes the kind of ingenuity a political engineer and, I think, a political scientist ultimately have to have if we are broadly to define the ultimate role of political science as one of improving the human condition.

These are some disorganized comments, but they reflect a feeling, and feelings are probably as important as reason and analysis in the particular science with which we are concerned. Professor Morgenthau's paper is heavily charged with feelings— among them, the anguish of a man who has chosen what he too quickly concludes is a lonely and unpopular position on Vietnam. Frankly, I am more taken with his feelings than with his analysis, and I would venture to say that we have more to learn from the whole man than from what he has attempted in this case as an exercise in pure reason.

DE GRAZIA: As Paul talked I was thinking of the problem of the Morgenthau temperament and then the Scandinavian temperament, and I recall being in the University of Gothenberg last year and meeting a young instructor who had been waiting for two years for housing. It is presumably the best organized, most advanced, and most prosperous country in Europe, if not the world, so that I had the feeling that maybe the instructor had become too used to *smörgåsbord*, and picking up whatever happened to be left on the table after everybody had filed through, with labor unions going through first, of course, taking what they wanted (*laughter*).

I was going to denounce Morgenthau's position. Professor Morgenthau is really being blasted by his own petard, I think. He gave me some diabolic satisfaction in the reading of his paper. He has been talking about the national interest so brazenly and so long in terms which are essentially meaningless to me that I am glad to see that the "national interest" has finally caught up with him and is "giving him what for." It has always been a rather amoral concept, it seems to me, a concept of a medieval kind. My predecessors mentioned the old-fashioned character of his theories, of his book, and I quite agree—the search for ideal truth that exists somewhere is like the search for the Holy Grail.

Because of the rather military conversation at our table at lunch time, I was reminded also of Cassino one day in 1943 when we were removing several newly taken German prisoners from the line in order to interrogate them. The outfit was the Thirty-sixth Division, the Texas National Guard Division (not a very well-organized division, because Lyndon Johnson had been sent to the Pacific, I guess), and a lieutenant wanted to kill the prisoners because, as he said, we had been getting artillery fire from them all afternoon. Well, how does one explain to such a person that, really, one cannot expect honied words from the enemy? I mean, they are there for a reason, too, and if one is going to have a war, one has to expect to get hurt. I feel that Morgenthau's complaint here is in slightly bad taste. If he is going to get into this war, he had better expect to get hurt.

The national interest has always been to me whatever the policy-makers have at any given moment decided that it should be, and so it never bothered me as a concept, and I have always discouraged students (I hope that I do not offend too many of you here) from concentrating upon it. It is a Platonic concept. I would much rather that students simply make empirical statements about who believes what, among the elite and among the masses, if they can measure it, and who has the power to carry out what they believe in—and whoever that may be can be conceived to have a kind of monopoly of the national interest insofar as their propaganda may be rendered effective. Any concept of the national interest beyond that, so far as political science is concerned, I would regard as rather medieval.

If there is one problem raised by Professor Morgenthau's paper (which in other respects does not raise problems), it is again the ancient but yet unresolved problem: the duty of statesmen to pursue truth as opposed to the ruling formula. We waver as a profession in assuming a position on this issue. We recognize, although sometimes we try to hide it from ourselves, that one has to be somewhat of a liar, a cheat, and all of that, in order to carry out policy.

This necessity is partly owing to a basic conflict between truth, or truths, or the search for the same, and the myth which is necessary for ruling a society, and partly a sheer matter of technique. One cannot reveal truth with the same phasing, same timing, and same pattern as one can reveal policy. Regarding the present moment, I, for one, am rather doubtful about the thought that our own leaders, on the question of Vietnam, may really be sharing my opinion about the situation, but I have no way of knowing it, and, in fact, I may feel that I should have no way of knowing it, and if I were in their position, I would not be telling persons such as myself that I had such a policy.

Professor Morgenthau does not direct himself to that question, but it seeps out of his pages. We need to know, as political scientists, what kind of ruling formula is demanded if we are to have certain stable social conditions or certain conditions for political equilibrium (however you want to use that term). We have to know or to have some idea of what it should be, I suppose, in order that we may build an applied political science, because we have never quite solved this problem of applied political science, concerning the *ruling myth*, which is a series of practical fictions, and the necessity to work on *truth* within that framework. As political scientists, we tend toward the position which Professor Morgenthau takes in a whole-hearted and rather exaggerated way—that whatever truth is must come out; it must be public property—while, on the other hand, we recognize a secret knowledge, which, I think, political scientists possess more than any other field of the social sciences, knowledge of certain things that cannot be told lest the whole society should fall apart.

EULAU: I do not want to address myself to Professor Morgenthau's paper directly, but I am rather astounded. On the practical research level, is it not the falsification of hypotheses that should be our concern in the search for truth?   From this it would seem to follow that our knowledge is always partial knowledge. Necessarily, we always have to start with an assumption, but under modern technological conditions, we can attach some calculation of probability to the statements of truth which we make. I do not have to make a statement of absolute truth in order to understand certain facts. This should be of interest to the social engineers who are willing to use our knowledge. Whether they are willing to use it or not would seem to depend on the degree of confidence that they have in the probability statements which the political scientist makes. It is at this point that the linkage takes place between our function as scientists and our other functions. The social engineers will try to establish the linkage, that is, the political corner where the specification of goals, the calculation of probabilities, and the building of policies have to take place.

At this point, quite clearly, I read something into Professor Morgenthau's paper, but it is so dogmatic actually, in spite of its emphasis on the contemporary and the significant. I think that it is far removed from what actually takes place in the relationship between scientists, on the one hand, and social engineers and social philosophers on the other. Perhaps this is the reason why he is finding himself so much at the margin of the discipline. I think that this kind of analysis is almost hopeless. I think that there are certain criteria or procedures of science; whether one believes in God or does not believe in God, whether one is an optimist or a pessimist, makes no difference at all. The physicists can make all kinds of assumptions about reality; yet in the laboratory they are collaborating. It seems to me that it is the task of political science increasingly to move away from the kind of rosy ideological blinkers which Professor Morgenthau advises us to put on.

SPITZ: May I venture a few comments in defense of Professor Morgenthau?   I did not come with that intention because I share many of the reservations which have been articulated about his paper. I do not, for example, fully accept his conception of power. However, I think that the representations of his views that I have listened to today are not altogether accurate. Let me try, then, not by speaking for Morgenthau but rather by speaking for issues that Morgenthau raised, to argue in defense of at least some points in his position.

Surely all of us recognize that there is a difference between appearance and reality. Not being a quantitative political scientist, I shall not venture any statistics here, but certainly it is true that a great many people accept the established ways without inquiring into them. Many of our colleagues in political science are content to teach from the established books without challenging what is in them, and what Morgenthau or any serious person can properly say is that the job of a scholar—whether he be a political scientist or a political analyst (if you do not want to call him a scientist)—is to expose the ever-present difference between appearance and reality. Morgenthau's concern for Vietnam is only one manifestation of this assumption of responsibility —and whether he is right or wrong does not interest me at the moment; it is enough to recognize the validity of his plea that we operate at the level of reality, and not at the level of appearances.

It may be that de Grazia is correct in emphasizing the need for a government or a statesman to utilize myths or deceits in order to accomplish certain purposes, but the job of the political analyst is different from that of the political activist. The analyst must rationally comprehend the use of the irrational; he must rationally understand how and why one uses myths, and he must make it clear that myths are, in fact, being employed; so that it does not argue against Morgenthau to say that we need a ruling formula. His reply would surely be that the business of the political scientist is the rational understanding of the irrational, and the articulation of that understanding with respect to the reasons or causes, the patterns of conduct, and the probable consequences of the resort to and exploitation of the irrational.

Now, there is a line somewhere in Silone's *Bread and Wine* where his chief protagonist says that to be a man is to fight against one's limits. I would prefer to read Morgenthau's exposition of the need for political scientists to be critics in that sense. The political scientist is the man who must not only seek the limits of our understanding, but must try to break through those limits. He seeks to discover his limits, not in order to surrender to them, but in order to combat and transcend them. This is the meaning, if you will, of the human condition. If he does not do this, he becomes simply an automaton who surrenders to the world as he finds it. The political scientist, if he is also a man, is of necessity a critic. True, he must look at the world as he finds it; but unless you are prepared to argue that the world in which we live is a just and good world, that there is no evil and no injustice, then the political scientist's understanding of that world includes an understanding of those shortcomings. His job, then, is (among other things) to expose the nature of those evils, those injustices, those wrongs, and even, perhaps, to suggest ways of correcting them.

In these terms, the political scientist is not simply a man who communicates what we already know, who transmits what is already accepted. He must be a critic; he must measure what we are against what we say we are or what we say we ought to be, and he must try to point out the ways in which we can move from where we are to where we ought to be. This is the least that we as political scientists can contribute to the human situation. And from this standpoint, it is altogether clear that the job of the political scientist is indeed to be a critic of society, that a "respectable" political scientist must be a critical political scientist, and not a conformist political scientist.

Now, if one is a critic rather than a conformist, one is obviously going to annoy a number of people. Alfred de Grazia had a sentence in his paper—that we do not punish people for being heretical, but for annoying others—which I think is fundamentally true. The fact of the matter is that a lot of people are annoyed by heretical views. I come from a very peculiar city—Columbus, Ohio—in which the utterance of truth is often construed as heresy. More than this, it is a heresy to be denounced. Given this situation—and I do not think that it is altogether unique to Columbus—to be a critic and to speak as a critic is to run the risk of unpopularity and retributive action. Again, I cannot measure this; I do not know how many people have become famous because they were rebels and how many have been struck down for essaying that role. But I think that Morgenthau is largely right. The people who are trouble-makers, who annoy

other people, are going to suffer for it.   Those of you who have
said that Morgenthau is now suffering for what he is doing—that
is, about Vietnam—are probably correct.   But I do not see that
one has to be a European to suffer this.   I have suffered it in
other ways, and with respect to other issues, and perhaps some
of you have, too.   If one is a critic, if one attacks the McCarthy
proceedings, if one justifies civil disobedience, if one tries to defend the students who are demonstrating, one is going to get
slugged by people; one is not going to be cheered—though one
will undoubtedly be cheered by some, by those one defends or
whose principles one espouses.

EULAU: Is one functioning as a scientist in this role?

SPITZ: I tried to anticipate that by saying that I prefer to
use the term "political analyst" rather than the term "political
scientist."   I do not think that Morgenthau is concerned with
political science in the limited sense in which you want him to
define that term.   If you conceive of science simply as a matter
of reducing ignorance to more and more knowledge, Morgenthau
would say, I think, that this is but a part of the activity of politics.   It is an important part, I think he would say, and certainly
I would say, but it is not the whole of political science—because
political understanding (or political science) is always but a
preface to action, a preface to what we can do with this kind of
knowledge.

This, of course, raises the old question of whether the political scientist should simply tell us what is, or whether he should
also make recommendations, or whether (if I may add another
dimension) he should concern himself with the correct principles
of good conduct.   In this context, when Morgenthau talks about
the unity of theory and practice, it is perhaps "old hat."   If one
takes someone like Robert Dahl, who works in an empirical or
behavioralistic vein, one is dealing with a political scientist who
comes to his empirical investigations via a rich background.   He
knows what he is doing; he operates within a humanistic context.
I regret that the same thing cannot be said of those (especially
students and younger colleagues) who purportedly pursue the
same type of inquiry.   There are places where students learn
how to manipulate IBM cards and run computers; but if you ask
the larger questions, their answer all too often is: "Oh, we just

gather the data, and then somebody, someday, will put them together." It seems to me that Morgenthau's plea is the obvious
yet necessary reminder that practical activity, empirical work,
has no meaning unless it takes place within a theoretical context.
You [Eulau] surely would not dispute that. Hence, when Morgenthau argues for the direction of practice by theory and the
correction of theory by practice, he asserts what any intelligent
man must assert. In the same way, when he speaks of *the* truth,
I would contend that a strong case can be made for maintaining
the distinction between appearance and reality, and for insisting
upon the importance of theory, and the unity of theory and practice, as essential to the effort to reduce ignorance, to discover
greater and more searching truths.

Some of you were disturbed by Morgenthau's use of the
number three. I do not understand why. One does not need
to make a great case for the number three to recognize that in
the history of political science—as of philosophy—the number
three is a customary, even venerable term. Plato used it as a
basic concept, as in his famous tripartite division of the soul and
in his division of the Republic into three classes. Bacon constantly stressed tripartite organization, as is shown in the first
book of *The Advancement of Learning* and in the *New Atlantis*.
And if one takes it at a most commonplace level, are not alternatives usually two extremes and a middle? I do not think
that Morgenthau was saying much more than that. We are
regularly confronted by a set of alternatives: two extremes, and
between them a middle range. Now, you are going to tell me
that there are twenty alternatives in between. Of course Morgenthau knows that; he is not a fool. All he is saying is that,
with respect to any issue, this is the way one must approach the
problem. No thinker can examine, or even anticipate, every
conceivable alternative. He can most profitably consider the
two opposing extremes and the most representative intermediate
ground and explore the consequences and assumptions involved
in each of them. So I see nothing wrong with his use of the
number three.

Whether he is an optimist or a pessimist does not seem to
me a cause for excitement. So far as the scientific aspect is
concerned, the label is irrelevant. What matters is only the

rightness or wrongness of his position. However, there is a sense in which I see nothing wrong in being a pessimist. For those of us who had great hopes in the 1930's—for example, in the labor movement as a positive force in creating a better world, or in some of the more venturesome efforts of the New Deal—but who have since been disillusioned, or for those of us who think of people as motivated by justice, but see them driven by self-interest, is it easy to be other than pessimistic? This pessimism need not affect one's understanding of reality, though it may affect one's orientation as to what is likely to happen in the world. Nor do I understand why Morgenthau's pessimism needs to be explained (or can be explained) as a result of his European origin. Clearly, there are optimists and pessimists in all nations. I think that it is enough to say that his pessimism derives from his evaluation of the world as he sees it in terms of his experience and in terms of his ideals.

Finally, I would have thought that your criticism of Morgenthau as holding to a very narrow range of political science should have been precisely the opposite. Morgenthau speaks in terms of power. He contends that the business of political science is not the state, nor is it process or policy content alone. We face instead a more important phenomenon: the fact that in the world in which we live, there are always men subject to the commands of other men. There are men at the top and men at the bottom; there is indeed a whole range of hierarchy. How did this come about? Why is it so? What, if anything, makes it legitimate? The business of the political scientist is to explore the nature of this power, the forms it takes, the ways in which men acquire it, how it is distributed, how it is used, how it may be controlled and directed.

Now, to take power in that sense is not to narrow but greatly to expand the reaches of political science. In fact, the proper criticism—if criticism there must be—is that it unduly explodes the whole area, because there is power of some sort in the economic sphere, in the religious sphere, in the schools, in the military forces, in the political system, however defined. One of the problems that Morgenthau would then have to resolve for us is where we should focus our concerns as political scientists. If it is power, is it all forms of power? Is it, for example, power in the Ecumenical Council or in the Roman Catholic hierarchy? That, I think, is where the real question and the burden of your criticism should lie, not in the allegation that Morgenthau is improperly narrowing the field. In fact, he is doing just the opposite. He is making allowance for all your interests—for structures, processes, systems, call it what you will. He is demanding recognition of the fact that power exists in the economic sphere, and not merely in the political sphere; that men are making decisions in economic life which affect our destiny; and that these decisions are frequently as important as are political decisions. This opens up the field of political science. If you are going to criticize him, do not say that he is narrowing it; it is wide open.

EULAU: How is he going to make those decisions?

SPITZ: However they are made, they must deal with these issues.

EULAU: I think that Dahl or Lindblom, who have written a very nice book on the political process, would say that decisions are not made in this way.

SPITZ: I do not know that Morgenthau said that they were made in any one way. He was talking about objectives, not how decisions are made.

EULAU: There is evidence of how decisions come about, but they do not come about in the way that Morgenthau says that they do. The budget process, for instance, is extremely complicated, and the positive identification of the power relations involved is extremely difficult. Policies are cumulative and incremental. There is much give-and-take; there are compromises, and there is frustration involved in discovering power when the flow of communication relevant to policy-making is upward. The difficulty is that the power concept, once we try to use it, does not tell us anything significant about policy-making. Some men are still trying to develop some kind of systematic theory of power, but as Jim March has discovered, there is the end of power. I am not saying that it is a concept that should be given up, for it is probably useful for everyday language. But I think that maybe there is a difference between us still. The difference is that you use power or influence in vernacular terms and we deal with these concepts in empirical or laboratory or survey research. It is extremely difficult to identify the whole set of influence relationships among various other things that affect policy outcomes. Power may be extremely dispersed and factionated, and it may be functionally distributed. The whole interpersonal setting is such that it is extremely difficult to identify something like power turnover and power relationships. Now, I think that once you bring all of these terms down to the operational level, they are just like the early concept of state sovereignty. Can we explain something by thinking in terms of power? Does the word power explain outcomes?

SPITZ: The answer, of course, would require me to articulate a whole theory concerning the nature and systems and processes and ethics of power. I cannot do that here. There is a considerable literature just on the meaning of power. People have written on the ends of power and on power as an end-in-itself. They have talked of fragmenting or consolidating power, of limiting or expanding it, of controlling it, and so on. All I think that one need argue to sustain this general line at the moment is to observe that whether one argues that men lust for power and this is the end, or that they take power as a means to other ends, one cannot avoid discussion of the fact that men must occupy certain positions in order to do certain things. *How* they get to those positions determines in part *who* gets there; *who* gets there determines in part *what* will be done. The things that you are talking about may qualify or even correct Morgenthau's or another's conception of power, but they can be incorporated within a general theory of power. I do not think that to define a power system one must point to the way things are done at this conference table. That is not the function of a political theory. A political theory is not a prescription of do's and don't's or a description of any particular setting. It is rather an attempt to set up certain broad categories within which these and other things can be subsumed, and which can thus make sense of the general situation.

I would emphasize that I am not arguing here that power should be *the* focus of political science. I am simply saying that it is inconceivable to me that a man like Morgenthau—or anyone else who deals with this power concept—is oblivious to the kinds of considerations that you have put forth here. If this is so, the obvious question must be: Why does he cling to these notions in the face of all these criticisms which have been made for so many years? If you tell me that he is an obstinate man who does not listen, I can only say, so much the worse for Morgenthau. But if he is an intelligent man, and if there are other able and intelligent people working in the field of power, and if Morgenthau and these others are aware of these criticisms, then there must be a good reason for their persistence in clinging to that concept. Yet you have been proceeding here on the assumption that Morgenthau is completely unaware of all these criticisms. I frankly do not understand you.

EULAU: The only point is, I think, the utility of a concept. A concept is useful only so long as it is useful.

SPITZ: Useful for what?

EULAU: For explaining relationships among people. Now Robert Dahl, for instance, suggested that you can apply common notions of power in the study of social relationships only as long as the concept has payoff for comparison. It seems to me that Professor Morgenthau, by way of contrast, imposes the concept on the phenomena, rather than analyzing the phenomena by the use of the concept.

CHARLESWORTH: I would like to raise a little question with you, David. You were defending Morgenthau's defense of the political scientist who speaks out and becomes unpopular?

SPITZ: This is one aspect of the political scientist, that is, there are political scientists who do this.

CHARLESWORTH: Then you were defending his defense of that?

SPITZ: Oh, yes, absolutely.

CHARLESWORTH: Well, there was a French professor who, at the close of his lecture to his students, said: "The best political science that I can teach you today is that I'm going out and vote against Napoleon III." So he went out and voted against Napoleon III, and that was the end of his professordom. Now, for every courageous man like that who makes a magnificent gesture, I wonder how many servelings we have, for example, like those who played up to the cause of the Nazis? I wonder if we encourage political scientists to conform, or do we advise them to speak out? I wonder how many critics we have, against how many of those who simply serve the current leading interest? What do you think about this?

SPITZ: Well, you would have to ask the quantifiers in our midst, but I would guess very few, because I think—if I may speak generally—most people want to be successful, which means to be accepted and approved.

CHARLESWORTH: I will accept your answer, very few.

EULAU: I never concern myself with the problem of whether the result of research is critical or conformist; let us not confuse our role of responsible citizen with our role of scientist.

HARTZ: If I may cut in, it is a poor thing to teach a student that he is not a good political scientist until he is unpopular.

SPITZ: I am sorry, but that is not what I take Morgenthau's message to be. There are things in his paper that I disagree with, and I do not want to defend Hans Morgenthau right down the line. My assumption, however, is that one should generally try to take a man at his best and try to find the real meaning in what he is saying. If he says some foolish or debatable things, one has to disagree with him. If Morgenthau were here, you could so challenge him, and he might modify some of those statements. He might have written this paper in a hurry. I do not know.

CHARLESWORTH: No, he did not write it in a hurry.

SPITZ: I certainly am not defending his every word, but he could still have written it in a hurry—even while he was in the hospital. I want to make one point about what it is that a teacher does. What he tries to do is to get the student to understand. He does not recommend that the student go out and lead a picket line, but he does want him to understand why the picket line is there. Similarly, if he wants him to understand the political process, he may have to raise questions and to tell him things that go counter to, let us say, the conventional understanding of the community of which he is a part. He frequently has to introduce facts and considerations to college students that go counter to what they learned in high school. Certainly, one of the most common experiences that I have had as a teacher, and that my colleagues have also had, is that we find ourselves compelled to disabuse our students of misconceptions that they have brought with them. Now, the job of the teacher is to teach the "truth" as well as he knows it. If you do so, you may run the risk of being a critic. This does not mean that you tell the student that *he* must be a critic; it means only that you, as a teacher, are trying to make him understand the nature of the real world.

VAN DYKE: By the same token, in doing this kind of thing you may be saying things that will produce a sounder appreciation of the system.

SPITZ: Yes, by all means.

VAN DYKE: And Morgenthau leaves that out entirely. He seems to be going on the assumption that the world is out of joint. The extreme inference is that if we were really honest and sound in our analyses of it, we would all go out and shoot ourselves.

SPITZ: But not everything is wrong. There are certain things that are wrong.

EULAU: The world is always out of joint.

VAN DYKE: Well, in some respects, yes, but it seems to me that critical analysis may lead either to a positive appreciation or to a negative judgment, depending upon circumstances.

SPITZ: That is the essential point of Mill's essay on civilization, where, in discussing creativity, he argued that the original mind is not necessarily the rebellious mind. The man who arrives at a judgment independently and autonomously may well come out in favor of an existing practice or arrangement.

WATKINS: It seems to me that we are talking about qualities of life and growing up in the world, rather than political science. The quality of growing up consists in teaching yourself unwelcome things all the time. Life is not just being a political scientist, and there is no magic in political science to give faith in the qualities needed for maturity. I suspect, and this might be worth testing, that some very great thinkers and activists have gone through the chastening experience of theory, which is disillusioning, and then have gone into orbit as humorists, poets, novelists, and the like. They grasp at another medium for the communication of truth, a medium which goes beyond the quantitative and the theoretical, combining reason with the intuitive and the emotional. I think that one of the greatest political scientists going is Herblock. He makes his points with a deft touch and a simplicity which says, in effect: "I can't do this in words; words are an imperfect means of communication. You really can't pin this one down." But he gets it down to something almost as basic as Einstein's $E = Mc^2$, by means which evoke a total response from the human being. I would like to include some of these people in the ranks of political scientists.

Spitz: There is a line somewhere in Paul Klee's writings that you might like where he defines modern art as an effort not to reveal the visible but to make visible the real. This, I think, defines Herblock's school.

Charlesworth: I should like to switch our conversation onto another track here if you would allow me to. Remember now, we are talking about objectives. Why are we political scientists? What are we doing? If we are doing something, we must have a reason for doing it. Let us take a surgeon. He practices surgery and he teaches surgery, and he teaches surgery by showing his students how he practices it. An engineer deals in books, and he also builds bridges, and he teaches his students by showing them how to do things. In the old Puritan churches, they used to have a pastor and also an instructor. Now the pastor and the instructor are combined in most churches, and we teach people by telling them what they ought to do. I wonder if we could address ourselves to the question of whether the political scientist in the United States ought merely to watch a football game, so to speak, or whether he ought to play football? Now, in the field of public administration where I happen to have a certain exposure or contact, the great majority of the people who presume to do the teaching are always talking about administration as if it were esoteric or literary or remote. Almost none of them show students of public administration how to organize a Sunday School picnic or something a little more difficult. Now, I am aware that I am on a rather low practical level here, but if you will forgive me, I would request that you put something on the record as to whether the political scientist, if he is teaching public administration, for example, should know how to organize a Sunday School picnic, and, if not, whether he should shut up about that subject (*laughter*). And if he is teaching international politics, does he know anything about the temper and mood of the little people spread around the world? Could I

persuade us to discuss that? Surely there must have been something important said at lunch time; let us get it on the record.

EULAU: Well, I do not know. I do not have any problems
in this regard. I mean, I am a person, but I play a variety of
roles. I happen to be active in the local Democratic club where
I voice my opinions and participate in policy-making and so on,
but I would never claim to participate in these things as a political scientist. I am a father, but I do not run my family the
way I would run the post office. It seems to me that if we are
asked what the objective of political science is, I would have to
say that I happen to take the word science very seriously and in
a very limited sense, in a sense of the tradition of science as
being concerned with reducing ignorance. This does not mean
that you do not start off with certain critical views of the environment in which we operate. I happen to be very interested in
metropolitan problems. For some reason, because of my scientific orientation, it had occurred to me that we ought to look at
some of the activists in this particular environment. I happen
to have picked on city councils and city councilmen, because of
their metropolitan and regional setting. What these city councilmen do or do not do, what their aspirations are, what their
attitudes are—that will, in the long run, affect the metropolitan
environment.

This does not mean that I have to commit myself toward
some idealistic utopian view of what the metropolitan environment might be. It seems to me that there is another role. You
may want the social engineer and the utopian and the scientist
to come together. But I want to be very clear about my role
in the relationship. Hopefully, I can tell them, under certain
conditions, what kind of consequences will occur. I can as a
scientist make certain assumptions about certainty or uncertainty. Economists continue in this way, and in political science we build models in which we can assume complete uncertainty, or complete certainty, or anything we can think of. We
can specify the degrees of certainty or of uncertainty with regard to conditions under which a given body of knowledge might
be used if we regard certain policy goals. But the specification
of policy goals seems to me a function which is not necessarily
that of the scientist.

CHARLESWORTH: Do you think, Heinz, that all political scientists should be scientists?

EULAU: No, I do not.

CHARLESWORTH: Cannot we have some normativeness?

EULAU: Yes, of course, but let us not call normativists scientists. You see, I think that Professor Morgenthau would claim that the particular function which he performs as a critic is that of the scientist. I think it is very interesting the way that Professor Morgenthau publishes. He seems to prefer the popular or semipopular journals. I am not aware of having read an article by Professor Morgenthau in one of the professional journals in the last ten years. Why not? Obviously, his material is not acceptable to the scientific fraternity.

VAN DYKE: As I understand it, our purpose is knowledge of the general rather than knowledge of the unique. Cardinal Newman's book on the nature of a university is one that I would recommend in this connection; it was written more than a century ago. One of his themes was that we are not after knowledge of a detailed situation, a detailed problem, a unique event. We are trying to get at general knowledge, knowledge that will be applicable to a whole category of cases. Now, I think that there is a relationship between the particular and the general, and I suppose that the person who has the general knowledge should be able to organize a school picnic. At the same time, there may be some unique circumstances connected with picnic problems that the generalist would not know about, so, really, my stress would be on development of general knowledge, and if the person who develops the general knowledge can also apply it, well that will add to my respect for him.

CHARLESWORTH: Do you think he should teach about organizing a Sunday School picnic if he has never organized one?

VAN DYKE: I hope he would not try it. He should have studied the problems of organizing Sunday School picnics if that is what the subject of his inquiry is.

CHARLESWORTH: Where does he study Sunday School picnics, in the library or out in the park?

VAN DYKE: Well, if one spends one's life getting firsthand information and collecting all the data firsthand, one may not get much done in one's life.   One has to use the experience of other people.

CHARLESWORTH: The men who wrote the books in the library—many of them have never been in the park either.

PALMER: It strikes me that you are trying to narrow this too much, or to get a clear-cut answer to something which does not admit of a clear-cut answer.   I do not see any particular value in the ability to organize a Sunday School picnic unless one has to organize a Sunday School picnic.   There are various kinds of talents; there are various kinds of contributions that one needs. In this country, above all others, I think that there is no doubt that we have been enriched by a considerable cross-fertilization between people who have done things, presumably, and those who have stood back and watched how things are done, so that this kind of dichotomy does not exist in many cases.   Now, maybe this fellow who has done things has not organized a Sunday School picnic, but has learned the techniques of organization in a more basic sense.   Even a first-class technical school is more concerned with a broader approach than with how you run a lathe in a particular factory.   A first-class university, I should think, is more concerned with some of the basic principles and concepts and approaches.   As some of my professional colleagues in Washington have pointed out, many people who are involved in decision-making studies have probably never made a political decision in their lives, but it seems to me that they still have something to contribute, as long as one takes what they have to contribute for what it is worth.

CHARLESWORTH: What are they teaching?   Are they teaching how to give advice or are they teaching how to make decisions?

PALMER: I think that they are providing some of the basic data by way of case studies or other approaches rather than——

CHARLESWORTH: You mean a McGeorge Bundy relationship to Johnson?   He tells Johnson everything that Johnson ought to know to make a decision.

VAN DYKE: But not in his capacity as political scientist.

PALMER: Exactly.   This is an example of something else I wanted to bring out: McGeorge Bundy's service, whatever it may have been, to Kennedy and Johnson was not as practitioner of the arts, but more as co-ordinator and idea man.   I recently looked at Iklé's book on *How Nations Negotiate*. Now, I do not imagine that Iklé ever got close to a decision in his life. It really does not make any difference. If this kind of exercise is useful, then I think that he has made a contribution.

CHARLESWORTH: We are nothing like engineers, clergymen, or surgeons?

PALMER: Even an engineer, for example, may have to possess broad qualifications and skills, and not just the technical qualifications to design a bridge, because he may find himself designing not a bridge but something else, getting involved in some other kind of skill.

CHARLESWORTH: But if he is supposed to teach how to build bridges, somebody has to teach him to build bridges.

PALMER: No, if he is supposed to teach how to build bridges, then he ought to know how to build bridges, surely, but I do not think that that is necessarily the greatest thing that is needed——

CHARLESWORTH: So a professor of public administration does not need to know how? Let me give you an example. During the 1930's we had a gigantic program to institute—unemployment compensation, old-age assistance, and public assistance. Now, there was a professional group who felt that they had a vested interest in this. They were the social case workers who, as you know, are trained to work on individuals, not to study mass needs to be administered on a mass basis. They get inside of you; they crawl around and look at all your innards, and they decide what you need and then prescribe. They might dislocate six other people in order to fix you up, but they do not care about that; they are individual case workers. There was a heavy battle in every jurisdiction that I know about between what we call the public-administrator people and the social-case-work people, and the case-work people lost. The law specified that one did not have to have this degree or that degree, and so on. I somewhat modestly advance the position that if we had had a core of political scientists who were trained public administrators, who knew about public administration from the standpoint of how to do it, we never would have had that battle. We would not now have the battle on these poverty fronts and the like. We would have people who know how to do things. If you will excuse me for repeating, we need people who do not stand off and watch a football game but go out and play football. Now, I know that you are going to get mad at me. I think too many political scientists are somewhat emasculated; they do not feel that a man should experience at firsthand what he is teaching. I submit that we have gone too far toward the literary, the abstract, the esoteric, and the irresponsible.

PALMER: I do not think that it follows that the fellow who is going to write and teach about football has got to be able to go out there and be an All-American center by any means. In fact, we know that even in this game some of the best students and coaches have not been of that type, but the main point——

CHARLESWORTH: Coaches?

PALMER: Yes, sir.

CHARLESWORTH: A coach who has not played football?

PALMER: There have been coaches who have had very little to do with actual playing or who have been only minor players. It is the science of the game really as much, perhaps, as anything else. But I come back to my main point—that what we need is broader skills and insights, the ability to organize as well as technical competence.

CHARLESWORTH: Now let us switch it around; let us take a fellow who teaches political parties. Should he have practical experience in a party situation or should he merely read Ostrogorski, Michels, and the rest of them and speculate about European ideas on the American scene?

VAN DYKE: The alternatives are too extreme; you should have a third one in there.

YOUNG: There are so many roles to be played in the whole political process that no one can play very many of them. We cannot all be a dictator or an African chief or a political boss, although there are roles we can play. The English have a traditional office called the Queen's remembrancer, who remembers certain types of events. In certain primitive societies, there are people whose duty it is to remember what has happened and the way things are done. Our function is similar. We keep the political tradition alive; we examine ideas of how society is governed and perpetuate them from one generation to the next. We have a creative role to play, not only in examining how government operates, but also in developing new concepts for the organization of society. As for practical experience, the point of accumulating knowledge is to try to abstract as clearly as possible the maximum knowledge with the minimum of effort so that the various experiences which one cannot have in fact will, nevertheless, be meaningful. This can be applied to the world of art, to novels, plays, operas, ballets, and the like. A political scientist, however, is not quite like a lawyer, who not only has a theoretical background of how the legal and political systems operate, but also participates in their operations, that is, he acts as a buffer between his clients and the government and between his clients and other people with whom they are involved. The political scientist does not participate in the process except at a rather higher level of abstraction in the sense that he determines what issues——

CHARLESWORTH: Do you think, Roland, that he is principally a spectator?

YOUNG: I should think so, yes. The fact is that people who can acquire power are not always those who can use it effectively. What Professor Morgenthau apparently wants is for political scientists to acquire power on the political side as opposed to the administrative side. There is certainly a good deal to be said for having practical experience, providing it adds to one's knowledge, but that is not always the case.

CHARLESWORTH: I am very unhappy about your acquiescence in this business that we are spectators.

YOUNG: Yes. I am not sure that if any of us were senators——

VOICE: Let us fall back on the third choice we have somewhere between the spectators and the actors.

YOUNG: Well, we are not only spectators; we certainly do play a part, but it is not the activist part.

VAN DYKE: There is a distinction between being a spectator and an advisor. There is another category in addition to that of spectator or advisor or participant, at least one other category: the one I have in mind is that of provider of knowledge needed for the decisions that have to be made. We can help provide the knowledge that is needed without serving explicitly as advisors and certainly without actually participating in the process. Now, I would suppose that our role as political scientists is mainly to provide the knowledge that will, hopefully, be useful to those who have to make the decisions.

YOUNG: If we could all be Bob Dahl's, that, in your sense, would be a desirable goal of a political scientist—that is, to know how the process operates and to know what will happen if one does this or that to it.

YLVISAKER: I would go after the quality of a man's mind. For example, Shakespeare had a tremendous perception into the way man governed himself and governed others. Shakespeare was probably a sideline observer, but he had the capacity to penetrate the formalities and to see the whole human being and the rich complexity of the governmental process. Those who have this capacity, whether from experience or insight, exercise great power over those who act. Where does one get this capacity? By participation? Maybe so, maybe not.

CHARLESWORTH: Well, Paul, I am sure that you would subscribe to the actuarial approach to all these problems. If you do not base your judgments on exceptions, should we not try to train our people so as to attain a majority skill, a majority objective, and not talk about geniuses or exceptions? One cannot do anything about geniuses anyhow.

YLVISAKER: Generally, I agree, and the Ford Foundation has been taking a very strong line that apprenticeships, internships, or the like should be a very vital part of political science. These internships have not really been integrated into the study of politics, because they have not really been accepted or taken seriously by the high priests of the profession.

Direct exposure, by whatever device, should be concentrated on policy-making—and on the heart of policy-making, which is man's struggle to survive his differences and to improve his condition, when all the criteria and all the objectives lie in the realm of the uncertain—which is the reason Bill Elliott, I guess, always wanted his students to wrestle with the ultimate sophistication of the Grand Inquisitor.

PALMER: There is no uncertainty there, Paul.

YLVISAKER: Well, there is. It is the Inquisitor's exploitation of uncertainty that we resent. The point that I am making is that political science finds its stuff in the realm of the uncertain and how man survives and contends with it. Now, I think that it is terribly important to expose young minds, analytical or professional or practical, to men who have to sweat through these uncertainties and resolve their differences. Maybe they resolve their doubts and their differences by circuses, bread, programs, war, a whole lot of devices, and a political scientist ought to know about all devices that mankind uses. Sometimes you can get out of it with a technical solution, an economic alternative, a political bargain, with violence or without it. But I think that it is terribly important for a young man who is going to be a political scientist to get in there, see it, feel it, live it. And I do not think that he has to come to it with any technical or managerial skill, whether it be to build bridges or to organize a Sunday School picnic, though if he has that first quality of perception, it would help to have that extra of a special skill.

CHARLESWORTH: Then he should not spend all his time in the library?

YLVISAKER: No, unless he happens to read the right books. Look at all the professions: those who are getting the highest pay, the greatest acceptance, I suppose, are those who are farthest away from the level we are talking about; they live and prosper in a cozy corner of certainty and full control where they can act in certain prescribed ways. But take the specialist—the doctor or the surgeon. Send him into Calcutta or send him into a hospital in Harlem. Certainly, he knows how to take out an appendix, but what help is his skill in facing the decision of whether he ought to let this man live or that man die? The old question is: Should we be curing more people in India, merely so they die of starvation? That is the decision that the political scientist has to make, and he does not have nearly as much prescription to offer. It is not a technique that everybody will accept and say, yes——

PALMER: A political scientist does not have to die in order to be involved in a certain situation.

YLVISAKER: Take the question of Vietnam, which is a moral problem that we are trying to solve by technical means. The irony is that the one piece of hardware that might "win" it is morally not available to the President. And consider the other half of his dilemma: he is still faced with the fact that he has all those poor people in Harlem and billions more poorer people out there in the next generation that he may have to help before he helps Harlem, and he does not have enough resources to go around. What solution is available to him? Here is where invention and ingenuity come in, where a political scientist has to be more than a historian (and certainly more than a critic). If he is purely a historian, he can go back and ascertain how they handled it in the past (and usually, I suppose, they did not handle it). But, for the future, what is man's alternative to war? Is it doing what the Japanese of the middle ages did by creating a sealed and hierarchical and static society? That is a doubtful remedy today, because people will not accept it—they can vote and they can veto. History does not offer any ready-made solutions; so a political scientist has no option but to be something of an inventor as well as an historian, forward-looking as well as learned in the past. I do not advocate encouraging our students to be so sure of their technical skills that they miss the need and lose their capacity for invention.

WATKINS: Well, Jim, I would like you to answer your own question. It seems that in terms of what you are after we have a fairly large establishment already. In the field of public administration there are rafts of schools and departments which are specifically trying to train people for the job of working in administration. Now you claim that we do not have people who know how to administer and that that is one of our problems. What has been going on in all these schools? Why have they not provided the necessary know-how? Have they been taught by people who have never organized a school picnic—or what *is* the trouble?

CHARLESWORTH: You ask what is going on in these schools? What is going on in these schools is a gigantic fraud. Now, here again I am making a damaging generalization. I admit that there are notable exceptions: there is a notable exception sitting right next to me [Sweeney]. He brings in practitioners to teach; he sends men out into the field, and when his graduates are ready they take a job starting at 9:00 on Monday morning, and at 9:00 on Monday morning they are ready to produce. They do not have to be trained any further, as is the case with the administrative class in Great Britain and many other places. I do not know whether this is correct or not (I think that it is correct), but I understand that this particular program [Fels Institute of State and Local Government] now has more city managers functioning in the United States than have come from any other single training program. We ought to have more of them.

PALMER: Since you have brought up this excellent local example, I might point out, just as an observer and not a doer in the Institute, that it seems to me that over the past several years there has been a great broadening of the curriculum and approach at the Institute, in exactly the direction that you are talking about as wrong, which has made the program more significant.

CHARLESWORTH: Well, the basic parts are unchanged—the field work and the bringing in of practitioners.

WATKINS: Do you think that all this ought to be transferred to the political science department?

CHARLESWORTH: Fred, what I have been saying is a kind of exordium to another question. Should we not separate public administration from political science and teach it in an entirely different way, in an entirely different school, with an entirely different objective? Let us take, for example, the field of economics. When Adam Smith wrote *The Wealth of Nations,* he was a professor of moral philosophy (that was slightly less than two hundred years ago). Well, we do not think of economics as moral philosophy any more. In the early part of this century, especially in the United States, economics was divided into one major part and a lot of subsidiary parts. One is what used to be called economic theory, and the other included finance, transportation, money and banking, management, industry, industrial geography, and the like. I used to have an administrative post in a graduate program that had to do with this, and we thought that this was a pretty good development. The student who wants to learn how to run a railroad does not get mixed up with the economic theorist, and both of them are trained to perform a useful but quite different service.

Now, we are aware that the economic theorist looks down his nose at the man who wants to run a railroad, but we still have to have men in the United States to run railroads. We cannot all sit around and contemplate economic theory. Indeed, many of us have been persuaded that the best economic theory comes from activists like Keynes and Heller and the rest of those who tell the government what to do, who do not just stand off and talk *about* economic policy. They are *in* economic policy, and that is how they justify their existence. I submit that the political scientists in the United States are lacking in courage and clear purpose.

SPITZ: Careful now, you are talking as a political theorist, not a political scientist. You are talking the language of at least some political theorists; you are advocating a retreat from what our behavioralists call political science.

CHARLESWORTH: Well, I do not want to advocate anything here. I am just raising questions. Do you think that it would help our total discipline if we separated public administration and all the *do* subjects from the *think* subjects?

DE GRAZIA: It depends a lot on whether you know what you want to do in public administration. I would be very much against the separation as long as public administration is essentially an antiquated army type of discipline——

CHARLESWORTH: Will you let me try to define public administration for the purposes of this discussion? In my opinion, it is the realization of legislative intent.

GUETZKOW: As long as we separate public administration—"do" contents—from political science—"think" contents—we shall be giving a rather routine kind of treatment to public administration, as is current among many who have been practicing and teaching over the decades since the two contents were prematurely separated. I do not wish to subscribe to such a public administration, and therefore I would not separate this child from the parent until it is better instructed—if ever.

DE GRAZIA: I wonder if public administration has not, to a very large extent, departed from small-group work and from the organizational theory that is being done in business groups and international development programs.

GUETZKOW: I think that we fail to make critical distinctions, especially the one between the degree of generality and particularity, and the distinction between pure and applied. I believe we can have pure theory—a "think" theory—about particulars as well as an applied science—a "do" theory—about these same particulars.   Conversely, we can have both a pure theory of subject matter at a high degree of generality *and* an applied theory at the same high degree of generality.   It is not fruitful to believe that there can be a long-enduring separation between pure theory or generalities—"*think* subjects"—and applied theory of particulars—"*do* subjects."

DE GRAZIA: I was only referring to the development of organizational theory outside of political science.   It has been my impression that more sophisticated theory along that line comes quite outside of political science's sponsorship.

VAN DYKE: I would like to mention a question that has not been mentioned here this afternoon.   I do not know whether you would be interested in discussing it or not.   I would be interested in hearing a discussion of it.   David Easton takes the view that the purpose of political science, if I understand him correctly, is to study the conditions of the persistence of the system.

EULAU: And changes.

CHARLESWORTH: You mean as a spectator?

VAN DYKE: No, not as a spectator, as an analyst, a person who tries to identify the conditions of persistence and change.

EULAU: I shall go back and pick up a few things.   You said [Charlesworth] that the economists are telling the government what to do, but we should ask: Why do the economists tell the government what to do?   Because the economists over two hundred years have developed a highly refined set of models in terms of which they can make reasonably reliable forecasts with regard to outcomes, given certain conditions, and we political scientists do not have these.

DE GRAZIA: May I suggest a more underhanded kind of explanation here?   It is that the economists are used because the government is hoodwinked; people are hoodwinked by the economists.   The believe that the economists are giving them answers, practical answers, but in many cases the proof is quite absent, just as the psychologists are called on to give advice on international tensions and the like, and they will put on their white coats and do so.

EULAU: Put two psychiatrists in a corner and they disagree, obviously.   I think that a discipline is made up of discipline;

130   A DESIGN FOR POLITICAL SCIENCE

if one had no discipline, one would have no hope. Obviously, this is why I would say that alternative models are desirable. The model which ultimately explains or gives new explanations is a reasonably reliable policy device for the time being, at least until overborne by a new model or by a new finding. I do not see anything wrong with this, because the whole task of science is to clear away ignorance.

GUETZKOW: It may well be, too, that the role of the economist since World War II in our culture has been enlarged by the prosperity of the times rather than the other way around.

EULAU: No, take the interest rates and the increased rates of the Federal Reserve System, which I assume are very unpopular. Now, these economists have reasonably allowed their calculations, on the basis of empirical evidence as well as in terms of their theoretical knowledge, to be projected into the future. Yes, we have to raise the interest rate, to prevent something from happening in the future. Now, this may become a self-fulfilling, or self-denying, prophecy in policy matters. One can never really say that something is right or wrong on the policy level from the scientific point of view.

Continuation of conference discussion on objectives (next morning)

CHARLESWORTH: Hans, we thought that since you were not here yesterday to hear the comments on your paper we would meet early this morning. In order to apprise you of our sentiments of yesterday, we have asked Norman Palmer to summarize those sentiments.

PALMER: I shall try to be as brief as possible because I know that we are eager to hear what Hans Morgenthau has to say. I would call attention to the fact that I am the only one of the commentators who had the courage to come this morning (*laughter*). We applied the adage that when the cat is away the mice will play, and it is particularly appropriate because according to Professor Morgenthau's rather rigorous definition, political scientists are all mice. As Morgenthau already knows, David Spitz proved to be a very stout champion of his approach. Spitz started out by saying that he disagreed with many points in the paper and then ended up acclaiming the positions taken, with proper comments on the lack of wisdom of the people who made certain criticisms.   I can assure you that he out-Morgenthaued Morgenthau in his eloquent presentation.

We raised a number of points with respect to the paper.   I tried to develop the optimism-pessimism theme and was chided for it.   It seemed to me that your paper reflected a characteristic European intellectual pessimism.   Some of us wanted to go over to an American optimistic view, but I was properly put in my place.   Pessimism-optimism has very little to do with what we are talking about here, and it does not necessarily follow that the approach is dictated by intellectual or cultural background.   Some of us were rather disturbed by what seemed to be lapses into authoritarianism and dogmatism.   (There are a few comments to that effect in one of the papers.)   We are a little uncertain as to what you mean by some of your more general and sweeping terms, for example, "moral commitment," "the truth of society altogether," "the perennial truths of politics," and the like.   I was intrigued, as I think some others were, with your reference to the fact that the range of rational choices seems generally to be three.   The significance of the number three is something which deserves some further explanation.

There were some who felt that your view of theory was too limited, especially as you applied it, in at least one instance, to the international field, in the light of the rather exciting prospects for the development of "new" theories as portrayed by Karl Deutsch's paper.   In fact, there were some who suggested that your whole approach was traditional.   I take it that that is a criticism, but I am not sure.   The term "antiscientist" was used in one connection, and the word "ideologue" was also referred to, although you yourself tried to cover your tracks pretty well on that one.   Many of us thought that your statement at the beginning of your paper of the purpose of political science was too limited.   One of the discussants said that certainly a purpose, among other purposes, of political science should be the reduction of ignorance, and others suggested that there were certain broader purposes and themes which should be considered, especially in the light of the thinking going on in our profession recently.

The whole question of theory and practice actually came up for its usual yes-and-no approach. Paul Ylvisaker, in particular, described himself as a social engineer. I assume that a social engineer is a practitioner who still tries to be respectable theoretically. In any event, the whole matter of the problems of applied political science with reference to some of these broad theoretical purposes and objectives came up. Paul had quite a lot to say about Robert Dahl with reference to the second round of reform effort in New Haven.

We were all somewhat concerned about this business of respectability in political science and your comment that political science ought to be an unpopular undertaking. This would suggest that an almost necessary criterion for effective political science is a lack of respectability and considerable unpopularity. Now, David pointed out that that is quite justified in the sense that, obviously, a political scientist should be, perhaps he must be, a critic and that any critic who feels impelled to say that the king has no clothes on will attract a certain amount of criticism. But we wonder whether this hair-shirt approach is not going a little too far with respect to the role and the position which our profession has. Is it not possible to think of a political scientist making some rather significant and useful contribution to a social or political system which is not that bad and which, perhaps, deserves some help in a positive way, as well as negative criticism?

Naturally, we discussed this matter of power in politics and international affairs. I thought that your approach was a very broad one, but some felt that it was rather limited. On one occasion, the remark was made that the national interest has caught up with you and that you are getting "what for" because of it: something which, I assume, takes us to a more immediate matter.

One final point was that your paper seems to suggest a profound feeling, a profound commitment, perhaps a considerable emotional disturbance with some of the problems of our time. At least one commentator suggested that this whole question of the place of emotional feelings, irrational feelings generally, with respect to political science, should have been mentioned a little more than you did. Well, these are some of the points that were brought out, and I am sure that they will provide enough basis for comment.

MORGENTHAU: Let me say first a word about the optimism-pessimism argument which is immortal but has to be slain from time to time. The two terms are completely without significance for any theoretical discussion. What does it mean to say that a man is an optimist? What does it mean to say that he is a pessimist? It means that his expectations either go beyond or fall behind what somebody else believes. If a doctor tells me that I have cancer, and I say, "Doctor, you are a pessimist," what I am saying is that my expectations go beyond his expectations, that his expectations fall behind mine. From a theoretical point of view, it is a completely irrelevant statement.

I remember very well, looking back on my life, how often I have been called a pessimist. At the beginning of 1932, when I left Germany because I thought that Hitler would come to power and it would be impossible for me to live under Hitler, my parents and everybody else said: "You are a pessimist." In 1933, after Hitler had come to power and I was out of Germany, I called my parents and advised them to get out as quickly as possible. My father said that these were the disturbances typical of any revolution, that it was only necessary to sit tight and in a few weeks all would be over, and then he said: "You are a pessimist." In 1935, I said to myself that World War II was inevitable; so I did not stay in Central Europe; I went to Spain where nothing was going to happen. I was a pessimist with regard to World War II and an optimist with regard to the Spanish Civil War, and lost everything I had in the process. I could go on and on in order to show that the juxtaposition of the two terms is completely meaningless in theoretical discourse.

The only question that counts is whether you are right or wrong. If you are right, it is irrelevant that the right proposition you propound falls behind or goes beyond the emotional expectations of your contemporaries, that, in other words, in the eyes of your contemporaries you appear as an optimist or pessimist. But I am fully aware of the fact that in spite of its obvious theoretical irrelevance, the optimism-pessimism argument will never be laid to rest, because the propensity to use it is too deeply rooted in our emotional predispositions. While I am saying this, I am aware that, on other occasions, I shall probably use the same argument, not being aware of its irrelevance. But I think that one ought, at least as a kind of introductory remark, make it clear that this kind of juxtaposition is really meaningless.

Now, let me come to the problem of political science. It is, of course, obvious that if one outlines one's position in, you might say, a dogmatic manner, one inevitably oversimplifies. Obviously, I am not expecting an organized political science in a country such as the United States to take to the hills and oppose or criticize American political society. The point that I was trying to make, in an admittedly oversimplified and, if you wish, extreme fashion, is that, throughout history, and inevitably in view of the nature of a true political science, all relevant political science has been relevant to the burning problems of the political society in which it operated—either by justifying and elaborating or improving the political status quo in a positive way or else by opposing it and then becoming the kind of unpopular political science to which I have referred.

What I was opposing implicitly, or perhaps not so implicitly, was the very strong tendency within our profession—which, again, I think, is inevitable since we have a mass profession, and not a small elite—to retreat from the burning political problems of the day into a kind of methodological or factual irrelevance. This tendency is, I think, very strong because the results are socially very attractive. On the one hand, the position is perfectly respectable, for it allows those who embrace it to engage in an activity which appears to be intellectually useful. On the other hand, the position is protected from direct contact with the so-called controversial problems of the day. This detached position, if I may say so, again in a somewhat exaggerated form, is the enemy against which I was trying to argue: this kind of intellectual playfulness, dealing with the irrelevant or extremely minute or, at best, minor problems of society—or with no problems of society at all, but with mere intellectual concepts—in order to create a wall between one's self and those problems of society which might force one to take a stand one way or the other.

Obviously, I have not come to this conclusion by reading books, but by living. Again, I am not apologetic about my cultural background, for it is obvious that I was brought up in Europe and that most of my formative experiences were there. I saw in Germany, before 1933, a great number of academics who were in their majority extremely able, intelligent, and honorable men, concentrating upon their own irrelevant but intellectually respectable specialty and turning their backs upon the burning problems of the day. I remember very vividly in 1935 when I came back to Germany for a few days and met, at the University of Munich, with a number of outstanding members of the faculty, who were all opposed to the Nazis, and with a number of church leaders. I listened to their discussions, and I was quite amazed at the parochialism of these intelligent and morally committed people. Each opposed the Nazi regime, not on general grounds but on the ground of particular infringements of their particular domain. Thus, the Protestant leaders said that they were against the Nazis because they infringed upon the freedom of the churches. The academics opposed the Nazis because they infringed upon academic freedom.

After the meeting was over, I mentioned to a world-famous scholar the experience I had had that same morning (I am still moved thinking about it) when the body of a close friend of mine had been delivered to his mother from the concentration camp of Dachau. This great scholar, who was also a great man, was obviously annoyed by what I was saying and cut me short with the remark: "I'm not dealing with politics; I'm a scholar." This is, perhaps, one of the experiences which have led me to believe that it is the moral obligation of a political science worthy of the name to be involved with, and to make an intellectual contribution to, the political problems of the day, and that, by doing this, it is bound to expose itself to the risks and liabilities of political controversy.

In a minor way, what this means has been brought home to me in recent months through my involvement in the debate on Vietnam. I became involved without any intention on my part, but by force of circumstances. I was simply saying what I thought had to be said, as I have done before on other issues without creating a stir, and all of a sudden I found myself in the eye of the storm.   This is a liability which, I think, a political scientist has to face.

Connected with this point is the problem of truth which Norman Palmer has mentioned—the truth of society.   On one side, there are the propositions which society regards to be true out of necessity—which it must consider to be true in order to maintain itself.   On the other side, there are the propositions which political science holds to be true and which may or may not be opposed to the truths of society, and which, in any event, are independent of them.   A political science thus conceived necessarily constitutes a political force, either in favor of the status quo or against it.

This is not an invention of mine, nor is it the result of special pleading in favor of a particular kind of political science. I have simply looked at the history of political thought, and I have found that those political thinkers whom we remember, and whom we regard to be great because we remember them, have all been political thinkers who were directly involved in the concrete political issues of the day.   From the prophets of the Old Testament and Plato and Aristotle to Marx and Lenin, this has always been the case.   So the innocuous political scientists, the political scientists who created a respectable methodological wall between themselves and the political problems of the day, are forgotten today exactly because they were, in their own times, irrelevant to the political problems with which men tried to come to terms, and they are irrelevant today.   We remember Hobbes and Locke, but who remembers the professors of theology or moral philosophy at Oxford and Cambridge in the seventeenth and eighteenth centuries who dealt with the problems which constitute what we today call political science?   Nobody does, because they were, as we would say today, conformists.   They were too timid, too much concerned with their standing in society and their academic respectability to deal creatively with the political problems of the day.   They were not even willing and able to deal creatively with the political problems of the status quo.   They were irrelevant then, and, for this reason, they are irrelevant now.   Thus, it is really a plea for relevancy in political science which has motivated those propositions which some of you have obviously found somewhat extreme.

The accusation of traditionalism I accept without any quali- fication, for I do not believe that the history of social thought in general and political thought in particular shows the kind of necessary and linear progression which could create an assump- tion in favor of that which is new, and to the detriment of that which is not new. I still believe that the greatest accumulation of political wisdom which the Western world, if not any civiliza- tion, has achieved is to be found in Plato and Aristotle, and that what came later has elaborated their fundamental propositions. Their successors have created some new ideas, discovered some new subject matter, and developed some new insights. But es- sentially we are all—whether or not we know it and whether or not we want it—the heirs of that great and unsurpassed accumu- lation of political insight and wisdom.

So I am a traditionalist and make no bones about it, and I think that the search for newness, for novelty for its own sake, is itself a misunderstanding of what politics and political science are all about. For the basic political issues, the very roots from which political life springs, are really inherent in human nature and therefore are immutable within the historical perspective which is open to us. We can understand, for instance, an In- dian political philosopher by the name of Kautilya who lived in the fourth century before Christ, without knowing anything about Indian political philosophy and history. One reads his most minute and intricate analysis of the balance of power and can understand it perfectly well, and one can apply the models which he developed in great profusion and with great subtlety to the present-day or any other historical configuration and find them relevant.

I do not need to run in open doors by belaboring the argument, for it is obvious to me and must be obvious to you that the issues and basic problems of political science are perennial—the problem of freedom, the problem of authority, the problem of order, and the issues arising from the acquisition, the accumulation, the limi- tation, and the control of power. These being perennial issues and problems of human existence, newness for its own sake is, in a sense, an alien element in the reflection on these perennial issues and problems. If one wanted to play with words, one could make a presumption in favor of tradition rather than in favor of novelty. In any event, it is in the very nature of the subject matter with which we are dealing that one cannot really maintain a presumption that something which is new, which has never been done before, for this very reason has an advantage over something which has been done before, which is traditional.

As far as those new approaches to politics are concerned, I should also say that I have no prejudice against them, only I am strictly from Missouri—I have to be shown. I am not at all willing to accept a methodological promise as the equivalent of the delivery of the goods. I remember that the first article that I ever wrote was on the place of methodology in the study of law. I wrote it in my early twenties when I was a law clerk. I have never been impressed with the importance of methodology. I think that the first and most important thing in any science is achievement. What does it tell us? What truth does it tell us about things we want to know something about? How it gets there, what techniques it uses, is an afterthought which is interesting, but it is by no means the essence of what we want to know. And if somebody develops a methodology and says that this is the thing that is going to save us, as it were, without applying it to the concrete issues of the day, I am simply unimpressed.

I read a great deal of the contemporary literature in this field, and I read it, I must say frankly, without being persuaded. I would like to be persuaded, and read too much of it, considering how limited our time and our energies are. But I simply cannot see that here is a new opening which shows us new vistas of political life and the possibility of the solution of political problems which have not been available to us before. Here I am not really dealing with a problem of theory, but, you may say, with a problem of intellectual perspective. If somebody can show me that he has found a way to solve a problem—by applying a new method to an old problem—I shall be convinced. If he can show me a way to predict the decision of the Hanoi government with regard to peace negotiations which is more reliable than those upon which nonmethodologically inclined scholars must rely, I shall embrace him and congratulate him. But this has not happened yet, and as long as it has not happened, I would say that the traditional methods have at least one argument in their favor, and that is tradition itself. They have been used since times immemorial, and they have given us insights and wisdom. They seem to be the best we have, and nobody has come up with something which is superior to them either in theoretical insight or in practical application.

This being the case, I find it revealing that one of my critics here has, for all practical purposes, read me out of the profession of political science altogether. But fashion is not identical with truth, and the history of the social sciences in general and political science in particular is replete with fashions which have been discarded and forgotten because, after their original impetus was spent, it became obvious that they had nothing to contribute to the discovery of relevant truth. This critic makes a point of not having read an article of mine in one of the professional journals during the past ten years, the implication being that there have been no articles to read. I must accept the statement of fact, but the record invalidates the implication. To mention only American journals: from 1956 through 1965, I have published three articles in the *American Political Science Review,* three in *The Annals* of the American Academy of Political and Social Science, and one each in the *China Quarterly,* the *Columbia Law Review, International Organization,* and *Problems of Communism.* Thus, empiricism, too, appears to have its limitations.

The same limitation of empiricism is obvious in another critic's statement to the effect that I find myself "so much in the margin of the discipline." Yet in the "Ranking of Great Men," derived from a questionnaire distributed to members of the profession (Albert Somit and Joseph Tanenhaus, *American Political Science* [New York: Atherton Press, 1964], p. 66) I rank third while one of my critics ranks seventeenth, and the other does not rank at all. "Some margin," Winston Churchill would have said.

CHARLESWORTH: Would you like to comment?

PALMER: I notice that you said in your comments that the basic problems in political science are perennial, whereas in your paper you talked about the perennial truths of political science.

It seems to me that there is a vast difference between problems and truth, certainly in time.

MORGENTHAU: In other words, while you might admit that problems are perennial, you are raising the question as to whether the truth is perennial. I would say that the truth is perennial insofar as you have only a limited number of possible solutions, let me say, to the problem of freedom and authority. When we take the different types of governments which Aristotle developed, we have here, one might say, a perennial truth. It is, of course, true that there are other types of government which Aristotle overlooked. It has been said, and I have said myself, that modern totalitarianism is a new form of government. But if one looks at it closely, one realizes that totalitarianism is a combination of forms of government which were known to Aristotle and that what is new is really the availability of modern technology for the purpose of exercising political power.

So I would say that there are truths in politics which are eternal, which are perennial in a very general way and which have to be applied to each individual historical situation and have to be filtered through the concrete character of the situation. In other words, the truths of politics are not essentially different from the truths of morality. Here you have, too, a number of basic postulates, such as justice, equality, and the sanctity of human life, but those perennial postulates have to be filtered through the concrete circumstances of each historical period, and this is what we call prudence. They receive concrete content through their contact with the concrete historical circumstances of the day. This is really also the task of political science: to rediscover the perennial truths of politics and to apply them in a theoretically valid fashion to the concrete issues of the day. This is probably as good a definition of political science as one can find.

CHARLESWORTH: Also in your paper you say, essentially, that a respectable political science is a contradiction in terms.

MORGENTHAU: Let me say right away that this is an over-statement. If you put me on the witness stand and let me take a holy oath, I would surround the statement with qualifications. Political science, in order to be true to its calling, must always run the risk of lacking in respectability and under the condition of political conflict is bound to be lacking in it.

CHARLESWORTH: I was rather intrigued by this statement. I was wondering if you would take a position on this. Does that mean that scientists and scholars everywhere all the time are essentially victims of their ecology or does it mean that a scholar is a person who is lacking in virility?

MORGENTHAU: I would admit that scholars of the latter type exist, but this is not a definition. The former statement is certainly correct. We are all in different ways children of history and society. Nobody can transcend the place on which he stands in history and in society.

VAN DYKE: May I inject a question here? As you well know, many people make a distinction between truths on matters of fact and truths on matters of value. Do you make this distinction? What significance do you attach to it?

MORGENTHAU: I think that this is one of the curses which a misunderstood Max Weber has inflicted upon us. The distinction between facts and values in the social sciences is, I think, extremely tenuous. Every fact in the social sciences which has any relevance is permeated with value; otherwise we would not have chosen it. The very perception of something as a relevant social fact presupposes a value-determined choice among a multitude of facts from which one chooses certain facts which are, for some reason, interesting to one, that is to say, which have a positive or negative value, as the case may be. The problem with which Max Weber dealt was not this problem of values or facts objectively considered, but rather the attitudes which the individual scholar takes toward society in either dealing with it in an explanatory fashion or dealing with it in a value-oriented fashion. But I think that even this distinction is very difficult to maintain, so I really do not accept the distinction.

VAN DYKE: The point would be that one's social environment influences one's decision about which facts to give importance to, which facts to notice.

MORGENTHAU: This is correct. This is what we all do.

SPITZ: It is not simply the social environment. It is the individual's judgment as well.

MORGENTHAU: His judgment as to what is or is not important. Let us look at the problems which interest us now—let me say, the conditions of the poor. In times past, the conditions of the poor were not interesting intellectually because their condition was traced to their natural environment which everybody took for granted to be immutable. Thus, it is a value judgment which has brought about this radical change in our intellectual perspective, in what we see as being important to society and, secondly, in our reformatory, our practical purposes, with regard to those facts which, all of a sudden, we have recognized to be intellectually relevant.

GUETZKOW: I should like to change the topic. You mentioned that one of the important differences in contemporary times versus older times is in terms of technology and how it has influenced political processes. Do you think that it has influenced them in any important way, or are these just like the effects of the speed of communication, as, for example, now we do not have a plenipotentiary, but we have a cable to the office?

MORGENTHAU: It has influenced them in a qualitative way.

GUETZKOW: You really feel so? Give us some examples.

MORGENTHAU: Look at the relations between government and people within a political society and the drastic shift of power which has occurred in favor of the government. It is not by accident that the rise of totalitarian government is coincident with the development of modern technology, because without modern technology, without the ability to control the flow of communications and transportation and without a near-monopoly of the most potent weapons of warfare in the hands of the government, totalitarian government could not establish and maintain its rule. It is not by accident either that in the technologically advanced societies, there are no longer popular revolutions; instead there are *coup d'états*.

DEUTSCH: Was this the case in the revolution in Budapest?

MORGENTHAU: The revolution in Budapest lasted two days, and it did not succeed. Certainly, there could be a revolution in the United States. You and I could take whatever weapons were handy and start shooting. But it would not last very long. In other words, a popular revolution is impossible in a modern state which is in full possession of modern technology. Look at the problem of race relations in this country.   A hundred years ago, it could lead to a civil war, because there existed an approximate equality, in terms of the technology relevant to a civil war, between a segment of the people and the government. Today, the superiority of the government is so enormous that the possibility of civil war is eliminated at the outset.   For this reason, the so-called Fascist revolutions were not revolutions; but, if they were a break with the constitutional continuity at all, they were *coup d'états,* because the controllers of modern technology seized the government and used that technology for the purpose of exercising governmental power.   For this reason, even in the technologically backward nations, when there is a so-called revolution the first thing that the revolutionists do is to try to control the airport and the radio station, because these are the sources of political power—modern political power. The qualitative influence which modern technology exerts upon the distribution of political power within a state is enormous, and I do not need to refer to international relations where it is, of course, obvious.

PALMER: I can understand the point, especially the responsibility of the political scientists who focus on the perennial problems of the day and perhaps even attempt to be of some assistance in solutions; but, in some ways, is this not too limited an approach?   In the physical and natural sciences, a great deal of research is not immediately applicable; in fact, some of the more significant in the long run may be the most abstract at the time.   I was thinking of this when I read the account of the speech which Walter Millis gave yesterday at the American Historical Association.   He said, as quoted in the *New York Times,* that "if a policy-maker read every title listed in the bibliography on peace research in history, I doubt that he would be much better equipped than he now is to arrive at the heart of immediate decisions that he must make."   I, of course, would be willing to accept that as probably valid, but does that mean that all the peace research is completely useless?

MORGENTHAU: I am trying to catch the relevance of your point derived from Mr. Millis' point.

PALMER: What is the value of background research in seeking solutions?

Morgenthau: I think that the point that Mr. Millis has made is perfectly obvious; it is obvious to scholars like ourselves. We cannot read everything that is published in our field. The policy-maker cannot read everything that is relevant in his field. I really do not see what your point is.

Palmer: Suppose he could?

Morgenthau: Well, if he could, he would learn something. He certainly would. This morning I thought about the importance of diplomatic negotiations, especially about negotiations with regard to Vietnam. While our government is sincere in the profession of its willingness to negotiate, it misunderstands the problem. Of course, everybody wants to negotiate provided his terms have a chance to succeed. So it is not a question of the willingness to negotiate in the abstract, but of the concrete issues of negotiations. I was thinking of what I had written in *Politics Among Nations* about the conditions of negotiation, a statement which is directly applicable to this concrete case, and I thought that if Mr. Johnson were to read those two pages, he might learn something. If a policy-maker could learn nothing from the contributions that scholars have made to the problem with which he is dealing, such failure would shed a rather dim light upon the value of scholarly enterprises for the solution of political problems.

Guetzkow: Earlier you mentioned that the immutable nature of human nature has important implications as to why the problems of politics are perennial problems and the truths of politics are perennial truths. What kind of impact do you expect that the psychopharmacological advances that are being made now and the genetic advances that will be made in the next fifty years or so will have then in terms of this changing human nature? I do not know if you would be willing to say that this will, therefore, have terribly important implications for us as political scientists.

Morgenthau: This might be the case, but again we are speculating. This has not happened yet, and nobody knows whether or not it will happen and, if so, in what form it will happen. It has already been proven in psychiatry that one can change the behavior of people through the application of drugs. But this does not mean that one can change their nature, that is, their basic aspirations and the social configurations to which the conjunction of those aspirations in different individuals leads. They remain what they have always been. One may change the modalities through which human nature reveals itself; one may limit the violence toward which it inclines; one may increase or decrease certain social tendencies to which it gives rise. But no drug is likely to extirpate the basic aspirations of human nature, such as the desire to be loved, the desire to have power, and the aspiration to immortality. At least, there is no indication that it has or that it will.

DEUTSCH: Thirty-five years ago, economics was much less well developed than it is today. Nevertheless, a thousand American economists thought that they knew enough about economics to write and to sign the declaration to President Hoover on the Smoot-Hawley Tariff, saying that it would, on the whole, make things worse and not better. The American general public has become used to the idea that, though the economists have been by no means infallible and though government officials at times may have confidential information about commodity movements that ordinary people do not have, on the whole, the opinions of economists are worth listening to. The economists have the civic duty to make known their views, when they have views, on matters of public policy. But, of course, the government can always find an economist who will say that a decision of the treasury is a wise thing and another economist who says that he thinks the treasury is making a mistake. They have every right and every duty to say so publicly even if there is the possibility of undermining public confidence. Their warnings may have an effect on the stock market, or they may give aid and comfort to communism.

Nonetheless, we have come to the accepted proposition that the professional judgment of the economist, though fallible, and though sometimes divided, is, on the whole, doing more good for the American community than harm and that economists should speak freely and should be defended in their rights. Would it be good if we said political scientists are probably as fallible as economists were thirty years ago? We have some experience and have made some studies, so we should come out either defending or criticizing what the government does, and have something to debate at least. In this sense, we ought to take a stand on the side of what Hans Morgenthau has put before us on the question of relevance. I would go beyond immediate relevance, however. Just as in economics a technical paper could be written on some mathematical problem which has no immediate policy relevance—you could say that of many of the technical works in economics or in political science—so a seemingly very abstract paper in politics may resemble a seemingly useless little experimental gadget in the laboratory. Faraday, when asked by a statesman what was the use of the dynamo, said, "You may tax it yet." So, eventually, I do think that we will end by defending the right of the political scientist to do research on topics which have no immediate policy relevance.

CHARLESWORTH: Einstein, you know, was asked why it was more difficult to make an agreement not to use the atomic bomb than it was to make the bomb itself. He said: "The answer is simple—politics is more difficult than physics." Do you think that politics is more difficult than economics?

DEUTSCH: Somewhat, but the difficulties are not likely to be overcome by shrinking from them.

MORGENTHAU: Jim has a very good point. Wealth is much easier to analyze quantitatively than power.

CHARLESWORTH: Yes, politics is infinitely more difficult.

MORGENTHAU: I am reminded of what William Graham Sumner said about sixty years ago. He said that the amount of superstition in the world has remained constant, only it has moved from religion to politics. This is a profoundly true statement. As long as the emotional commitments of contemporary men continue to attach themselves to politics, it will remain enormously difficult for this reason alone to make dispassionate scientific analysis prevail in political decisions—again, look at Vietnam, at least from where I sit.

DEUTSCH: Thirty years ago, the emotional commitments were made to balanced budgets.

MORGENTHAU: I know—even less than that. I remember periods in the 1950's when this was gospel. What was the President's name?

DEUTSCH: I was very much impressed with the comment of Fred Watkins on economics. In about one sentence Watkins has pinpointed what economists are studying—the allocation of scarce resources. I would be glad to think that one effective scholar has been studying for a long time the allocation of scarce resources for influence. There are scarce, limited capacities to persuade and to enforce the guidance of human habits of voluntary compliance and human habits of co-operation. Any government has limited resources in the society—limited resources for persuasion and limited resources for enforcement. This is influence or power, and politics deals with the allocation of these limited resources for persuading people or for pushing them around. It is perfectly true that it is hard to measure these things quantitatively, but economics truly deals not only with the quantifiable unit of money but with a very subtle problem: Are people willing to work? Are people willing to work hard, or are they lazy? Are they secure?

MORGENTHAU: But in particular it deals with the problem of how human beings react in terms of other values, let me say power, to certain economic phenomena. And while economics deals only with one particular phase of it, politics deals with all of it, and this makes politics much more difficult. For instance, take the current issue of raising or not raising the interest rate. In a sense, this is a political problem because it deals with the reactions—one might almost say the emotional reactions—of people to this problem in terms of the sum total of their social values. So the very examples that you have given show that what is true in economics to a certain extent is true in politics to an infinitely greater extent, because politics deals professionally with those irrational or not quantifiable aspects with which economics deals only marginally. As you know, in economics a great deal is quantitative and mathematical and can therefore be figured out with precision, but in politics there is very little that can be quantified.

CHARLESWORTH: Hans, do you think that the modern breed of econometricians are taking economics out of the social sciences?

MORGENTHAU: Certainly, if they think that there is nothing more to economics than that—that, in other words, econometrics is the core of economics. I think that we are dealing here with the same kind of intellectual exercise to which I referred before when I talked about political science. I have made the point somewhere in my writings that there exists a parallelism between this kind of abstractionism in economics and abstractionism in political science. I even made the point that there is a relationship between abstract art and abstract political science. Perhaps it is because they are equally incomprehensible to me.

CHARLESWORTH: When we measure two test tubes in the laboratory, it is pretty easy to say that one has $3\frac{1}{2}$ cc. and the other has $3\frac{1}{4}$ cc., but if I say to you that this man is stronger than that girl is pretty, that is the difficult kind of comparison one gets in a political world. Does it ever occur to you to despair of ever making a science out of this whole business?

MORGENTHAU: I think that you are falling into the same error that I have been falling into: you overstate your case. As far as the strong man and the pretty girl are concerned, I have no problem. The issue does not arise for me!

CHARLESWORTH: I mean that in matters political we have to compare things that are not comparable—the hardness with the wetness, with the bigness——

MORGENTHAU: If one wants to make it into an exact science, one has to despair, but if one wants to illuminate the political scene with theoretical insights, I do not believe that one needs to despair.

Recent Trends in Research Methods in
Political Science

By Karl W. Deutsch

IN the field of political science, the last decade, and particularly the last five years, have been marked by a large increase in the resources for political research that have become available. There has been an increase in the range, diversity, and effectiveness of empirical methods of investigation; an increase in the amounts, variety, and accuracy of quantitative data; and an increase in the breadth, versatility, and power of the available mathematical and statistical methods of data analysis and interpretation. All these resources have been further enhanced by the greater availability of electronic computing equipment and of IBM-type equipment for tabulations.

Together, these various new resources have permitted a new kind of theory about politics. The classic theories of politics— from Plato and Machiavelli to Marx and Pareto—had involved at bottom deterministic models which stressed one or a very few variables as supposed "causes." Each of these theories then relegated most of the other conditions surrounding the outcome into a large and ill-defined residual category of other factors. These other factors were treated as too numerous and complex to be dealt with explicitly by the theory, but also as too important to be completely disregarded. Accordingly, they were left to be summed up more or less vaguely by the intuition or judgment of each analyst. In the theory of international politics, comparable simplifications were employed. Nation-states in a balance-of-power process were treated as single actors comparable to the planetary "point masses" and hard billiard-ball-like corpuscles of Newtonian astronomy and physics. The simplicity of the basic models of all such theories and the paucity of major variables explicitly dealt with was thus matched by the diffuse multiplicity of minor factors and the insightful unreliability of the resulting interpretations and predictions.

The new theoretical approaches to politics permitted to dissolve each of these hard oversimplified entities of "nations," "classes," or "leaders" into a much larger array of components and subsystems within it.   At the same time, they replaced a very few deterministic "causes" or "forces" by a much larger number of relevant conditions or significant variables.   All of these were held to interact in a probabilistic manner, which could be analyzed statistically, by such methods as correlation analysis, so as to permit the calculation of the average contribution of each such condition or variable to the distribution of outcomes.[1]

Causality was thus replaced by probability, and the search for single causes and for master keys to prediction or control gave way to multivariate analysis.[2]

This change in approach had occurred in the natural sciences and their applications before it came in the social sciences.   About the time of World War II, the most probable trajectory of the shell from a heavy naval gun was computed at the Massachusetts Institute of Technology by computer procedures which took into account numerous conditions for each shot, including the elevation and aiming of the gun; the powder charge; wind strength and direction; the course, pitching, and rolling of the ship; and the rotation speed of the earth's surface at the particular latitude. Each of these conditions could be thought of in deterministic terms as a "cause," but the outcome of their interplay was viewed probabilistically.   Some of these conditions obviously had greater influence on the distribution of outcomes—here the scatter of shots around the target—than had others, but each factor produced a sufficient improvement in the prediction so as to be worth taking into account.

In the social sciences, an analysis of this type might show that

[1] On the significance of this change, see Seymour Martin Lipset, *Political Man* (London: Mercury Books, 1963), pp. 72–75; on the significance of the shift to probabilistic models, see Karl W. Deutsch, *The Nerves of Government* (New York: Free Press, 1963); Harold and Margaret Sprout, *The Ecological Perspective on Human Affairs with Special Reference to International Politics* (Princeton, N. J.: Princeton University Press, 1965).

[2] For extended discussions of techniques, see Paul F. Lazarsfeld and Morris Rosenberg (eds.), *The Language of Social Research* (New York: Free Press of Glencoe, 1955), esp. pp. 206–283.   For a knowledgeable discussion of some of the difficulties of the older viewpoints, cf. Robert M. McIver, *Social Causation* (Boston–New York: Ginn, 1942).

the strongest condition making for more isolationist behavior by the voters of a congressional district and by the congressman representing it was the habitual Republicanism of the constituency. A weaker but still significant factor might be the rural—as opposed to urban—character of the district. A possible third and fourth constituency characteristic favoring isolationist behavior might be the percentage of voters of German or Irish stock and the distance of the district from the sea, but these last two conditions turned out to matter very little, if at all. Each condition thus contributed something to the outcome—the frequency of isolationist behavior—but none determined all of it, and where several or all of these favorable conditions coincided, the frequency of this outcome was much higher.[3]

What has just been recounted is merely one example of what is now a standard technique of multivariate analysis in political research. Yet, as has been suggested, this is more than change in technique. It is a change in basic viewpoint, replacing single overriding "causes," simple "ideal types," and implicit and irretraceable "judgments" by increasingly explicit images of complex processes, with many quantitatively measurable variables, each making its measurable contribution to the probability distribution of outcomes.

This joint change in basic outlook and method, however, could not have occurred without a large increase in the pool of available specific techniques of research and analysis, the pool of available data, and the pool of skilled personnel in political science and in the social sciences, and a substantial increase in the budgets required for research. As in other fields in the natural and social sciences, ranging from biology and meteorology to psychology and economics, the capitalization ratio of political science has been increasing, that is, there has been a substantial rise in the amount of capital, equipment, resources, and clerical and technical support required to give full effectiveness to the average professional scholar or social scientist in this field. Even so, political science will continue to need the labor of lonely men, thinking and writing at their desks, just as physics will continue to need the work

[3] Leroy N. Rieselbach, *The Roots of Isolationist Behavior: Congressional Voting and Presidential Leadership in Foreign Policy* (Indianapolis: Bobbs-Merrill, to be published in 1967); and "The Basis of Isolationist Behavior," *Public Opinion Quarterly*, 34 (Winter 1960), pp. 645–657.

of individual thinkers of the kind of Albert Einstein. For a substantial proportion of political scientists, particularly of the younger generation, the age of the hand-loom weavers is ending, but in all age groups the need for individual discoverers, creators, and designers will remain.

THE CONTRIBUTION OF NEW DATA

New data are becoming available on a rapidly increasing scale, and the availability of data categories particularly relevant to political science could be increased further by special efforts. Nine broad kinds of such data have been developed in recent years by political scientists who have made them more available, more comparable and accurate, or more meaningful in the context of more advanced interpretation.

The first of these are elite data, including data on elite positions, incumbents, recruitment, and attitudes. The gathering and interpretation of such elite data has been developed in recent years, at the national and international level by Harold Lasswell and his associates, and at the level of community elites by a number of investigators ranging from Floyd Hunter to Robert A. Dahl.[4]

The second category includes data on mass opinion, gathered in over forty countries by sample surveys of the general Gallup- or Roper-poll type, many of which are now stored at the Roper Center of Opinion Research at Williamstown, Massachusetts. It also includes less voluminous but still extensive data developed to further refinement by the techniques of such organizations as the University of Michigan Survey, directed by Angus Campbell, Philip Converse, Warren Miller, and Donald Stokes, or in the survey of Negro voting and registration in the South by James W. Prothro and his associates at the University of North Caro-

[4] Cf. Harold D. Lasswell, Daniel Lerner and C. E. Rothwell, *The Comparative Study of Elites* (Stanford, Calif.: Stanford University Press, 1952); H. D. Lasswell and Daniel Lerner, *World Revolutionary Elites* (Cambridge, Mass.: M.I.T. Press, 1965); Robert North, *Kuomintang and Chinese Communist Elites* (Stanford, Calif.: Stanford University Press, 1951); Suzanne Keller, *Beyond the Ruling Class: Strategic Elites in Modern Society* (New York: Random House, 1963); Donald Matthews, *The Background of Political Decision Makers* (New York: Doubleday–Random House, 1954); *U. S. Senators and Their World* (Chapel Hill: University of North Carolina Press, 1960); Karl W. Deutsch and Lewis J. Edinger, *Germany Rejoins the Powers* (Stanford, Calif.: Stanford University Press, 1959).

lina.[5]   Related data on political attitudes at the mass opinion
level have been developed through extended depth interviews of
smaller samples of voters by Robert E. Lane,[6] and through repeated panel-interview methods by Paul F. Lazarsfeld and his
associates.[7]

The third and fourth categories of data are formed by voting
statistics, similar to those gathered for the United States by
Richard M. Scammon, and by legislative voting data, such as
those analyzed for the United States Congress by David Truman.[8]
The fifth category are data from content analysis, developed early
for political science by such scholars as Harold Lasswell and Ithiel
Pool, and more recently by Richard L. Merritt, and adapted to
powerful semiautomatic computer methods by Philip Stone, Robert North, Zvi Namenwirth, and others.[9]

The sixth category consists in aggregative data, such as social,
economic, or demographic statistics, census data, and the like,
which are gathered by governments or private organizations for
operational purposes of their own, but from which one can learn
by suitable and critical analysis a great deal about the social

[5] Angus Campbell, Philip E. Converse, Warren E. Miller, and Donald E.
Stokes, *The American Voter* (New York: John Wiley & Sons, 1960); Ralph
L. Bisco, "Social Science Data Archives: A Review of Developments," *Amer-
ican Political Science Review*, 60: 1 (March 1966), pp. 93–109; and the
special section "Data in Comparative Research," *International Social Science
Journal*, 16:1 (1964).

[6] Robert E. Lane, *Political Ideology: Why the American Common Man
Believes What He Does* (New York: Free Press of Glencoe, 1962); see also
Political Life: Why People Get Involved in Politics (Glencoe, Ill.: Free Press,
1959).

[7] See the articles on "Panel Analysis," in Paul F. Lazarsfeld and Morris
Rosenberg (eds.), *The Language of Social Research* (New York: Free Press
of Glencoe, 1955, 1962), pp. 231–259.

[8] David Truman, *The Congressional Party* (New York: John Wiley &
Sons, 1959); Richard M. Scammon (ed.), *America at the Polls: A Hand-
book of Presidential Election Statistics* (Pittsburgh: University of Pittsburgh
Press, 1965) and *America Votes*, Vol. 1 *et seq.* (New York: The Macmillan
Company, 1966).

[9] Philip J. Stone, Robert F. Bales, J. Zvi Namenwirth, and Daniel M.
Ogilvie, "The General Inquirer: A Computer System for Content Analysis
and Retrieval Based on the Sentence as a Unit of Information," *Behavioral
Science*, 7 (1962), pp. 484–494; Dexter C. Dunphy, Philip J. Stone, and
Marshall S. Smith, "The General Inquirer: Further Developments in a Com-
puter System for Content Analysis of Verbal Data in the Social Sciences,"
Behavioral Science, 10 (October 1965), pp. 468–480.

structure and process of a country, and particularly about their rates of change in different periods and conditions. Such aggregative data have been gathered in the *United Nations Compendium of Social Statistics* (1963), the *Cross-Polity Survey* by Arthur S. Banks and Robert Textor, and the *World Handbook of Political and Social Indicators* by Bruce M. Russett and his associates.[10] Major issues arising in the use of such data are discussed critically in the volume *Comparing Nations,* edited by Richard Merritt and Stein Rokkan.[11]

Closely related to aggregative data are the historical data which form the seventh category. Many of these are aggregative data for earlier periods, permitting the construction of time series and their study for possible trends, cycles, or secular changes. A handbook of such historical trend data for recent decades is in preparation at the Yale Political Data Program. Other historical data consist in lists of historical events, such as the list of the number and duration of wars and the number of fatalities in each compiled by Lewis F. Richardson, Quincy Wright and J. David Singer or the lists of deaths from domestic political violence, in the 1950's compiled by Rudolph Rummel and by Raymond Tanter.[12] The preparation of carefully checked, consolidated, and revised lists of such historical data, as in the lists by David Singer and his collaborators, greatly enhances their usefulness for political analysis.

An eighth source of data are the other social and behavioral sciences, which are yielding increasing amounts of knowledge about the conditions and effects of communication and communication overload; the formation of images, attitudes, and motiva-

[10] Arthur S. Banks and Robert Textor, *A Cross-Polity Survey* (Cambridge, Mass.: M.I.T. Press, 1963); Bruce M. Russett, Hayward R. Alker, Jr., Karl W. Deutsch and Harold D. Lasswell, *World Handbook of Political and Social Indicators* (New Haven: Yale University Press, 1964).

[11] Richard L. Merritt and Stein Rokkan (eds.), *Comparing Nations: The Use of Quantitative Data in Cross-National Research* (New Haven: Yale University Press, 1965); cf. also Raymond A. Bauer (ed.), *Social Indicators* (Cambridge, Mass.: M.I.T. Press, 1966).

[12] Rudolph Rummel, "Testing Some Possible Predictors of Conflict Behavior within and between Nations," Peace Research Society (International), *Papers,* Vol. 1, Philadelphia, 1964 (Chicago Conference, 1963), pp. 79–111; David Singer and Melvin Small, "The Composition and Status-Ordering of the International Systems: 1815–1940," *World Politics,* 18: 2 (January 1966), pp. 236–282.

tions; the behavior of small groups; the patterns of decision-making in organizations; the changes in social roles, mobility, and structure; the interplay of child-rearing patterns, personality, and culture; and, generally, a large array of data about human behavior, gathered from skillful observation or sometimes even from controlled experiment. The broad survey by Bernard Berelson and Gary A. Steiner, *Human Behavior*, contains much information significant for political science, and so do the studies on *Communication and Persuasion* initiated by Carl Hovland, Irving Janis, and H. A. Kelley and the studies on communication overload by James G. Miller and his associates.[13]

The ninth and last group of new data is in part derived from the preceding eight. It includes the new analytic, mathematical, and statistical routines and computer programs that are now being developed for use in political and social science, and it also includes the new secondary data, such as ratios, rank-order profiles, statistical distributions, correlations, and the like, which have been computed with the aid of these methods.[14] Such secondary data also include series of processed or "cleaned-up" data, derived from raw data but categorized according to relevant discriminative variables, with gaps in the data filled in, and with known biases or errors adjusted so as to make the residual error as nearly random—or even normally distributed—as possible. Such "data-making" is itself an essential step in the conversion of raw data to analytic usefulness, and its results are usually worth storing and retrieving for later analyses.[15]

It is difficult to estimate the total volume of existing political science data from these nine sources and the volume of new data that is being added each year, but a rough guess may be at-

[13] Raymond Tanter, "Dimension of Conflict Behavior within Nations, 1955–1960: Turmoil and Internal War," Peace Research Society, *Papers*, Vol. 3, Philadelphia, 1965 (Chicago Conference, 1964), pp. 159–184; James G. Miller, in D. McKenzie Rioch & E. A. Weinstein (eds.), *Disorders of Communication*, Research Publications, Association for Research into Nervous and Mental Disorders, 1964, pp. 42, 87–100.

[14] Cf. some of the points raised in K. W. Deutsch, "Theoretical Bases for Data Programs," in Merritt and Rokkan (eds.), *Comparing Nations, op. cit.*, pp. 27–55.

[15] Cf. J. David Singer, "Data-Making in International Relations," *Behavioral Science*, 10: 1 (January 1965), pp. 68–80; see also Raoul Naroll, *Data Quality Control: A New Research Technique* (New York: Free Press, 1962).

tempted.[16]   The largest single source by now are probably the opinion polls from many countries.   About ten million standard IBM cards, or their information-carrying equivalents on tape or film, may be in existence, with perhaps 0.5 million being added each year.   The second largest source are voting statistics the world over, which may amount to about five million IBM cards or card equivalents, with another 0.5 million accruing annually. The third largest category is much smaller: present stocks of quantitative historical data, other than the relatively recent poll and voting data already included in categories one and two,

TABLE 1—EXPECTABLE INFORMATION REQUIREMENTS OF POLITICAL SCIENCE
(IN MILLION CARDS OR EQUIVALENTS)*

Activity	Data Stock			Annual Additions	
	1965	1970	1975	1965	1975
1 Elite Data	0.1	1.0	3.0	0.2	0.4
2 Mass Opinion	10.0	12.5	15.0	0.5	1.0
3 Voting Statistics	5.0	7.5	10.0	0.5	0.5
4 Legislative Voting Data	0.05	0.2	0.8	0.05	0.05
5 Content Analysis	0.1	0.6	1.6	0.05	0.2
6 Aggregative Data	0.1	2.5	7.5	0.5	1.0
7 Other Social Sciences	0.15	0.4	0.9	0.05	0.1
8 Mathematical Routines & Secondary Data	—	2.5	7.5	0.5	1.0
9 Historical Data	0.7	2.1	4.1	0.4	0.8
Total	16.20	29.3	50.4	2.65	5.05

* All these figures merely illustrate orders of magnitude. Some of them may well be subject to an error margin of up to 50 per cent.

amount to no more than 0.7 million, with perhaps as many as 0.4 million card-equivalents of new historical data becoming available each year.   The remaining six categories of data are much smaller at present, amounting to perhaps no more than 0.5 million cards in existence, but growing fast enough to contribute the equivalent of 1.25 million new cards each year.   A more detailed presentation, with a tentative projection to 1975—with a stock of fifty million card-equivalents existing by that time, and a total annual growth rate of perhaps as much as five million—is presented in Table 1.

The cost of storing and processing these political science data

[16] K. W. Deutsch, "The Information Needs of Political Science," International Federation for Documentation (FID), *Proceedings of the 1965 Congress on Documentation* (Washington, D. C.–London: Spartan Books–Macmillan and Company, 1966), pp. 199–203.   The figures given here are from a revised version of this paper which will be published in due course.

for easy retrieval and secondary analysis, by means of an inter-connected network of data repositories and centers for data proc-essing and analysis might run to about one million dollars at the 1965 level of such data, rising to perhaps as much as an annual cost of five million dollars by 1975.

A more extended discussion of the data needs of political sci-ence will be published elsewhere.[17]   Here it may be more useful to deal with the question: How are the data from all these vari-ous sources to be co-ordinated to best effect?

THE CO-ORDINATION OF DATA FROM DIFFERENT SOURCES AND TECHNIQUES

The diversity itself of the new data and techniques of repro-ducible—and hence verifiable—empirical research is creating a major research method through the mutual confrontation of dif-ferent data and research results.   In dealing with a major po-litical science problem, it is becoming increasingly possible to plan at one and the same time for several convergent research attacks. Has European integration—and particularly integration between France and Germany—increased, decreased, or remained substan-tially at the same level from 1955 to 1965?   To answer this question, a recent study sought evidence from aggregative data of the results of actual behavior in trade, travel, mail, and stu-dent exchanges, together with data from the content analysis of elite newspapers and a broader range of periodicals, results of a large number of mass opinion polls, and a special survey of French and German elite opinion, gathered through extended in-terviews.[18]

In a case study of this type, these diverse data are then con-fronted with one another, in their bearing on the problems under study; the results of these confrontations are then evaluated criti-cally by the investigators in the light of their general historical and descriptive knowledge—so to speak, their "clinical" experi-ence—of these particular problems and of problems related or similar to it; and these confrontations and evaluations then serve as the basis for the investigators' judgment.

[17] *Ibid*, p. 203.

[18] See K. W. Deutsch, L. J. Edinger, R. C. Macridis, and R. L. Merritt, *France, Germany, and the Western Alliance* (New York: Scribner's, 1967); and K. W. Deutsch, *Arms Control and the Atlantic Alliance: Europe Faces Coming Policy Decisions* (New York: John Wiley & Sons, 1967).

More generally, this emphasis on the problem-oriented confrontation of several streams of evidence should help us to get away from the familiar controversies as to whether one kind of data, such as survey data, should be preferred to some other, such as aggregate statistics either in general or in dealing with some particular class or problems.[19] The truth may reside not so much in any one kind of data, or in the result of any one technique, even if these data and techniques are used not naïvely and unskillfully, but in the most highly skilled manner. Rather, truth may be thought of as a relationship between different streams of evidence. A statement is the more likely to be true, the larger the number of different classes or kinds of evidence that confirm it. Also, a statement contains the more truth the larger that part of the information contained in it which will have to be included in any successor statement to it, reformulated or revised, by which the original statement will have to be replaced in the light of new evidence. Improved methods for the multiple confrontation and correlation of diverse bodies of evidence bearing on the same problem deserve, therefore, a high priority in our attention.

In order to make progress in this area, it might be desirable to collect systematically the various relevant empirical-observational or experimental techniques, survey instruments, questionnaires, and questions that have been used in the social sciences and to record:

1. Which of these have been applied repeatedly, under what conditions, with what results, and with what indications as to their replicability? [20]
2. What is the correlation among the results of different survey instruments, questions, or experimental techniques bearing on the same substantive problem or class of prob-

[19] For a useful discussion of some of the problems involved, see Ralph H. Retzlaff, "The Use of Aggregate Data in Comparative Political Analysis," *The Journal of Politics,* 27: 4 (November 1965), pp. 797–817, esp. pp. 798–799; Austin Ranney, "The Utility and Limitations of Aggregate Data in the Study of Electoral Behavior," in Austin Ranney (ed.), *Essays on the Behavioral Study of Politics* (Urbana: University of Illinois Press, 1962), pp. 91–102.

[20] For a provisional list of about two hundred test instruments or questionnaires relevant to the relationship of personality to political behavior, see Leroy N. Rieselbach, "Personality and Political Attitudes: Available Questionnaire Measures" (Ann Arbor: Mental Health Research Institute, University of Michigan, 1964), multigraphed.

lems? How do mass opinion data generally correlate with the results of content analysis of mass media, or of school textbooks, or of other supposedly "representative" sources?

3. To what extent can the results obtained from different techniques or data sources be interpreted as indicators of a common underlying structure or process? To what extent are such indicators then interchangeable? On what grounds and by what procedures should preferred indicators be selected, or joint indicators be constructed?

4. What is the correlation between different aspects of reality, each of which is associated with its own indicators, but each of which is also linked to other aspects of reality, in some manner and to some degree? What, for instance, is the correlation between overt or salient attitudes, expressed "off-the-cuff" in response to brief opinion-poll questions, and latent and more deep-seated attitudes, that are revealed only in prolonged depth interviews? [21] Or what is the correlation between expressed attitudes or intentions on the one hand, and actual behavior, on the other? Could these correlations between attitudes and behavior be improved by including explicit data on such major discussions of each attitude as its salience, intensity, and the respondent's involvement and his closure of mind, as suggested by Louis Guttmann? [22]

5. What is the correlation between panel responses and the responses elicited from comparable fresh samples interviewed at the intervals in time? [23]

In recent years, however, questions of this kind about empirical data sources and data-gathering techniques have been exceeded in interest by another group of questions: those about better mathematical and statistical methods of analysis and about new sources of theories and models.

[21] Cf. Some of the material reported in footnote 10, above; see also Russett, *et al., World Handbook, op. cit.*, pp. 192–195; and David McClelland, *The Achieving Society* (Princeton, N. J.: Van Nostrand, 1961).

[22] Louis Guttman, "The Principal Components of Scalable Attitudes," in Paul F. Lazarsfeld (ed.), *Mathematical Thinking in the Social Sciences* (Glencoe, Ill.: Free Press, 1954), pp. 216–257.

[23] The correlation may vary with the length of time over which the panel is being interviewed. For a survey designed to compare over a decade the responses of a large panel with those of comparable fresh samples, see Chikio Hayashi *et al., A Study of Japanese National Character* (Tokyo: Institute of Mathematical Statistics, 1961, in Japanese with English summaries of tables).

SOME NEW METHODS OF ANALYSIS

When we speak of "new methods" of mathematical and statistical analysis in political science research, we are rarely if ever referring to such methods invented by political scientists. Ordinarily and expectably, such methods are being developed by statisticians or mathematicians spontaneously or in response to some request from some field of natural or social science. What is new is usually only the application of this or that method to some problem in the field of political science followed by the increasing acceptance and application of this method or its results by other political scientists.

In this manner, the use of statistical distributions for the analysis of political and social phenomena was pioneered by George K. Zipf and developed further by Herbert Simon and by Hayward Alker, Jr. and Bruce Russett and their associates. Zipf applied such distributions to the study of the relation of capital cities, nation-states, and empires. Herbert Simon applied it in a more advanced manner to the study of processes that give rise to new organizations, such as business firms, or possibly—at least in principle—new states or other political groupings.[24] Alker and Russett surveyed a number of statistical measures of inequality, which were applied to the unequal distribution of such politically relevant variables as income, land holdings, voting representation.[25] Russett and his associates also presented, in their *World Handbook,* international distribution profiles for seventy-five politically relevant variables so as to make them available for further analysis.[26] Work is underway to prepare similar profiles of the distribution of many of these variables within par-

[24] Herbert A. Simon, *Models of Man* (New York: John Wiley & Sons, 1956); George K. Zipf, *National Unity and Disunity: The Nation as a Bio-Social Organism* (Bloomington, Ind.: Principia Press, 1944). For a criticism of Zipf's Approach, see Karl W. Deutsch, "Communication Models in the Social Sciences," *Public Opinion Quarterly,* 16: 3 (Fall 1952), pp. 356–380; and for the whole field, see Hayward R. Alker, Jr., *Mathematics and Politics* (New York: The Macmillan Company, 1965); and "The Long Road to International Relations Theory: Problems of Statistical Non-Additivity," *World Politics,* 18: 4 (July 1966), pp. 623–655.

[25] Hayward R. Alker, Jr., and Bruce M. Russett, "On Measuring Inequality," *Behavioral Science,* 9: 3 (July 1964), pp. 207–218; see also Bruce M. Russett, "Inequality and Instability: The Relation of Land Tenure to Politics," *World Politics,* 16: 3 (April 1964), pp. 442–454.

[26] Bruce M. Russett, Hayward R. Alker, Jr., Karl W. Deutsch, and Harold D. Lasswell, *World Handbook, op. cit.*

ticular nations, such as over the fifty states—or sometimes even the three million counties—of the United States. This would make it possible to compare the international and intranational distribution patterns of important variables, and thus to learn something about the possible effects of a particular nation-state either as an equalizer among its constituent districts or regions, or else as a promoter or stabilizer of inequality; and such comparisons could then be used to test some of the existing theories—such as that of Gunnar Myrdal—on this subject.[27]

Distribution patterns of variables can be studied not only among states or territories, but also among organizations, firms, or social groups or classes. Even a preliminary survey suggests that Vilfredo Pareto's well-known generalization—that in the long run the inequality of income distribution over different countries and periods does not substantially change—is incorrect. In the mid-1950's, the gini index of inequality for income distribution before taxes ranged from 0.54 for Mexico to 0.35 for Australia; and it may have dropped for West Germany from 0.47 in 1950 to 0.32 in 1959. The differences in inequality over time, or between nations, are quite substantial. It seems plausible that to a significant though not unlimited extent they are subject to the processes of political allocation and decision.[28]

Even more interesting are time series, that is, distribution patterns of variables over time. Under appropriate conditions and with the help of suitable techniques, such time series can be used to interpolate data for missing dates written the period they cover, and they can be extrapolated back into the past or forward into the future. For many purposes of analysis it would be desirable to develop a standard notation for reporting time series. Such a notation should include the trend line of the series, that is, more technically put, the monotonic regression line best fitted to the data; and with this, it should also give the standard deviation, that is, the distance from the regression line within which 68 per cent of the actual cases or data can be found in the case of a normal distribution. If the trend line measures the central statistical tendency of the time series—for example, how fast it is rising or falling over time, and at what rate its change is accelerating or slowing down—the standard deviation measures the extent of the

[27] Gunnar Myrdal, *Rich Lands and Poor* (New York: Harper, 1957); and *An International Economy* (New York: Harper, 1956).

[28] Russett, *et al., World Handbook, op. cit.*, pp. 243–247.

scatter or variance of the actual cases around this trend.

Knowledge of this variance is often a matter of both theoretical and practical importance. Impecunious gamblers are often ruined not by the steady but small trend of the house odds against them, but by the large transitory fluctuations in their losses which may soon wipe out their meager capital so that they cannot stay long enough in the game to recoup some or all of these losses in a later winning sequence. And what happens to the limited resources of gamblers can similarly happen to the limited following of politicians or parties, or to the limited troop reserves of armies locked in fluctuating battles or campaigns.

In addition to the secular trend of a time series, its other major compounds should be reported. A cyclical change may be superimposed upon the trend, somewhat as a business cycle has been superimposed upon the trend of American and European economic growth during much of the nineteenth and early twentieth century. There may even be more than one such cyclical movement, for a short-wave or short-term cyclical movement may modify further the combined result of the secular trend and of a long-term cycle or long-wave process.

Another component of the time series may be a stochastic process, that is, the interplay of a random factor at each relevant instant with the present position or state of the system, as determined by its past. Thus, a drunkard on a level field might take a random step of equal length in any direction, but at any time he could only move one step away from where he just had been. If the drunkard is walking on a slope, gravity will add a long-time bias to his progress. The probability distribution of any such "random walk" and the probable fate of the drunkard—for instance, his likelihood of overstepping the brink of a nearby precipice—can be calculated by a mathematician from the relevant data. Conversely, a time series of data can be analyzed for the possibility of fitting to it a relatively simple mathematical random-walk model or similar stochastic model, and thus improving its simulation and prediction significantly beyond what a relatively simple combination of cycles and monotonic trends could accomplish.

If an analysis of this kind should suggest the presence of a random input element or factor in the process by which the time series was generated, it may be desirable to separate this random element further into two components. The first would be that part of the random input which could be matched readily by a relatively simple normal distribution, i.e., a Gaussian curve, or by some other well-known distribution, such as a Poisson or a Yule distribution, and which, therefore, would lend itself to easy computer simulation. If so, that part of the random process that could be readily simulated by any such well-known distribution would be described in these terms, and the residual amount of randomness reported separately—as irrelevant "noise" or as intriguing mystery, depending on the interests of the investigators.

In this manner, the analysis of any time series will lead us to search for one or several process models. In examining a time series—such as an increase in literacy, or in political participation, or in some indicator of political stability or instability, we ask what process could have produced such an outcome. We are apt to be led to a similar search when we ask what could be the result of the interplay of the time series in which we are interested with another time series with which it connected by some underlying political, social, or economic process. We are all familiar with cross-over effects which occur if one variable or time series grows beyond some other variable by which it had been balanced. Thus, if the manpower losses of an army come to exceed its recruitment, it will start to dwindle; if the expenditures of a firm continue to exceed its earnings, it will become unprofitable and may go bankrupt; and if the number of persons angered or alienated by a government continues to grow faster than the number of persons attracted to its support, this government may be headed for political bankruptcy and eventual collapse, unless it can reverse its loss of domestic popularity or else bring in foreign support in adequate amounts.

Other thresholds or cross-over points may occur in relation to the proportions of people on one side or another of a single indicator. Thus, by 1950, urban Negroes for the first time had come to form the majority of the American Negro population, which, as late as 1940, had been in its majority rural. In some sense, this shift of balance within the American Negro community might well have alerted social scientists to the subsequent change in Negro political behavior, which occurred in the 1950–1960 decade. In all such cases, however, we are still dealing with some balance or interplay among two or more magnitudes or elements, which requires for its study some implied or explicit process model or mode of process analysis.

A very primitive method for keeping track of a larger number of different variables of states or political systems to be compared consists in specifying a configuration of variables relevant to our analysis for each case, and in specifying for each variable anywhere between two and ten different gross states or levels, separated by cut-off points suitably chosen for each variable. In this manner, it is possible to construct a simple configuration code, with each digit corresponding to a variable, and each numerical value of that particular digit corresponding to a state or level of that variable. Such a notation can then be used as a mnemonic device in constructing an inventory of interesting trends and patterns in comparative and international politics.[29] Even as primitive a technique as the use of configuration codes permits us to identify frequent configurations, and to single out for special study deviant cases and the particular dimensions and degrees in which each such case is deviant.

Another technique for identifying a deviant case has been developed by Michael Hudson, with the help of the rank-order profiles of some of the standard variables in Russett's *World Handbook*. In studying the case of Lebanon, Hudson noted the ten countries closest to it on the rank-order profiles of several indicators of social mobilization and economic development. He then repeated this procedure for such political indicators as the ratio of government expenditure to gross national product, and the ratio of votes cast to total adult population. He found that Lebanon ranked close to relatively advanced countries in its social and economic development, but close to far less well-developed countries in its indicated levels of government services and of political participation, and he related this contrast between Lebanon's society and its politics to the observed political instability of the country.[30]

A more extended method of analysis consists in computing correlations for each pair of a set of variables selected as salient for a given collection of countries, units, or cases. For the 75

[29] K. W. Deutsch, "Toward an Inventory of Basic Trends and Patterns in Comparative and International Politics," *American Political Science Review*, 54 (March 1960), pp. 34–57. For some critical points, see Retzlaff, *op. cit.*

[30] Michael Hudson, "A Case of Political Underdevelopment," *Journal of Politics* (pub. sched. Fall 1967).

variables in Russett's *World Handbook,* this procedure produced about 2,800 correlations. The computer was then programmed to print out all correlations with coefficients of correlation of 20 per cent or higher, with interesting results.[31] In another adaptation the computer was programmed to print all correlations, but to rank for each variable all other variables in descending order from the strongest positive to the strongest negative correlation with it. It was possible, therefore, to see whether some particular theory was confirmed not only by the strength of each correlation but also by its rank order among other theories. In this manner, some useful information could be extracted even from weak correlations in terms of their rank-order distribution.[32]

It is well known that a pair correlation often is not very informative, but the introduction of a third, discriminating variable may reveal a much stronger or much weaker relationship among the first two variables for some or all of the subgroups created by the introduction of the third.[33] This being so, it should be possible and worth-while to develop computer programs for the rapid searching of large fields of pair correlations so as to identify for each pair correlation those third, discriminating variables the introduction of which would produce, in at least some of the new subgroups generated by the third variable, the greatest changes from the original correlation between the first two variables. Differently put, it might be desirable to find rapid computer search methods to find the most interesting "triplets" of variables and to compute and print out the relationships to which they give rise.

Other computer routines for searching large numbers of correlations among variables have already been used, such as the "pattern search technique" employed in the *Cross-Polity Survey* by Banks and Textor (which would further gain in usefulness if some of its coding procedures could be confirmed by additional research and retesting).[34]

[31] Russett *et al., op cit.,* pp. 261–292.

[32] Karl W. Deutsch, unpublished research, Yale University, 1965.

[33] Cf. Paul F. Lazarsfeld, "Interpretation of Statistical Relations as a Research Operation," in Paul F. Lazarsfeld and Morris Rosenberg (eds.), *The Language of Social Research* (New York: Free Press of Glencoe, 1955, 1962), pp. 115–125; and Russett *et al., World Handbook, op. cit.,* pp. 323–340.

[34] Arthur S. Banks and Robert Textor, *A Cross-Polity Survey,* footnote 10, above.

Beyond the correlation techniques used thus far at all widely by political scientists, there are the broader possibilities of using methods of multiple-regression analysis, so as to compute and rank more accurately the contribution made to our prediction of the value of one variable by our knowledge of each of several other variables correlated with it. In addition to multiple-regression analysis, the method of factor analysis and the various techniques comprised within it all appear suited to the treatment of a wide range of problems in political science.

Factor analysis in essence replaces many variables by a few "factors" each of which is more or less highly correlated with a group of the original variables which are highly correlated among themselves, but have much less or no correlation with other groups of variables. In this way it is not necessary to compare, say, sixty countries in regard to, say, twenty indicators of economic and social development, such as per-capita income, steel production, newsprint consumption, literacy, industrial employment and the like, but it may suffice to compare these countries in terms of a single factor, "economic and social development," which is highly correlated with all the special indicators in this particular group. Factor analysis has been applied effectively to regional analysis, to voting patterns in the United Nations General Assembly, and to West European mass opinion data.[35] Eventually, it should be possible to use factor analysis, or else multiple-regression analysis, to find out whether the nationality of respondents—for example, French or German—has not a much stronger bearing on the distribution of political attitudes expressed than do such familiar conditions as age, income, socioeconomic status, occupation, religion, or socialist or nonsocialist party affiliation. Preliminary work at Yale suggests that this may be the case, and may lead in time to quantitative measurement of the relative influence of each of these conditions.[36]

[35] Hayward Alker, Jr., and Bruce M. Russett, *World Politics in the General Assembly* (New Haven: Yale University Press, 1965); Bruce Russett, "Discovering Voting Groups in the United Nations," *American Political Science Review*, 60: 2 (June 1966), pp. 327–339; Donald A. Puchala, *European Political Integration: Progress and Prospects* (New Haven: Yale University Political Science Research Library, 1966), multigraphed.

[36] K. W. Deutsch, work in progress, Yale University, 1965–1967; and "Integration and Arms Control in the European Political Environment: A Summary Report," *American Political Science Review*, 60: 2 (June 1966), pp. 354–365, esp. p. 364.

A different but intellectually related set of techniques of analysis is based on estimating with what probability an observed distribution of outcomes would be produced by some random process, and then searching for special influences or determinants only to account for the observed deviations from the results expectable from random probability.   Such probabilistic "null-models" have been applied to the analysis of the appearance in large bureaucracies, of small numbers of "wise men" who made a seeming sequence of correct policy choices, or foresighted adjustments to some changing party line.   The null-model would then predict how many spurious "wise men" would be produced by random probability among a given number of bureaucrats making a given sequence of choices, and how many additional "wise men"—that is, makers of a correct sequence of choices—would have to appear in an organization of this size in order to justify the presumption of some genuinely high competence in making such choices.[37]

Other uses of the null-model technique combine it with the matrix analysis of transaction flows among a plurality of actors. Here, each row in one matrix represents the actual transactions initiated by one actor or else a subtotal of such rows for all transactions initiated by a group of actors, while each column in the matrix represents the transactions terminating at one of the actors, or at a subtotal of such actors.   The righthand marginal column then contains the total of all transactions initiated by each actor, and the bottom row contains the total transactions terminating with each actor.   The cells in the matrix then contain the actual transactions flowing from each actor to every other.   A second matrix is then constructed from the same marginal columns and totals, but replacing the actual transaction figures in each cell with an expected figure computed from the marginal data with the help of a null model based on random probability. A third matrix then contains in each cell an index of relative deviation of the actual from the expected value for each pair of actors in each direction of the transaction flow between them.[38]

[37] K. W. Deutsch and William Madow, "On the Appearance of Wisdom in Large Bureaucratic Organizations," *Behavioral Science,* 6 (1961), pp. 72–78.
[38] A technical description of the method is given in I. Richard Savage and K. W. Deutsch, "A Statistical Model of the Gross Analysis of Transaction Flows," *Econometrica,* 28 (July 1960), pp. 551–572; and a computer program has been published by H. R. Alker, Jr., in *Behavioral Science,* 7: 4 (October 1962), pp. 498–499.   For suggested improvements in the method, see

The method has been applied to studies of integration in colonial empires and in regions of sovereign states; to a world matrix of exports in 1938 and 1954; to exports and trade integration patterns in the North Atlantic area between 1890 and 1963; and to the flow of mail, travelers, and university students among the six states of the European Common Market for the period 1925–1963; and it has been developed by Harrison White for application to the analysis of matrices of intergenerational social mobility, in which the fathers' social status or class forms the rows (or origins), and the sons' status or class forms the columns (or destinations).[39]

The more extended such methods and techniques become, the more they attempt to come to grips with the complexities of social processes, the more they drive their users to search for new sources of broader theories and models. Here the development of new methods leads back more to a strengthened interest in theory.

Some New Sources of Theories and Models

"New" theories, in the context of the recent developments in empirical research methods, are any theories that can be tested operationally, that is, by procedures and evidence that can be reproduced impersonally, regardless of the political or cultural preferences of the observer, and that can also be tested, at least indirectly, against "nature," that is, against some aspect of physical reality. The community of social scientists is then the community of persons who can agree upon a growing body of interpersonally verifiable methods and data, and who through this use of reproducible evidence remain connected with one another and with the larger world of nature.

The first source of new empirical theories, then, are many of

Leo A. Goodman, "Statistical Methods for the Preliminary Analysis of Transaction Flows," *Econometrica,* 31 (1963), pp. 197–208; and "A Short Computer Program for the Analysis of Transaction Flows," *Behavioral Science,* 9: 2 (April 1964), pp. 176–186.

[39] Harrison C. White, "Cause and Effect in Social Mobility Tables," *Behavioral Science,* 8: 1 (January 1963), pp. 14–27; see also Karl W. Deutsch, "Toward an Inventory of Basic Trends and Patterns in Comparative and International Politics" (see footnote 29, above), pp. 34–57, esp. pp. 46–48; Hayward R. Alker, Jr., and Donald A. Puchala, "Trends in Economic Partnership in the North Atlantic Area," in J. David Singer (ed.), *Quantitative International Politics* (New York: Free Press, 1967).

the old nonempirical theories of the classic tradition of political science. *Implication analysis* can be used to examine each such theory for those of its implications that can be empirically tested. A classic example of this technique is ascribed to a nine-year-old boy, young Heinrich Schliemann, who reportedly remarked one day at the family breakfast table that if Homer's account of the eight-foot-thick stone walls of Troy was true, then these stone walls still were likely to be in existence, and that he, Heinrich Schliemann, some day would dig them up—something which subsequently he did. Similarly, if certain of Plato's theories in *The Republic* are true, there ought to be born a certain proportion of highly gifted children among the total population, and there ought to be a corresponding proportion of jobs or social roles of leaders of either the "philosopher" or "guardian" type in the society. If these quantitative implications of Plato's should be confirmed by empirical data about the actual statistical distribution of intellectual ability and of social leadership roles in all societies, or, at least, in some particular society, then Plato's theory might, of course, still be found in error in other grounds; but if already these relatively simple empirical data should contradict it, then the theory certainly could not be accepted even provisionally without substantial modification. A systematic search could be made of major existing political theories—both classic and modern—to find implications that can be confirmed or disconfirmed by verifiable data.

A related technique might be the construction of a *propositional inventory*, which would gather and exhibit all or at least many of the relevant and verifiable propositions that could be found in some particular political theory or in several such theories. Harold Lasswell's and Abraham Kaplan's book, *Power and Society,* would lend itself admirably to this procedure.[40] Many of its propositions are already explicitly labeled in the text, so that they only need to be put side by side, and each of them confronted with a file of data and testing procedures relevant to its verification.

Attempts to verify a specific proposition or a broader theory usually lead to its restatement. Discriminating variables or critical conditions have been overlooked and must now be provided for. Distinctions and qualifications must be added, or even more

[40] H. D. Lasswell and A. Kaplan, *Power and Society* (New Haven: Yale University Press, 1950).

drastic reformations may be necessitated or at least suggested. The explication and testing of old political propositions and theories thus leads to the formulation of new ones.

A similar procedure can be applied to propositions, theories, and methods of inquiry drawn more broadly from the social sciences. Sociology, psychology, anthropology, and economics all can be searched for patterns of thought and for specific propositions or theories that could be applied with suitable modifications to the study of politics. J. David Singer's recent collection from the behavioral sciences of materials directly relevant to the analysis of international politics is an important step in this direction.[41]

Another source of new theories and models for political research is found in *general systems theory*. Here attention is drawn to relations that may be similar at different systems levels: Why do many suburbs in metropolitan areas defend their "sovereignty" against mergers with, or encroachments by, either the central city or else some proposed metropolitan federation or authority? What similarities and what difference does this suburban struggle for quasi-independence show to the resistance of many sovereign nation-states against the pressures and attractions of their larger neighbors, or of proposed regional federations or projects for world government? When does integration prevail, and when does separatism, at the metropolitan and at the international levels, respectively? A recent joint study by experts in metropolitan planning and specialists in international relations has tried to make a beginning toward answering these questions.[42]

General systems theory, however, has broader implications for the development of political and social science theory. The use of common terms and concepts drawn from general systems theory has been studied by Oran Young, both for a group of political theorists and for a group of scholars drawn from a wider range of disciplines.[43] Some specific concepts and models widely

[41] J. David Singer, *Human Behavior and International Politics: Contributions from the Social-Psychological Sciences* (Chicago: Rand, McNally, 1965).

[42] Philip E. Jacob and James V. Toscano (eds.), *The Integration of Political Communities* (Philadelphia: Lippincott, 1964).

[43] Oran R. Young, "A Survey of General Systems Theory," and "The Impact of General Systems Theory on Political Science," *General Systems*, Vol. 9 (1964), pp. 61–80 and 239–253; cf. also Klaus E. Knorr and Sidney A. Verba (eds.), *The International System: Theoretical Essays* (Princeton, N.J.: Princeton University Press, 1961); Charles A. McClelland, *Theory and the International System* (New York: The Macmillan Company, 1960).

used in general systems theory—such as cybernetic models and the feedback concept—are at the heart of some recent efforts by contemporary political theorists.[44]

Cybernetic models stress not only systems but also processes, particularly the processes of communication and control. In a broader sense, general systems theory is also a theory of processes, that is, of changes over time. James G. Miller has pointed out, however, that general systems theory does not neglect the research advantages that can be reaped from the study of structures, that is, of systems considered at a single instant or relatively brief period of time. Studying both structures and processes permits us to pay attention to the location in space of relatively persistent nodes of interaction which are embodied in relatively stable, enduring, or recurrent arrangements in space, that are then available for many different processes of interaction and that can be located, and sometimes manipulated, by investigators.[45] Models of particular processes, with direct or potential relevance to politics, have been proposed in regard to political power systems by Morton Kaplan, to arms races by L. F. Richardson, to "peaceful coexistence" by G. F. Gause, and to games of strategy by John Von Neumann and Oskar Morgenstern, by Thomas C. Schelling, by Anatol Rapoport, and by others.[46]

[44] David Easton, *A Systems Analysis of Politics* (New York: John Wiley and Sons, 1965); and *A Framework for Political Analysis* (Englewood Cliffs, N.J.: Prentice-Hall, 1965); K. W. Deutsch, *The Nerves of Government* (rev. ed.; New York: Free Press, 1966); John Burton, *International Relations: A General Theory* (Cambridge, Eng.: Cambridge University Press, 1965); cf. also Charles Dechert (ed.), *The Social Impact of Cybernetics* (South Bend, Ind.: University of Notre Dame Press, 1966).

[45] James G. Miller, "Living Systems: Basic Concepts," *Behavioral Science,* 10: 3 (July 1965), pp. 193–237; and "Living Systems: Structure and Process," *Ibid.,* 10: 4 (October 1965), pp. 337–379; and "Living Systems: Cross-Level Hypothesis," *Ibid.,* pp. 381–411.

[46] On process models, see Morton Kaplan, *System and Process in International Politics* (New York: John Wiley & Sons, 1957); and "The New Great Debate: Traditionalism vs. Science in International Relations," *World Politics,* 19: 1 (October 1966), pp. 1–20; L. F. Richardson, *Arms and Insecurity* (Pittsburgh and Chicago: Boxwood Press and Quadrangle Books, 1960); G. F. Gause, *The Struggle for Existence* (Baltimore: Williams and Wilkins, 1934); and "Verifications experimentales de la théorie mathématique de la lutte pour la vie," *Actualités Scientifiques et Industrielles* (Paris: Hermann, 1935). On game theory, see John Von Neumann and O. Morgenstern, *Theory of Games and Economic Behavior* (2nd ed.; Princeton, N.J.: Princeton University Press, 1947); Martin Shubik (ed.), *Game*

A good deal of work also has been done on models of the process of learning, as derived from various theories of learning and tested against diverse experimental data.[47] Learning models —and perhaps particularly those making use of probability and of stochastic processes—in principle, should be applicable to various political problems involving behavior change or development over time. Applying such concepts and models of learning to the political behavior of individuals and groups, perhaps in combination with cybernetic models of self-steering, autonomy, memory, and goal-seeking and goal-changing feedback processes may well constitute a promising line of advance for political research and analysis in the future.

A particularly interesting class of such process models are the

---

Theory and Related Approaches to Social Behavior (New York: John Wiley & Sons, 1964); Thomas C. Schelling, *The Strategy of Conflict* (Cambridge, Mass.: Harvard University Press, 1960); and *Arms and Influence* (New Haven: Yale University Press, 1966); Anatol Rapoport, *Fights, Games and Debates* (Ann Arbor: University of Michigan Press, 1960); *Strategy and Conscience* (New York: Harper & Row, 1964); *Two-Person Game Theory: The Essential Ideas* (Ann Arbor: University of Michigan Press, 1966); and Anatol Rapoport and Albert Chammah, *Prisoners' Dilemma* (Ann Arbor: University of Michigan Press, 1966); Kenneth E. Boulding, *Conflict and Defense* (New York: Harper, 1962); Edward S. Quade, *Analysis for Military Decisions* (Chicago: Rand McNally, 1964); Martin Cyril McGuire, *Secrecy and the Arms Race* (Cambridge, Mass.: Harvard University Press, 1965); A. V. S. deReuck and Julie Knight (eds.), CIBA Foundation Symposium on *Conflict in Society* (London: Churchill, 1966).

[47] Cf., for example, Ernest R. Hilgard (ed.), *Theories of Learning* (Chicago: University of Chicago Press, 1964); and Ernest R. Hilgard and G. H. Bower, *Theories of Learning* (2nd ed.; New York: Appleton-Century-Crofts [rev. ed.], 1956); Ernest R. Hilgard and D. G. Marquis, *Conditioning and Learning* (2nd ed.; New York: Appleton-Century-Crofts, 1960); Patrick Suppes and Richard C. Atkinson, *Markov Learning Models for Multiperson Interactions* (Stanford, Calif.: Stanford University Press, 1960); Merrill M. Flood, "Stochastic Learning Theory Applied to Choice Experiments with Rats, Dogs, and Men," *Behavioral Science*, 7: 3 (July 1962), pp. 289–314; Robert R. Bush and W. K. Estes (eds.), *Studies in Mathematical Learning Theory* (Stanford, Calif.: Stanford University Press, 1959); cf. also Bernard Berelson and Gary A. Steiner, *Human Behavior: An Inventory of Scientific Findings* (New York: Harcourt, Brace, and World, 1964), pp. 133–235; B. F. Skinner, *Walden Two* (New York: The Macmillan Company, 1948); Otto Klineberg, *The Human Dimension in International Relations* (New York: Holt, Rinehart, and Winston, 1964); and *Tensions Affecting International Understanding: A Survey of Research* (New York: Social Science Research Council, 1950).

stochastic processes, the models of gambler's ruin and of random walk between barriers, mentioned earlier in this paper.   Another version of stochastic-process analysis can be applied to several stages, states, or groups.   This method involves the construction of *transition matrices* in which each state or group, at one time— such as Republican, Democrat, Independent, and nonvoters—is represented by a row, and the same state or group at a later time is represented by a column.   Those individuals who did not change their state or group then remain in the cells on the main diagonal.   Each of the other cells then contains those individuals that changed from the state indicated by the row to the state indicated by the column.   Some transition probability for each cell can be assumed for each cell, or calculated from data for an early stage; and the probable future population of all cells can then be calculated for a number of steps ahead.   This method has been applied by Lazarsfeld and Anderson to the opinion changes of voters in Erie County, Pennsylvania.[48]

A similar method could be applied in principle also to the analysis of revolutions and guerrilla wars.   These processes could then be analyzed by means of a transition matrix, which might show in five rows the initial strength of government troops, active government-supporters, passive or latent government-sympathizers, neutrals and indifferents, passive or latent opponents of the government, active opponents of the government, and actual guerrilla forces or revolutionary troops.   The corresponding columns might then show the subsequent strength of each of these groups, say, a year later.   The transition probabilities for each cell then might indicate how many active government-supporters had joined the government troops and how many had lapsed into passivity, or how many of the initially indifferent or neutral had shifted to the rebel side or even joined the guerrillas.   A calculation might then show what the state of affairs in the country might be five years later, if these trends should continue.   How much of a government or a rebel army would then still be in existence?   The introduction of foreign troops on one or both sides

[48] T. W. Anderson, "Probability Models for Analyzing Time Changes in Attitudes," in Paul F. Lazarsfeld (ed.), *Mathematical Thinking in the Social Sciences* (New York and Glencoe, Ill.: Free Press, 1954), pp. 17–66; for the survey data used, see also Paul F. Lazarsfeld, Bernard Berelson, and Hazel Gaudet, *The People's Choice* (New York: Columbia University Press, 1948).

of the conflict would complicate the matrix—as it would the conflict—but could be covered in the same kind of analysis.

To gain data for our various process models we resort to *longitudinal studies,* that is, to studies of time series of behavior changes in the past. Sometimes, however, we can also use data from *cross-sectional analysis,* comparing at one point in time several individuals, organizations, or cases at what we believe or surmise are different stages of one and the same sequence of development. Thus, the development of kittens into cats can be studied by photography or studying one kitten day after day as it grows up, or else by photographing or studying on one and the same day, side by side, many kittens of different ages, ranking them by size and other presumed indicators of maturity. If we are dealing with a process similar to the succession of stages of biological maturation, then the results of longitudinal and cross-sectional studies should be closely similar. Insofar as the results of these two kinds of studies differ, however, it seems likely that the biological analogy does not apply. In comparing highly developed and underdeveloped countries in the world today, we may find sharper and more extreme contrasts between these groups than we find in examining the rise of any one of today's advanced countries from its lower levels of, say, a century ago to its present level of affluence. To the extent that this is the case, we may wonder whether today's developing countries in Asia, Africa, and Latin America are of a different kind than were their counterparts in Europe one hundred years ago, or whether the difference among the countries is less important than the difference between the periods. If so, the comparison of longitudinal and cross-sectional studies would have furnished some evidence that the world had changed in some relevant aspects, and it could even indicate something about the extent and direction of the change.

As models become more rich and more realistic, they lend themselves more readily to *simulation.* One approach to such simulation of processes is mathematical. A statistical or mathematical model is constructed that corresponds to the most important characteristics of the real-life process to be simulated. Various changes and contingencies are then represented by numerical inputs into the model, and the changes produced by them in the state of the model and in its outputs to its environment are noted. These output changes can be thought of as responses of the model to the changes in its various inputs or parameters.

Where data are too scant, processes too complex, or models too simple, complete mathematical or statistical computer simulation may not be practical. In this case, it may be possible, however, to limit the formal model to a very few structural relationships connecting in specific ways several actors—such as political groups or rival countries—and then have each of these actors played by a person, who uses his own mind, memories, and preferences to make moves and decisions and to respond to moves by other actors. Even if the players are high school or college students, such games may lead to discoveries; if they are experienced diplomats, or military or political experts, the likelihood of obtaining relevant new information—or at least to discover relevant and hitherto neglected contingencies—should be correspondingly higher. Some intermediate techniques also have been developed between the pure simulation by computer and the "war-game" type of more or less dramatic representation by human actors. These employ computation for some parameters, variables, and trends over time, but let human actors make the remaining decisions within their context. A rich literature on simulation has sprung up, and the work of Hans Speier, Harold Guetzkow, Richard Brody, Lincoln Bloomfield, and others has become a significant part of political science.[49]

[49] See Harold Guetzkow (ed.), *Simulation in Social Science: Readings* (Englewood Cliffs, N.J.: Prentice-Hall, 1962), and Harold Guetzkow, Chadwick F. Alger, Richard A. Brody, Robert C. North, and Richard C. Snyder, *Simulations in International Relations: Developments for Research and Teaching* (Englewood Cliffs, N.J.: Prentice-Hall, 1963). A concise but very useful statement is E. A. Robinson, "Simulation and Theory Construction," in his chapter "Recursive Decomposition of Stochastic Processes," in Herman O. A. Wold (ed.), *Econometric Model-Building* (Amsterdam: North Holland Publishing Company, 1964), pp. 147–151. See also the review article by Sidney Verba, "Simulation, Reality, and Theory in International Relations," *World Politics,* 16: 3 (April 1964), pp. 490–519; Ithiel de Sola Pool, Robert Abelson and Samuel Popkin, *Candidates, Issues, and Strategies: A Computer Simulation of the 1960 Presidential Election* (Cambridge, Mass.: M.I.T. Press, 1964); and Ithiel Pool and A. Kessler, "The Kaiser, the Tsar, and the Computers: Information-Processing in a Crisis," *American Behavioral Scientist,* 8 (1965), pp. 39–44. See also the important survey by Robert P. Abelson, "Simulation of Social Behavior (mimeographed), as well as his forthcoming study on the politics of fluoridation and the forthcoming comparative study on simulation methods by Hayward R. Alker, Jr. See also Herbert H. Goldhamer and Hans Speier, "Some Observations on Political Gaming," *World Politics,* 12 (1959), pp. 71–83; Leonard P. Bloomfield and Norman Padelford, "Three Experiments in Political Gaming," *American*

Simulation at best cannot be much better than our under-standing of the processes which we imagine we are simulating. Anatol Rapoport has proposed a broad distinction among three kinds of social and political processes, and particularly of proc-esses of conflict.[50]   The first kind of processes are *fights*.   Here the parties to the fight do not think or calculate effectively; they just react each to the other's behavior.   One dog growls, and the other dog growls louder; the first dog's hackles rise, and the second snarls, until the escalation ends in a dogfight.   A sover-eign state increases its armament; its neighbor tries to keep ahead of it by some margin, but the first tries again to keep ahead, and the arms race may end in exhaustion or a war.   Processes of this kind resemble blind processes of nature, and they can be simu-lated by pairs of differential equations in the case of two parties.

The second kind of processes are *games*.   Here the parties make rational decisions in the pursuit of their interest.   This is for each player the interest to win, and it does not change.   The outcome of each player's move also depends on the move chosen by his opponent.   Each player must try, therefore, to know or estimate the probability distribution of all possible outcomes, with the distribution of the corresponding possible payoffs to him-self; and he must choose his own moves accordingly, so as to in-crease his gains and cut his risks.   This behavior of rational players can be simulated in principle by the mathematics of game theory which were referred to earlier in this paper.[51]

The third type of processes Rapoport calls *debates*.   Here the viewpoints, intentions, and interests of the parties themselves may change.   They may become more or less hostile to each

Political Science Review, 53 (1959), pp. 1105–1115; G. H. Orcutt, "Simula-tion of Economic Systems," *American Economic Review,* 50 (1960), pp. 893–907; Thomas C. Schelling, "An Experimental Game for the Study of Bargaining," *World Politics,* 14 (1961), pp. 47–68; Andrew M. Scott *et al., Simulation and National Development* (New York: John Wiley & Sons, 1966); R. Brody, "Some Systemic Effects of the Spread of Nuclear Weapons: A Study through Simulation of a Multi-Nuclear Future," *Journal of Conflict Resolution,* 7: 4 (December 1963), pp. 664–753.

[50] Anatol Rapoport, *Fights, Games and Debates, op. cit.,* pp. 1–12.

[51] *Ibid.,* pp. 107–242; also *Two-person Game Theory: The Essential Idea* (footnote 46, above).

other; one actor may become converted to the viewpoint of another; or both may shift to a perception of some overriding common interest. A fair amount is known about such processes from studies of psychology and semantics—and presumably of religion —but there are no mathematical techniques available for simulating them.[52]

This shortcoming is not trivial. Much of politics, and generally of human conflict, involves a combination of all three kinds of process. The intellectual *style* of game theory—though not its actual mathematics—pervades much of the work of modern writers on strategy, while the style of the theory of the escalating "fight" processes can be seen in various writings on escalation, regardless of whether this process is viewed with favor or alarm. Hardly anyone, however, discusses international politics in terms of a debate in which not only each actor's tactics may eventually change, but also his viewpoint and interests—and they may do so autonomously or in response to what occurred in the debate. As a result, the topics of the debate may shift, as well as the roles and mutual attitudes of the opponents or partners.

This process is ubiquitous in politics and generally in human affairs. It is of crucial importance in domestic politics, and perhaps no less in the long run for international relations. Yet its nature is not well understood. Even the literature on international communication often deals more with propaganda, manipulation, and persuasion—all processes in which the views and interests of at least one partner in the process are expected to remain unchanged. Studies of genuine change in political images and goals in response to experiences and to autonomous processes within acting countries or governments are still few and far between, although the volume on *International Behavior,* edited by Herbert Kelman, represents an attempt to move some way in this direction.[53]

[52] *Ibid.,* pp. 245–309.

[53] Herbert C. Kelman (ed.), *International Behavior: A Social-Psychological Analysis* (New York: Holt, Rinehart and Winston, 1965). For several significant recent analyses of both historical and contemporary cases of cultural and attitude change of whole societies, see Carl J. Friedrich (ed.), *Revolution: Nomos VIII,* Yearbook of the American Society for Political and Legal Philosophy (New York: Atherton Press, 1966).

Here again, the search for models, data, and techniques for simulation leads us back to the age-old search for insight. Scientific techniques can only help to solve a problem that has been perceived. Ordinarily, they cannot overcome obstacles that have not been recognized. A failure of nerve to face these problems, a failure of heart to reach out beyond the politics of competition and manipulation to the politics of growth and new social learning—such failures could not be wiped out by improvements in methodology.

With the willingness, however, to confront all relevant political problems—even those that may be difficult and painful, such as the rigidities and blind spots in our own thoughts and practices—political science can use the new methods to make real progress. We need a cumulative political science where knowledge will grow and clearly improve in scope, amount, and quality, as it has done in so many other fields of human knowledge. Such a cumulative knowledge of what can and what cannot be done in politics under specific conditions should open the way to more effective applications of political science in the service of freedom and peace, within countries and among them. Medicine and economics have come a long way in developing from "dismal sciences" to humanistic sciences. Political science may yet move in the same direction.

Comment on Professor Deutsch's Paper

By Heinz Eulau

METHOD drives political scientists into warring camps, and perhaps more so than any other aspect of their discipline. There was a time when political scientists were rather vigorously debating the discipline's scope. But as political science expanded its substantive concerns and theoretical interests, a live-and-let-live attitude made for an era of good feeling. Indeed, boundaries are now seen not as something to be respected, but as something to be explored and extended. Similarly, mutual tolerance has come to characterize the discussion about the objectives of political science. While some political scientists are primarily interested in theoretical matters, others more in practical affairs, and still others in closing the gap between knowledge and application, no one would any longer venture to legislate another's motivations and purposes. What political scientists should do and for what reasons they should do it, are questions that do not excite the imagination. For they are stale questions that not so much promote as retard whatever pressing problems, whether of an ethical, theoretical, or practical nature, stimulate scholarly inquiry.

Not so with method. In matters of method, paradoxically, the issue is joined and the battle is fought between the ancients and the moderns. This is paradoxical precisely because it is in matters of method that one should cultivate a maximum of mutual esteem and tolerance. For method and methodology are the least developed and most misunderstood components of political science. Yet, where one might expect political scientists to tread with caution because their feet are made of clay, they stamp with violence as if they wore a storm trooper's boots. Not curiosity about what the other fellow is doing or trying to do, not empathy with his trials and tribulations, not sympathetic hope that he will succeed, but denial, defensiveness, and defamation are typical attitudes one encounters in discussions of method and methodology. More often than not, what takes place is not

a dialogue but a dispute.   And the disputants are more inclined
to issue manifestoes asserting their own righteousness than to
explore the sources and circumstances of their disagreement.[1]

Whatever virtues or vices one may find in Karl Deutsch's
"Recent Trends in Research Methods in Political Science," one
cannot deny its broad-minded approach to the problem of method.
Even those who may not share Deutsch's enthusiasm for the new
technology cannot but admire his generosity.   For the very
diversity of methods, techniques, and data that Deutsch discovers
and describes does not disturb him, as it often disturbs those less
tolerant of methodological ambiguity, but appears to him as a
new beginning: "The diversity itself of the new data and techniques of reproducible—and hence verifiable—empirical research
is creating a major research method through the mutual confrontation of different data and research results."   Truth, Deutsch
tells us, "may be thought of as a relationship between different
streams of evidence."   Undoubtedly, this epistemological and
methodological catholicity may be offensive to those who prefer
to invest in a single stock in the market of ideas.   But it suggests, to me at least, that perhaps a new spirit of methodological
liberalism has come to lead us out of a really unnecessary professional quandary.

Moreover, it is not only the basic orientation implicit in
Deutsch's "method of confrontation" that is significant; perhaps
more important is the possibility that this method may be useful
in shedding some light on our methodological problems.   For I
do not believe that our problems of method—*logos* notwithstanding—will be solved by logic, and surely not by logic alone.

---

[1] This state of affairs reached its high point, I think, with the publication
of Herbert J. Storing (ed.), *Essays on the Scientific Study of Politics* (New
York: Holt, Rinehart and Winston, 1962) and the ensuing attempt at debate
between the contributors to this book and Professors Sheldon S. Wolin and
John H. Schaar in the pages of the *American Political Science Review,* Vol.
57 (March 1963), pp. 125–160.   In some respects, this useless debate served
a useful function: many colleagues with whom I talked about it felt that the
debate represented a waste of good space.   And I also know, from being
privy to some unpublished correspondence between the editor of the *Review*
and some of the most maligned in the debate, that the latter, being genuinely
creative men, refused to join this ridiculous and unproductive controversy.

Logic is a powerful tool, but it is a tricky one if it is not related, in one way or another, to empirical reality.   It is Deutsch's position, if I understand him correctly, that our methodological difficulties cannot and will not be solved by logical analysis, but by the confrontation of masses of empirical research evidence that diverse methods and techniques are capable of dredging up. In other words, in the "method of confrontation" the burden of proof for the viability of a method is shifted from the method itself to its results.   Not abstract and logical analysis of methods as such, but the confrontation of the data "made" by different methods becomes the test of a method's utility.   There are some difficulties in this approach, but I cannot see how one can deny its plausibility.   For what Deutsch advocates is a kind of friendly competition among diverse methods.   Whatever method yields the most satisfactory results, presumably from the perspective of their relevance in testing theoretical propositions, would have to be accepted, at least until found wanting because another method makes for better results.

Of course, not every method is equally useful in studying every kind of problem.   Obviously, methods most adequate for data-making or data-manipulation on the macrolevel of analysis may not be useful at all on the microlevel or on intervening levels.   So banal is this statement that it does not, perhaps, deserve to be made.   I make it only because Deutsch's inventory of recent trends in research methods is predicated on it, and because much methodological disputation ignores it.   It is surely strange that political scientists, who would probably all admit that the microscope and the telescope serve different purposes, are prone to reject a method because it does not happen to be useful on the level of analysis on which they are carrying on their research.   Clearly, the analyses of power relations in the government committee and in the international system are likely to require different methods.   But, in this connection also, Deutsch's "problem-oriented confrontation of several streams of evidence" should go a long way in helping us solve the difficult question of transition and linkage between different levels of analysis.   For, ultimately, we hope to make theoretically valid statements about power, for instance, that can be tested on all levels of analysis and are relevant on all levels.[2]

All this is not to say that the confrontation of data collected and manipulated by different methods, whether on the macro- or micro-levels of analysis, will automatically solve our methodological problems. In fact, our difficulties may be confounded. For instance, it would be a mistake to assume that methodological ingenuity and technical finesse will free us from having to make partly subjective judgments about the reliability of our data or the validity of our measures. But subjectivity is itself a variable rather than a constant, as it is often conceived to be. All too often, we still contrast subjectivity with "objective truth" as if objectivity were written with a capital "O" and truth with a capital "T." And this goes for all parties, on whatever side of the subjective-versus-objective controversy they are located. I would argue that rather than denying subjectivity, we affirm its possibility, but accompany this affirmation with the conviction that, as reasonable men, we can reach such intersubjective agreement as is necessary to approximate whatever objective reality may be. In this convergence of our traditional belief in reason and our scientific commitment to empirical verification, method is the bond. For the task of method, it now appears, is not to eliminate all subjectivity, which is probably impossible, but to maximize intersubjectivity. Knowledge is the process of knowing in which there is no "final analysis."

Though it may be written in different ways, if I read the history of scientific development correctly, the methods of science do not so much function to create knowledge as to reduce ignorance. This does not mean that what motivates us is not a quest for knowledge. But what motivates us must not be mistaken for what we actually do when we seek knowledge. If we knew, before testing a hypothesis, that it were either true or false, there would be little incentive to proceed with knowledge-making. It is for this reason that we prefer to assume ignorance as the context in which we undertake research. Formulated in this way, research can tell us what is false and leaves open what may be true. The role that methods play in this dynamic of the

---

[2] I have hinted at some of the difficulties involved in my *The Behavioral Persuasion in Politics* (New York: Random House, 1963), pp. 123–127.

research process should be evident: as methods develop, today's truth may be tomorrow's falsehood. Clearly, it is preferable to claim less for our methods rather than more if we want to avoid methodological rigidity.

This is the background, I think, against which Deutsch's "method of confrontation" must be assessed. It seems to me that it allows for both intersubjectivity in the evaluation of research results and for an open-ended research process. This is all the more necessary because it is as likely as not that the confrontation of research results may yield findings which, for the time being at least, cannot be reconciled. Truth and falsehood may coexist, and not only one truth and one falsehood, but several truths and several falsehoods. I share Deutsch's enthusiasm for the research opportunities which the new technology of the behavioral sciences has made possible in the study of politics. But our enthusiasm would be misunderstood if it were not placed in the context of what knowledge is all about. Otherwise, if the confrontation of research results is negative, the wrong conclusions might be drawn from it concerning the methods that were employed. It is important to keep in mind, therefore, that a result is always negative only from the perspective of the hypothesis we are testing, for the results may be seen as positive from the perspective of the counterhypothesis. The confrontation is, then, a kind of dialectic which, like the research process itself, must be seen as a continuing enterprise, perhaps with an identifiable beginning, but surely not with a foreseeable end. It is a process in which the results of research are subjected to increasing strain and stress, for the results are never final but always exposed to the subtle, cumulative interplay of theory, method, and data. It is the very diversity of research methods and techniques made possible by the behavioral sciences that makes Deutsch's "method of confrontation" an important strategy of investigation.

But if it is in the crucible of confrontation that our methods must meet the demands we make on them for reliable knowledge, it is incumbent upon us to respect all available methods, and not to reject them out of hand. Fortunately, no longer can it be said, as I had to say only a few years ago, that concern with methodology has not been a hallmark of political science. One seeks in vain in the vast literature of politics for the kind and degree of methodological awareness easily found in the work of economists, sociologists, or psychologists.[3]

Deutsch's inventory is indicative of a changed state of affairs (and his coverage is by no means exhaustive). Yet, I still find a good deal of resistance to "purely" methodological research—studies primarily concerned with inventing, developing, and perfecting methods and techniques. This is curious because it should be obvious that our knowledge is never better than the methods with which it is created. There was as much "method" in the older historical, legal-institutional, and philosophical political science as there is in the new political science. Only there was little awareness of the fact, if fact it is, that "method is the bond." Perhaps it was this unawareness and lack of self-conscious concern with method that has made the older studies so obsolete. Perhaps, had there been more interest in methodology, some of the recent disputes over method could have been avoided. At least I, for one, see no inevitable conflict between the newer methods of the behavioral sciences and the older methods of political inquiry. The problem is to determine just what a method can and cannot do in the quest for knowledge. If this is so, then Deutsch's "method of confrontation" is, indeed, a useful strategy, and concern with method may yet unite rather than divide political scientists. If method is *not* the bond, it should be.

[3] Heinz Eulau, "H. D. Lasswell's Developmental Analysis," *The Western Political Quarterly*, Vol. 11 (June 1958), p. 229.

Comment on Professor Deutsch's Paper

By Harold Guetzkow

DEUTSCH'S speculations about "Recent Trends in Research Methods in Political Science" suggest that the coming decades will be a nightmare for the scholars of political life. The "new data" are staggering in their amounts, even if they are somewhat "co-ordinated," as Professor Deutsch hopes, through the use of probabilistic, multivariate methods of analysis. And the "new sources" of theories can be expected to generate demands for data in even greater abundance.

How can the student of politics of the future handle such complexities—will he not simply be data-bound? In our historical roots we have two potentials which may enable us to transcend the burdens which Deutsch describes as emanating from recent methodological trends in political science. By tradition, political scientists continuously and insistently ask big questions, questions about the future. By tradition, political scientists have persistently focused upon political theory, as a way of handling problems impossibly large in scope. In my judgment, updating of these traditional tendencies may help to prevent us from being data-bound during the coming decades, as we test increasingly complex theories with growing mountains of data.

(1) Data may bind us by limiting our vision to political life as it is—not as it might be. Yet, in our past there has been some interest in the construction of new forms of political institutions, as when Augustine built his *City of God* and Harrington sketched *Oceana*. Were contemporary policy-makers and scholars to utilize this potential in the co-operative development of alternative futures for use in experimental field situations, new data might be generated to transcend the constrictions imposed by descriptive data drawn from institutions of the past and present.

(2) Data may bind us by overwhelming us, given the inadequacies of our natural languages for theory-building. Yet, in our past—even in our remote past with respect to mathematics, as Alker illustrates—there has been little willingness to employ more

formal languages for theoretical work. Were political scientists willing to utilize such rhetorics—including simulation—in the construction of political theory, perhaps we might overcome the constraints of complexity induced by the realities of data.

With the flowering of comparative research methods in politics during the last two decades, we slowly are releasing ourselves from the ethnocentrisms of our culture; we are less "culture-bound." Let us consider in turn each of the two potentials mentioned above, to ask whether such methods might enable us to be less "data-bound."

LOOSENING THE BOUNDS OF THE PAST: CONSTRUCTING ALTERNATIVE FUTURES

From Plato onward, as political theorists we have been given to the development of Utopias. As Americans, we are impressed particularly with the creativity of our Founding Fathers in constructing new political institutions, as they garnered the fruits of the political theorists of the Enlightenment. And the French again are at it, as we witness Betrand de Jouvenal's leadership in *Futuribles*. The envisioning of alternative arrangements for future states of political affairs by planners is in its infancy; as yet, there has been little systematic effort in comparing one possible future with another. In creating such alternative futures, we have been less than rigorous or systematic. We have tended to be advocates of a particular formulation—and in those rare instances when we have had power, we have often played the selected policy alternative to the hilt.

With increased resources, as Deutsch indicates, it is possible now to make multivariate analyses of alternative hypotheses, given the historical and contemporary data we are fashioning into data stores from which we then can make retrieval. This trend in our methods enables us to test hypotheses empirically, so that we may ascertain something of the validity of the multitude of arm-chair speculations which we have fabricated so elegantly over the past twenty-five centuries. With the coming of carrells equipped with computer consoles connected to international master data banks, we may have ways of sorting through the plethora of intriguing hypotheses. Easy access through our libraries to systematically stored data will free us from being overwhelmed by the data—it may even encourage data-use by those among us who have shunned systematic empirical work.

These developments in automated techniques for data-handling may be paralleled, as Milbrath, Janda, and I have explored, using techniques for searching our historic traditional literature—at least that part developed by our political geniuses—for propositions, which then may be retrieved. In fact, it may be that an ability to reduce the redundancy in our writings through computerized programs of content analysis may turn out to be as important a methodological tool as our rapidly increasing capability for developing, storing, and retrieving data. Each year the Office of Science Information Service of the National Science Foundaiton reports on "Current Research and Development in Scientific Documentation"; it would seem that there is no warrant for despair.

Given such computer assistance in the consolidation of our hypotheses—both in deflating the redundancy and in using data banks for winnowing—we are ready to construct alternative futures. As our experimental work in organizational sociology develops, it will be possible to apply the laboratory techniques presently employed in the study of face-to-face groups to the experimental study of institutional processes in politics. There is little reason why we cannot extend the laboratory work of David Barber in the study of county financial boards—a procedure involving even experimental intervention—to such political situations (like the reorganization of state legislatures) and to the renovations now underway in the procedures of courts.

As we push further into the latter half of the twentieth century, perhaps we must learn to work in tandem with our policy colleagues in political institutions, so that as they construct new political machinery and make new nations, they no longer need opt for but a single future. Instead, as the practitioners invent new political processes, it would seem possible that they may want us to design experiments with them, in which carefully searched hypothetical alternatives, grounded in consolidated data, are explored systematically in quasi-controlled situations. The recent experimental work of the Civil Aeronautics Board Authority on its organizational processes included appraisal of some six alternative formulations of administrative structures, each of which was made operative in two or more replications.

In addition to taking the data as they "came" and "are coming"—or even as they are synthesized in the process of "data-making," as David Singer so effectively pleads—might we not also conduct field experiments? In such situations, the manipulation of political structures and processes might be so designed as to yield empirical checks upon our alternative hypotheses about the future. For those which are short-range in time perspective, we might realize the experiment immediately. Then, final policy choice need not be made before the results of th alternatives have been systematically evaluated. Those alternatives of a longer time perspective might at least be carefully monitored, so that the data generated in their execution could become empirical data for those who plan the successive alterations of today's alternative futures.

Mastering the Data Crush through the Construction of Complex Operating Theories

Over the past centuries, political theorists have used our multitude of natural languages with some fruitfulness—from Greek and Latin to French and English. In early Western political thought, there has been a dabbling with mathematics. Will we find it advantageous to utilize the recent advances in the development of the logics—of which mathematics now is conceived as but one part—as aids in the construction of more complex political theory? Deutsch's observation of our shift from deterministic models to probabilistic ones is an example of what is possible as our mathematically inclined colleagues adapt tools originally designed for tackling problems in the physical and biological sciences. Should the mathematicians themselves become intrigued by our problems as expressed in multivariate theory involving less-than-precise measurement, we might hope for a flowering to give us, in theory-construction in the scientific study of politics in the twentieth century, something of the leverage which differential and integral calculus gave the physicists and engineers of the nineteenth century.

But more viable at the present is the trend in our research methods toward the formulation of political theory in computer languages.   As a number of our colleagues in political science are demonstrating, it is possible to express political theory in another variation of the artificial languages which men now contrive, namely, FORTRAN and its derivatives and dialects.   Cherry-holmes and Shapiro are building a model of the House of Representatives of the United States Eighty-eighth Congress, representing the attitudes involved in voting on both domestic and foreign bills, as well as communication processes which occur in foyers and "smoke-filled" chambers.   As our computer technicians complete the development of programs which can handle natural languages, perhaps we will have a theory-construction heuristic for use on stored data in our computer consoles in our offices, which will guide our theoretical formulations—just as the "Socratic System" of Swets and Feurzeig guides physicians in making their medical diagnoses.   With the future development of multipurpose analog computers, the contemporary limitations in simultaneous processing in multivariate models may be circumvented.   Our consortia will supply the data bases through which the propositions that we are typing in our offices may be empirically appraised within the limitations of existing data.   Through such computer assistance, our natural languages—with their redundancies and slippages—will be revoked into clear, well-formulated systems of propositions, with indications as to where data were found sufficient, wherein the data are but partially adequate (and more must be "made"), and when data do not exist as yet to permit falsification.   It is interesting to note the "verstehen" tone of Professor Deutsch's comment that "simulation at best cannot be much better than our understanding of the processes which we imagine we are simulating."   The ordinary classical forms of logic encourage the use of nonoperational definitions, and suffer from sequential limitations in not permitting us to say "everything all-at-once," as is necessary for handling systems characterized by large interdependencies.   The empirical base of most such "understanding" is embedded in anecdote rather than in systematically reviewed data.

Such theoretical constructions may be given operating form—developed as simulations—in which initial conditions may be explored as to their consequences, by permitting the system of propositions to function over time.   When the simulation is somewhat adequate, one gets a partial modeling of past as well as present political processes. Charles and Margaret Hermann simulated historical politics in their representation of the events of June and July, 1914, based upon the Stanford analyses of the exchange of diplomatic messages among the great European powers immediately preceding World War I. Pool's remarkably valid work on voting in the Kennedy election is a demonstration of the potential for this form of theory-construction in political science and is grounded in contemporary data. Abelson's recent survey of the development of all-computer simulations of both artificial intelligence and attitudinal processes belies Professor Deutsch's assertion that change in the "viewpoints, intentions, and interests of the parties" of a "debate" are not to be simulated.

Because political scientists do not want to be data-bound— that is, bound by the empirical realities which happen to have evolved in past and present political systems—we want theoretical vehicles for the examination of possible futures, eventually even for the long-range. Herman Kahn's work in the exploration of the problems of escalation through verbal scenarios is more systematic than the speculative Utopias of yore—especially in its consideration of the spate of alternatives. Richard Brody's exploration of the problems of the proliferation of nuclear capability through a man-computer simulation of the international system—in which human decision-makers assembled in quasi-bureaucracies are employed in conjunction with computer programs —seems to eliminate more of the vagueness of natural language analysis in handling multivariate formulations. Perhaps the all-computer simulation, in which the remarkable complexity of political futures may be examined for longer periods of time and with wider variation in initial conditions and ongoing processes, will provide us with a methodological tool for the construction of political theory with a rigor and fullness which the early Greeks sought to achieve in their pioneering use of natural language.

In perspective, how are we to cope with the complexities of the multivariate techniques involved in using abundances of data for the generation and testing of political theories, which Deutsch speculates will soon place a staggering burden upon both teacher and research in political science? By emphasizing our traditional interests in Utopian thought about the big questions of the future, we perhaps can free ourselves from being bound to the data of the past. Can we actually avoid being trapped in the "as is" by the utilization of experimental and simulational methods in exploring alternative futures? By emphasizing our time-honored interests in political theory, we perhaps can avoid being crushed completely by overwhelming amounts of data. Can we invent computer heuristics for theory-construction, so that our data-gathering abilities do not outstrip our ability to develop viable political theories in a new holistic style? With a balanced development of these tendencies, perhaps the "Recent Trends in Research Methods in Political Science" can be made manageable, so that we will not become data-bound. Then, with Professor Deutsch in the vanguard as always, we will have the capabilities for work in the "politics of growth and new social learning." Let us hope that our tools of the future will enable us to transcend the data bounds, as even now we are transcending the bounds of our cultures in the study and development of the political life of mankind.

Comment on Professor Deutsch's Paper

By Roland Young

THERE are many indications of a spirit of disquietude prevalent in the discipline of political science, and for evidence we need go no farther than the several conferences which have been held recently on the meaning of political science, the books which have been produced, and the papers we have been considering here. Professor Van Dyke has now told us that it would be "inappropriate" to make recommendations concerning the optimum scope of political science until, as he put it, "questions pertaining to purpose and method have been resolved"; yet I imagine that he would agree that the purposes set forth by Professor Morgenthau or the methods described by Professor Deutsch do not supply all of the missing criteria.

We are still on square one, for our view of the nature of politics and of political science has a direct bearing on the objectives of the discipline and our methods of inquiry. The search for a definition of political science may appear to be an esoteric endeavor which is quite harmless so long as it does not prevent us from getting on with our main business of teaching and research, and up to now the various conferences and discussions and books do not seem to have produced consensus and agreement. Communications within the discipline are often difficult; many of the research scholars in political science who are mad on method find no place for the older learning, whereas the more traditionally minded political scientists may feel, regarding method, very much like the stammerer who learned to say "Peter Piper picked a peck of pickled peppers" with great fluency, but could find no way to fit the sentence into his conversation.

After Professor Deutsch's strictures on finding simplistic causes, I am hesitant to use the word causes in searching for the roots of our discomfort, but the fact is that the discipline of political science has been subjected to a variety of external pressures in the postwar period which have not resulted in a well-integrated discipline, but have managed to shatter old forms and assumptions almost beyond recognition. There are, as I see it, three major external pressures which have influenced political science during this period (although the list is not necessarily exclusive). One pressure has been to co-operate with other social science disciplines in a variety of ways, such as area programs, joint seminars, and combined introductory courses. Political science is now less parochial than before the war, but this exercise in togetherness has demonstrated all too clearly that there is little difference between the social science disciplines, save only as they are shaped by their intellectual history, the vested interests of the departments and of book-publishers, and the budgets of academic deans.

A second influence has been the intellectual discovery of the new and largely undeveloped part of the world, the revelation that people can be organized in hundreds of ways unassociated with the modern state. In many cases, the family and the political system may be identical, and the political terminology of the West may be inapplicable in describing these complex, multifunctional units. All of this material has provided a rich ore for the political scientist, indeed, for anyone interested in the government of people, and in carrying on field research on common problems the barriers between disciplines have often disappeared. For a period, it appeared that political science might become culturally oriented and that it would supply an additional component to the nongeneralizing anthropologists. However, the rapid rise of the new nations has tended to block this approach, not for valid intellectual reasons, but because the concepts that can now be used (nation, political party, and army, for example) seem to suggest uniformities (which may not in fact exist).

A third influence has been the development of research techniques, which Professor Deutsch has so clearly described. As he has said:

There has been an increase in the range, diversity, and effectiveness of empirical methods of investigation; an increase in the amounts, variety, and accuracy of quantitative data, and an increase in the breadth, versatility, and power of the available mathematical and statistical methods of data analysis and interpretation. All these resources have been further enhanced by the greater availability of electronic computing equipment and of the IBM-type equipment for tabulation. The emphasis of these developments is not on co-operating with other disciplines, not on obliterating distinctions through a common approach to a common problem in a cultural area, but on utilizing methods (developed by other disciplines) in resolving a multitude of problems (only some of which are political).

Political training does not seem to be required; cultural variations are of little importance; the concepts are derived from the method, not from the vocabulary of politics; and the data required is more available in the technically developed countries. Professor Deutsch comments that "these various new resources have permitted a new kind of theory about politics," and it may well be that these techniques will be found to be the most economical method of gathering, organizing, and perpetuating a certain kind of knowledge in the future.

These various influences have tended to break down the insularity of political science, to make it one of the social science disciplines, but, strangely, at the same time there has been a movement to clarify the position of political science and to establish its uniqueness as a discipline. It is no wonder that it shows signs of schizophrenia! Unlike the economists (who, as Professor Watkins has reminded us, have built a discipline around the allocation of scarce goods), the political scientist has found no comparable lode-star to guide his efforts. Never mind: a number of other disciplines share the same difficulty, and it may be that this is not the goal we should seek.

The source of our discontent may also be found in the assumptions of political science, which, despite the intellectual roots which go back to Greek learning, is primarily the product of twentieth-century thinking and effort. While accepting the political system of the West as a starting point for its inquiry, it has not developed any systematic set of categories for its findings. It has accepted a public-private dichotomy which is often difficult to apply in practice. It uses the materials supplied by history, particularly the topics from more recent years, and applies many of the research techniques of sociology. It accepts certain legal categories, such as the jurisdiction of the State, which is the heritage from the feudal system of land-holding. Law is divided into public and private categories; public law is "made law," and political science thus identifies itself implicitly with the legal positivists. And politics becomes not only struggle, in Professor Van Dyke's terms, but also manipulation.

Political science has greatly simplified the nature of the political order, and the use of high-level abstractions (such as state and sovereignty) tend to conceal the structure of society. In the words of Ralph Linton, "Human beings are anthropoid apes attempting to live like termites," and there are no instinctual drives which determine how order is to be created. So order is a cultural creation which cuts through society and includes the individual, the family, group associates, and various forms of political and legal systems. Political science, accordingly (it seems to me), should be concerned with the creation and maintenance of order, and the various subdivisions and fields and disciplines are developed for convenience in handling the problem and are not inherently obvious or justifiable.

The various systems are, indeed, cultural achievements of a high order, and they are constantly being evolved to meet new demands. In many ways, the Western system is unique, partly because it is based on law, and based, too, on a particular type of law which permits great flexibility and movement and encourages individual creativity, and it is a system which, in one way or another, has challenged the more traditional systems throughout the world. The system is constantly interested in establishing justice—that is, in establishing rules which are morally defensible— in all of the areas where interests conflict. (The question raised earlier, whether political science should be interested in crime, seems to answer itself: the heart of the political system is to prevent internal disorder.) The various systems of order interact and overlap, and they may extend horizontally, encompassing activities beyond the territorial boundaries of the political unit. The public and private dichotomy may be useful for some purposes, but we may also conceptualize a pattern of legal and political order which has both public and private facets.

The constant problem facing society—any society—is to develop and maintain a satisfactory system of order, and this problem, it seems to me, is the particular concern of law and of political science, and perhaps of anthropology and sociology as well. Our theory has perhaps been too land-based, too culture-bound, too grounded-in-current-events, too little interested in concept formation, too little concerned with the great historical processes, too little interested in ideology, too little concerned with creating new forms of order, too much the prisoner of unrelated ideas, and all of these weaknesses become embarrassingly obvious as one examines the shortcomings of the discipline.   Nevertheless, the contributions of political and legal ideas to the creation of a system of order have been prodigious, and it is this system, with necessary ramifications and adjustments, which is creating such a stir in the world today.   The new pattern may be one of order or of disorder, but, whichever it may be, the older forms of control are being challenged throughout the world.

The various approaches described by Professor Deutsch certainly provide data not before available for understanding the operation of these systems.   They also raise the problem of the preservation of the autonomy of the individual, a topic on which Professor Deutsch has commented on another occasion.   In discussing the continuing debate between the optimists and pessimists in politics, he wrote:

Conceivably, we might emerge with the Augustinian viewpoint that the probabilities are still heavily against survival, and for the eventual self-destruction, of every autonomous unit.   Or we might arrive at the belief that an attitude of awareness of these odds in favor of destruction might in itself be a factor in changing them for the better. . . . At the present time we are at best barely beginning to understand a little of the working of human personalities and human organizations.   In our search for understanding, it may not be safe to disregard the individual and social insights of thousands of years, laid down in the great philosophic and religious traditions of mankind.   The day may come when social scientists who refer to some elements in these traditions will no longer automatically be suspected of obscurantism, or of a breach of professional standards.   Perhaps we may look forward to the time . . . when the study of the growth of autonomy, and of the responsibility of persons and groups, will be carried forward with the help of all the sources of relevant knowledge available to mankind.[1]

[1] Karl Deutsch, *The Nerves of Government: Models of Political Communication and Control* (New York: Free Press of Glencoe, 1963), p. 244.

Conference Discussion on Methods

YOUNG: I want to say, in the first place, that I have long admired Karl Deutsch's work and his intellectual insight, his versatility, and his willingness to adventure into new areas. I have particular admiration for his book on *The Nerves of Government*. The question then arises of how these new materials, these new techniques, fit into political science. And this raises the question whether we are developing a new kind of theory where we can state propositions scientifically, or whether these newer techniques can be integrated into the political theory which we have hitherto developed. This takes us back to the first question on the nature of political science. We talked about this yesterday. I do not think that we came to any conclusions, but my own conclusion is that political science is not unique; there is no political science as such; we are all dealing with the problems of power, or, more particularly, I would say, with problems of order. I say that because it seems to me that if we look at the problem of order we can see political conflict in all kinds of situations, ranging from the individual to the order of international relations. Order, I believe, is a more useful concept than power, and it has the merit of being applicable to the study of non-Western societies.

I am a bit alarmed—I say this with deference—at some of the assumptions, not in Karl's paper, but in that of my colleague Harold Guetzkow. It does not seem to be recognized that political thought is a cultural development over a historical period, and it seems to be implied that we are now, for the first time, getting rather clear statements of what political science is.

It seems to me that it is quite impossible to understand our system of government without looking at its historical roots, and I would look not only at Aristotle, as Professor Morgenthau has suggested, but at the tremendous impact made on our system by, say, the structure of Roman law and the implications of that system for the organizations of public and private authority which we have constructed. Indeed, if one were interested in computerizing a legal system, I would suggest that one examine Roman

197

law, where there are hard concepts with specific meaning which, in many cases, are still applicable in our own thinking.

Roman legal ideas have given structure to our political thought and to our institutions, and, added to that, of course, there was the great development in the Middle Ages when parliamentary forms of government were developed and law could actually be changed. Law has been developed into a significant and powerful instrument of control, and it is assumed that social conflict is an aberration from a pattern of order based on law.   But, in the modern age, we have arrived at a position where control by law has been supplemented by other kinds of control, and these controls may well be frightening, as Karl Deutsch points out.   One of the disturbing factors in this development is that techniques for research may also be used as techniques for control.   We proceed from law to policy, which is supposedly based on law, although the legitimacy basis for some official action may be quite tenuous. From policy one may proceed to communications, and it is possible to control action by controlling communications.   This brings us back to the earlier statement that politics is merely one form of control in establishing public order.   Some of the techniques of research described by Karl Deutsch are particularly applicable to the control of communications.

We are constantly creating new forms of order as the old forms change.   The institutions themselves do not change so readily, but we are constantly modifying our forms of order to take care of new situations.   The modification takes place, in part, through the development of new concepts and the modification of old ones, and the system of control is based on the control of words and symbols.   They can be computerized, and we find that our system of political control is really a big mathematical statement.

There are areas where the older forms of control continue to operate, and these are the areas, it seems to me, that especially require our attention as political scientists.   They present theoretical and intellectual problems of the nature of the order to be created as well as the problems of accumulating information through research methods.   The inadequacy of existing controls presents, first of all, an intellectual problem which apparently stems from the fact that existing controls are essentially land-based: that is, the jurisdiction of the legal and political system is based on land, and it does not take fully into account the nature of mobility in modern society. There are three areas, in particular, where the nature of the political order is especially contentious. One area is the city, where the population is constantly expanding. How are these people to be brought into the political system? What part are they to play in the process of government? The old theories and methods of participation seem to be inadequate, and we have not built up new types of representative institutions which will make it possible for the urban masses to participate meaningfully in the political process.

The second area relates to the development of a new system of political order in the new nations, so-called, and I am pleased that Karl Deutsch has been sending his students to some of these territories, applying the techniques that he has described to an examination of nation-building. In these traditional areas, the older methods of political control are truncated, inefficient, and inadequate, and the study of the creation of new systems of order seems to me to be very much a part of the problems with which political science should be concerned.

The third area relates to the great cultural regions of the world and the relationship between them. I would like to think in terms of interrelated systems of order rather than in terms of international political power, and the task ahead lies in creating and extending the systems of order in a comprehensive fashion. Here the goals and the vocabulary are important, and it naturally follows that they should influence the choice of methods. If we examine the historical development of societies we find a network of relationships, a network of controls, which need not be described exclusively in terms of power. It is not too fanciful to compare the relationship of world societies to the kinship structure of Africa, where there are multiple systems of order, variously interrelated. The international arena is a place where we can use comparative insights and historical experience to develop and maintain broader systems of interrelated control, based principally on law, which will enlarge the area of the political community. Our culturally derived political and legal concepts are, to a degree, relevant and appropriate to this act of creativity. We should be aware of our major assumptions of political and legal control and build on the idea which we have been developing over a long historical period. Our basic need, as I see it, is to develop theory with its roots in history and culture and to think of the learning process as a constant accumulation of knowledge and the political (and legal) process as a constant adjustment to new factors as order is created and maintained.

Some of my colleagues wish, I believe, to develop new statements on the nature of political behavior and to develop new theory based upon the empirical evidence produced by these various research techniques. They may be right. My emphasis, however, would be to build on existing theory, for I do not think that empirical evidence will necessarily have very much meaning beyond the conceptual framework of Western ideas in which it is implicitly grounded. With that, I will end my comments and listen to what Mr. Eulau has to say.

EULAU: Thank you. Well, I would like to address myself a little bit more to the immediate content of the paper—the problems of methods. Karl engenders an enormous enthusiasm. I think that this enthusiasm is something against which we must guard ourselves a little bit. Now, as I read Karl's paper, I think that the first criticism that I would make is that, very much like a child's, Karl's world seems to center in Yale. His footnotes are mostly related to eminent works which have emanated primarily from Yale, and I must admit that they certainly have not emanated from Harvard.

DEUTSCH: In the latest edition there will be a lot more reference to Stanford (*laughter*). I am aware of the work at Stanford.

EULAU: Most of the references are to international politics and international-relations literature. I find it very interesting that the three main papers at this meeting all came out of international politics. The most exciting and most solid advances have been made in the field of American politics. I think that one could write a much more solid paper there, because in the American politics field there is so much more methodology that has been used both for the accumulation and for the replication of hypotheses. We cannot afford to live in the same world as a child who is playing with toys. We must be very careful in the employment of all our gimmicks and gadgets, from the computer down to regression analysis, scaling and factor analysis, and mathematical models—in which some of us have trained ourselves and in which some of our students have certainly developed a facility.

Take, for instance, what Karl calls "the problem-oriented confrontation of several streams of evidence." Now, the burden of his paper is that this confrontation of evidence is secured by a variety of methods and that it is likely to have a positive outcome. Now, this sounds good, but in the American field, where we have confronted a variety of data secured by different techniques, the experience calls for some skepticism. Let me give an example—the Michigan Survey Research Center's study on representation. The confrontation of attitudinal and perceptual data, collected by interviews, with hard roll-call data proves to be rather disillusioning. Only one study has been reported so far, but it was found that the correlations between the interview data and the hard data were satisfactory only in the field of civil rights. When we get to foreign-policy and welfare issues, the correlations are very low or insignificant. So the confrontation of data acquired by different techniques may well turn out to be disillusioning. This, in turn, emphasizes what I tried to point out yesterday—that our main task is the reduction of ignorance, that is, the falsification of hypotheses. This does involve methodological ingenuity. Rather than "data confrontation," it seems to me that one of the most challenging things, at least in political science, is the relationship between macrophenomena and individual behavior. I think that the most interesting research in the next few years will be concerned with the problem of how one moves from the level of the individual to the level of larger units. The whole connection has been suggested by group theory, the relationship of the individual to the higher level, to the small group, and, partly, to the larger system. Now, what kind of data can be used here will determine, in part, how the dilemma of macro-microanalysis can be solved. The naked eye is a highly unreliable instrument, and this becomes quite obvious when we observe individual behavior.

The other major dilemma that I see today is that we do not, as yet, have a kind of training which allows people to develop a high degree of intersubjectivity. When I think of Harold Lasswell, I think of the great contribution that he has made. He has made us aware of the requirement of self-observation as a pre-condition for establishing intersubjective agreement. This is extremely difficult to work out, and I do not think that a reliable or new political science is possible until intersubjectivity can be attained. I think that this is a problem of training so that the observers, like the scientists in the laboratory, can observe the same thing.

I think that a third enthusiasm of the new technology, that is made explicit by Karl in the beginning of his paper, is that it might be the source of new theory. Now, I read this part of his paper very carefully, and I find that after a glorious beginning we are back to what I like to call the no man's land of methodology. Karl suggests that we can now pick out the old theories and, by implementation, extend them. I think that this should be the main thrust of the newer technologies. We have done it in our legislative work; we have picked up Burke's theory of representation, or his theory of parties, and this has turned out to be very fruitful. I think that this is why it is so important that the new younger men whose focus is on mathematics should be given very thorough training in classical political theory. Certainly, Karl suggests that we might develop inventories of propositions which are floating around. I think that this is rather a hopeless enterprise. I think that the propositions are too disconnected and disjoined. One cannot and should not immediately subject these to empirical tests. I think that propositions first have to be organized in terms of some kind of theoretical structure, and then we can contribute to knowledge by testing a particular proposition.

In Karl's listing of propositions, he slides very quickly over from these things, which I can buy, to general systems theory and related models. The point that I would like to make is that these are not models of politics *per se;* they are useful models for the organization of data. But I have yet to read—and that includes David Easton's new book—a systems analysis from which one can derive testable propositions about politics. In other words, while the systems framework is a form of framework, a useful mapping device which may help us to orient ourselves in the flow of political events, I do not believe that it is possible to derive propositions from it, at least I have not seen it, to derive testable propositions from general systems notions.

I say this with regard to my own work. I always see things in terms of inputs, conversion, and outputs. I do not want to fool myself into thinking that this is politics. I think that within this systemic mapping it is still necessary to advance propositions about politics. Then we find ourselves back in this listing of Karl's models, cross-sectional designs, simulations of games, and the like, which, I think, are really techniques for the testing of theories. I do not know quite how the theoretical problems of modern political science can be solved by technological expansion and know-how. It seems to me that the theoretical enterprise is autonomous and that all one can expect from theory is that intrinsically it be testable, although it may not be testable in fact.

Let me, in conclusion, just make some general remarks about the problem of method. It is not quite clear to me in Karl's paper, but he distinguishes, or at least makes the distinction which I make, between methods and technique. The method refers to all the designs of analysis by which inferences can be made. One is concerned with the degree of reliability of inferences. This always brings us back to the classical methods—the deductive method, the inductive method, and the like. In the inductive method we can have such things as the experimental design— in the laboratory, as James Barber has used it, or in the field, as Sam Eldersveld has done. We can have a factor-experimental design, and we can have comparative studies, case studies, and longitudinal studies. All these things are methodological problems in the sense that they involve different degrees of reliability with regard to the kinds of inferences which are to be made from the data.

I think that this is quite different from the problem of technique, which largely refers to the means of making observations and collecting data. To start research in political science today involves the selection of the means most appropriate to maximize the reliability of the inferences which are made, but regardless of whether one proceeds deductively (which very few political scientists do) or inductively, one tries to choose certain strategies which maximize reliability of the method, and then to choose the means or techniques. Tactics, on the other hand—I am deeply involved in them—involve the adjustment of the strategies, that is, the adjustment that is necessary day by day in the humdrum relating of the research design to the exigencies of the situation. Very often a maximal strategy may have to be modified because of the stubbornness of the data.

Let me suggest something.   Very often, we have to substitute. We may have to substitute aggregate data for survey data simply because the surveys cannot be executed, although it would be much more preferable to have survey data.   The choice of technique also depends, of course, on the level of analysis on which one tries to conduct the research.   We have had considerable difficulty in trying to make statements about individual behavior, using aggregate data, because we always have the obvious problem of the fallacy of ecological correlations.   In this connection, another interesting problem is to ascertain where comparative analysis ends and statistical analysis begins.   In the field of comparative government, the method has traditionally been comparative, whatever that means, because of the global unit of analysis that was employed.   Now, Karl, for instance, using aggregate data—I think, very bad data—tried to move from the comparative to the statistical method.

I am trying to do this right now in my own work.   We have been trying to study different types of city councils in the San Francisco Bay region.   You may think that this is hardly relevant to an important problem, but if one puts this into the context of a policy consideration, of the metropolitan problem and the obstacles which exist there for integration, one can rationalize the project in terms of its importance.   That is not my concern right now, however.   Quite clearly, we have eighty-nine units. We can deal with them statistically; we can rank-order them; we can make regression analyses on the basis of the whole range; we can develop typologies and the like.

PALMER: Are you trying to move from the comparative to the statistical or from the statistical to the comparative?

EULAU: Both—back and forth.   You see, in order to evaluate the kind of inferences which can be made in trying to divide eighty-nine cities into three types, we get a six-cell table which is basically a comparative analysis.

Deutsch: What is the objective standard on the basis of which you compare? I mean, with respect to what are you comparing eighty-nine city councils?

Spitz: Can you list a few specific variables? What are the things that you are comparing in these eighty-nine city councils?

Eulau: Well, we are examining such things as structural differentiation or institutionalization within the council. There are whole types, whole orientations, which come with different sorts of analysis, and we can categorize the councils in terms of these criteria.

Hartz: I wonder if you would elucidate that a little. I do not quite understand the role-structure principle. Can you explain that?

Eulau: Well, I do not want to go into this, but let me give you a simple example. We have pressure groups within the community. We are able to classify individual councilmen into three types—let us say we call one type "pluralists," another "antagonists," and a third "tolerants." Now, by aggregating the individuals or by some cluster analysis of roles, we can characterize the role structure of each council, which now becomes the unit of analysis, and we can relate, for the purpose of comparison, councils classified in various dimensions of role cluster.

Palmer: But do you not have to categorize relations—something like an ideal type or something of that sort?

Eulau: No, these are empirical types, not ideal types.

Palmer: And yet, you know, there is in that categorization a degree of ambiguity and complexity which would seem to me to raise very serious questions of classification.

Eulau: I do not wish to get into the problem of how the types are constructed. They are constructed out of a variety of empirical indicators, you see.

Charlesworth: What empirical indicators?

Eulau: We get perceptions and attitudes toward pressure groups, out of which we construct the types. This is beside the point. I am talking now about the fact that it is possible, just as one would categorize governments into parliamentary or presidential, to categorize city councils into certain role structures.

Morgenthau: May I ask you one question? Why do you

say that this is beside the point? It seems to me to be the only point which is relevant.

Eulau: I do not wish to go into my own research. I just want to make some comments on Karl Deutsch's work and the relationship between the comparative and statistical forms of analysis and the continuity of going from one or two cases to many cases. I do not want to go into my own research, because how role types are constructed is a long story. I am perfectly willing to send you the papers. Really, it is possible to categorize the councils in certain characteristic ways. We do it by sociometric methods, and then construct typologies, which makes possible rank-order correlations, regression analysis, and the like. In that sense, the point that I wish to make here relates to the methodological attack. I characterize as a tactic of research the substitution of one set of analyses for another and the different kinds of inferences which can be made from comparative analysis or statistical analysis.

Another problem, of course, is the replacement of direct observation by the interview. Probably many of you are satisfied with getting the data in the *New York Times*. It is, in my judgment, a very bad sort of information, but it may be all that is available. Yet, I believe that direct observation may become possible. It is being done in the laboratory already. Karl, in his paper, mentions Barber's work at Yale about the Boards of Finance. I think that one can obviously develop techniques of photography and recording in natural settings, not in the laboratory setting, where behavior can be directly observed, where the discussions can be taped, and political scientists can perform analyses.

Finally, I think that very often we substitute perceptions and attitudes for behavioral realities. One makes a full series of assumptions about the relationship between attitudes and behavior. The point that I would like to make is that I think that we are perfectly aware of the limitations of the data. Sometimes, coming back to my original charge of enthusiasm, we think that when we have psychological data we have behavioral data, but we certainly do not. Yet, very often attitudes and perceptions are the only alternative we have to behavioral data. In this connection, it is all-important that we recognize about whom we are going to make the statements. I would say that the role of political science has been simply outrageous in its confusion of levels of analysis. We shall not bring about the study of changes in international politics if we move from making a statement about the nation or about the international world back to the behavior of the individual decision-maker. It is just one big confusion of levels of analysis. In fact, the kinds of observations, the kinds of reliable judgments, that one can make about human behavior depend on the level of analysis and the method employed on this level of analysis.

SPITZ: May I ask just one brief question on your last point? Are you implying that each level requires a distinct method?

EULAU: It may.

SPITZ: It may, but you are not saying that it does; yet if you say that there is confusion, you are implying that we need a different method.

EULAU: No, I am saying that it may be necessary. For instance, I have grave doubts about the reliability of the use of aggregate data about individual behavior. This is what we usually call the fallacy of ecological correlation. Now, within certain limits of confidence and knowing certain statistical safeguards, I think that one can make certain inferences. We can measure averages or deviations. But even the standard deviation must not be confused with individual behavior; it is still only a range of behavior that is being discussed. So I think that this is the problem: How do we observe?

Let us go to the large system. I think that that is a problem with which David Easton does not concern himself at all. How does one observe whole systems? Well, I would say that, at the present time, it is impossible to observe whole systems. I think that one can make statements about whole systems, large systems, but that one cannot observe them. This is precisely the reason why one has to move on the individual level. This is the meaning, it seems to me, of what is called the behavioral movement in political science—that one has to move from the level of the individual to the level of the system. Now, admittedly, for the first twenty years, most of the analysis was on the level of the individual; I do not think that much was said about systems. I think that the development of the work of the Survey Research

Center in the electoral field is extremely interesting. When they started out in 1948–1952, they made statements only about the individual, about the American voter. But in the last two or three chapters of their second book, they make statements, based on individual behavior, about the kind of elections in which behavior takes place. I think that the Survey Research Center people have successfully moved from the level of the individual, and they are able to make fairly reliable statements about elections as global phenomena.

GUETZKOW: I came here because this conference gave me a chance to learn from some people with whom I had never talked before. I am glad that yesterday we established an area of tolerance with respect to the problem of subjective criteria, in terms of what should be the scope and purpose of our studies, because now maybe you will be willing to include me although I certainly seem to be out on the extremes, no matter what kind of survey is made of the discipline. I share with many of you the attempt to become highly relevant immediately. This is my fight against the limits, as we put it yesterday, and I am fighting hard. I tend to get enthusiastic—I suppose because I am so lonely and so often misunderstood, even by colleagues who usually understand me. Therefore, I have to make sure that my little autogiro works by itself, and I have to renew it by writing papers to myself like the little set of comments that I wrote after receiving but the first nine pages of Karl's paper.

I made two points about Karl's approaches. Even now that I have finally had the opportunity to read the remainder of his paper, I think that they are appropriate. They are simple points, and I suppose that they both bespeak my interest in having immediate relevance. One is that we should achieve relevance not just by doing experiments in the laboratory—although I think that this is an important thing to do—but by working with policy people and doing our experiments in appropriate arenas, for example, as in the negotiations at the Geneva Arms Control Conference, trying out some of the ideas in Hans's work and some of the contrary propositions which are also in the competing literature, as Sawyer and I have pointed out elsewhere.

The second point I make, and herein is where I am often misunderstood, although perhaps it is that I am just wrong, is in my concerns about simulation. Part of the problem of our mis-understanding among ourselves as members of a discipline is our inability to communicate well through ordinary language. I am ready for a more adequate language, and I do not think that we necessarily have it in the development of the more formal kinds of techniques that Karl describes. One of the ways in which I look at simulations is that they are a kind of formal theory perhaps adequate some day to handle the complexities of policy. I call them "operating theories," to try to distinguish them from operational theory, which is usually concerned with definitional matters. In constructing an all-computer model of an international system or of a legislature, as some people are now beginning to do, using many ideas from the empirical work, it seems to me that we shall have a more feasible way of making complex comparisons and of talking about the kinds of theories that are developing. Because of the limitations of our own human brains, it seems to me that computer assistance can help a great deal, potentially, in terms of handling the complexity of the kinds of theories that we are beginning to generate as we work empirically in the complexities of policy.

From all this I get to the notion that, although I agree with what Karl is saying, I think that we must make sure that we keep perspective. This way, you see, I feel very close to many of my colleagues who are very (as they put it) nonquantitative. I am trying to work with data in such a way that—and here again I am being premature, for here, perhaps, Heinz and I may disagree—the inventories of propositions can be built early, with data books available for testing which propositions are the adequate ones and which are the not-so-good. I want us to be empirical, but I do not want to be data-bound, I want us to be creative in our empiricism, in the sense that we can create new kinds of political phenomena in our real-life experiments by applying policy in different ways.

These are the reasons that I feel that Karl's perspective, in a sense, has its limitation. His suggestions are solid, as they are ways of trying to be more rigorous and systematic in ferreting out what is adequate about the kinds of theories that we are building. But they are also, in a sense, retrospective in terms of being anchored in "what is" and "what has been." Through my experiments in policy, I would like us to continue the tradition we have had (and it has been quite a vigorous one) of creating new kinds of political institutions. This is why I like the way Roland put his comments when he talked about the "creation of order-maintaining systems."

SPITZ: May I raise two questions on the meaning or implication of three sentences at the very end of your [Deutsch] paper? All of the previous comments have dealt with methodology. I shall not venture to comment on or question any of that. Throughout your paper you talk about ways and means, sources of data, and the like, but on the very last page you seem to make an astronomical leap into what the behavioralists like to call normative political theory. You say, for example:

Such a cumulative knowledge of what can and cannot be done in politics under specific conditions should open the way to more effective applications of political science in the service of freedom and peace, within countries and among them.

What I would like to ask is how you would relate your data to utilization for good ends rather than for bad ends, how, indeed, you would decide from your gathering of data which ends ought to be selected, or whether, since you are concerned only with the gathering of data, you do not think that the determination of ends has nothing to do with political science and therefore should not be considered a part of political science. But if you do consider this a part of political science, I would like to know how you make that kind of statement and how you will instruct your students or us to decide among alternative ends.

In the very next sentence, where you speak of economics, may I revise your statement and see if you will accept this rendering? I would like to revise your sentence to read: "Economics has gone a long way in moving from a humanistic discipline to a dismal science." If I read Adam Smith and John Stuart Mill correctly, the one thing that is clearly there is a concern for humanistic ends. No one can read Mill, whose book is called *Political Economy* and dealt with human values throughout, or read Adam Smith— who, as Mr. Charlesworth said, was a professor of moral philosophy and was concerned not with the allocation of resources or with how to become a millionaire, but with the wealth of nations—

and not be impressed by the fundamental concern of these men for human values.

Morgenthau: This was self-interest.

Spitz: Well, let me simply say that as I read the economic journals today—no, I cannot read them; I can only look at them, made up as they are of mathematical equations—I detect very little that has to do with humanistic concerns. Now, if it is true that economics has moved from a humanistic discipline to a dismal science, I would suggest that your last sentence is absolutely wrong, that our business is to reverse it. Far from following economics, we should move the other way, because if one is really interested in humanistic concerns, one should seek not to be like economists, but to be unlike economists.

Charlesworth: Karl, you have a lot of salvos to return here. We are all ears.

Deutsch: Well, I would say that this is an illustration of the human predicament. To Harold Guetzkow, I am a somewhat data-bound old fogy looking back into the past and cleaving and subscribing to past political systems rather than looking toward the future. To Heinz Eulau, I am an enthusiastic child playing with new toys and gadgets. In fact, I think that both of these critics have pointed out aspects common to all of our present states of research. At times, we all get excited or carried away with the possibilities of doing something new, and at times we all suspect that we are prisoners of the old, of our past, of our experience, of our data, to a high degree. I would say, in this sense, that this is an illustration of a general human condition, and I would certainly accept both criticisms—and it is very likely that I suffer these crucial indignities to a more intense degree than my colleagues.

I have one very general point which comes back to the earlier debate we had on Hans Morgenthau's views—and that is the question of the perennial truth. Years ago, Philip Frank made the point that if one has a philosophic system which asserts a perennial truth, independent of the results of empirical research, then actual observation will show that what began as substantive theory changes and becomes a language. Perhaps the best example is the concept of matter in Marx's discourse, which began as the matter of nineteenth-century chemistry with Marx. In the writings of Lenin it became, in 1914, what Lenin called "the electrical theory of matter," and by the 1940's and 1950's it became, in the Russian textbooks, of course, whatever modern physics said it was—that is, the word "matter" had become a counter in the language; it had lost any autonomous substantive content and got its substantive content from empirical science.

I would suspect, similarly, that when political science would speak of human nature, the term "human nature" becomes a residual category. Whatever observably changes in human behavior (for instance, human beings, at one stage of development frequently show a propensity to incest, while, at other stages, children show a disclination to love their mothers quite that much) we simply call a cultural change. Whatever cannot be accounted for by our psychologists, anthropologists, and others as being culturally determined we move to a residual category of "human nature." In this sense, what began as a substantive theory becomes a language.

Similarly, at one stage, one assumes that a certain fact of property relation is natural to men, but at length or longer it turns out that it is not quite clear. Should a telephone station be owned by American Telephone and Telegraph or should it be owned by the state? Property has been defined by the church as a natural right, limited by the particular habits and customs of different periods and countries. I would presume that we have a certain degree of perennial theory, but I would warn against overestimating it. A good deal of what sometimes appears to be a perennial theory of politics, is a perennial language.

I would add that when the classic models are applied in total, they are usually static or cyclic. We are now dealing, however, with the politics of irreversible and cumulative change. This does not mean that I am not tremendously concerned lest the political scientist neglect in his studies the great political tradition of the past. I would agree with Hans Morgenthau that much of the great political thought has been produced by good minds working on the burning issues of their time rather than with mere abstractions. Although, generally, the point that one should stress more is what is a source for order, I am in full agreement with the concept of law as a general concept for order, and I think that one can think of law as an operation of logic as a legal code. Roman law is a good example for this.

I would add to this, if Heinz Eulau will forgive me, that my preferences are for confronting evidence from different sources, that is to say, to try to simulate, as I call it, a particular legal code —to ask myself what, given a combination of contingencies, this legal code is likely to produce. Is it likely to produce clear-cut decisions? Is it likely to produce circular reasoning? Is it likely to produce decision conflict? A computer can try out in a few minutes a great number of contingencies that can arise in a legal system which it would take an individual years to go through. So the computer can be a swift and merciless instrument for exploring legal codes, including exploring them for hidden inconsistencies.

I would like to add to this, however, as much empirical data as possible—observation data as well as aggregative data. I would add to this some corrections, such as to what extent the law is actually obeyed and to what extent it would be obeyed if there were no law—in other words what the autonomous probability is of people not committing murder even if murder were not illegal. I would like to find out, in other words, what the difference is which a legal code makes to the probability distribution of behavior observed over long periods of time. Is there, for instance, a control process with an effective negative feedback pattern? If an illegal murder occurs and an outraged public demands the imposition of the death penalty, does this have as a consequence any observable drop in murder frequency, or does it turn out that changing the penalty from death penalty to non-death and back again has so little to do with the observed frequency of murders that the effects of the death penalty disappear in the long run? If one finds that the death penalty is simply not a controlling device of real effectiveness, one could then ask whether there are any other devices, other things that the government can do or has done, which have an appreciable effect on making murders more or less frequent.

I would agree that in nation-building the actual building of laws and institutions is, of course, of major importance. Laws at least have one great advantage: they are cheap. Enforcing them may be more expensive, but passing a law is one of the most inexpensive ways of thinking about influencing the behavior of the people.

SPITZ: Are you suggesting that we use law because it is cheap or because it is a matter of belief? Do people pass laws because it is cheap to pass laws or because they actually believe that laws will achieve certain intended effects?

DEUTSCH: Both beliefs and experiences reinforce each other.

SPITZ: How do you know which is which, your point or mine?

DEUTSCH: At the moment I do not. At the moment I would say that it is probably chiefly a process where the belief—the belief in the effectiveness of law—makes more people follow laws. The ease with which laws are passed, the relative ease, then, in turn, makes people think that it is a good experiment.

SPITZ: Yes, but easier is not cheap. Suppose it were very expensive. Do you think people would not pass laws?

DEUTSCH: I would ask you to find me a case where this can be observed and then——

SPITZ: You are the man who made the statement. I am asking you. How can you tell me this?

DEUTSCH: One cannot deal with precisely that in a calculable sense, with the cost of making certain——

SPITZ: No, but I am asking a specific question. If belief enters into the making of law, how do you know, empirically, that people would not pass laws if it were much more expensive to pass laws? If I believe that passing a law against murder will diminish murder, and you tell me that it will cost ten thousand dollars rather than ten dollars to pass the law, am I less likely to pass the law? Is that what you are asserting as an empirical fact?

DEUTSCH: Let me make three points. Generally speaking, many things in politics, in my experience, are overdetermined. That is to say, they happen not just because of one reason causing them but because of several things. Those elements already in a chain of causation are very likely to be circular, quite often they are in a feedback process. For this reason, I would not give a high priority to disentangling these elements unless I have some empirical data the help me disentangle them. We can probably find countries where passing laws is easier and countries where it is harder—a comparative look at constitutions might show this. It might then turn out that I could run a regression analysis and say that the outcome seems to be good aggregate attitude data on what people thought about the effect of law in different countries. Given this evidence, one could disentangle the question.

SPITZ: As of now, then, you cannot say that this is true.

DEUTSCH: I can say that there are methods for finding out the relevant differences——

SPITZ: Yes, but as of now you do not have the answer, so your statement as of now is not warranted empirically.

DEUTSCH: No, I said at the moment that the two factors are interrelated, namely, that the belief that laws work and the ease with which laws can be passed are interrelated and mutually reinforced.

SPITZ: That formulation I will accept.

DEUTSCH: That is what I wanted to say. Now, let us come back to the points raised by Heinz Eulau. His words made me imagine a play in which one figure in a minuet of political science, as he dances, from time to time says, "I have found something interesting and new." The other man who dances to the same sound of the same music steps two steps back and says, "Oh, we have seen a lot of those things. What about accuracy and reliability?" Here we have the discoverer and the skeptic. Haskins, in a handbook on research in industry, suggested that in a new field where a great deal or most of the needed knowledge is yet to be found, the attitude of hospitality to active research for new findings, of enthusiasm, is appropriate. In fields where most of the relevant discoveries have been made, as in a great many fields, the discipline is old. In such disciplines there are a large number of very-well-trained practitioners in all the techniques. Skepticism, says Haskins, is appropriate to such diciplines because almost anything worth finding has probably been found already and almost anything that anybody says is new is probably not very good, because if it were good it would have been found before. I am anxious that we in political science shall not end up combining the skepticism of an old discipline with the ignorance of a new one. We have, on the one hand, the 2,500-year traditional body of knowledge about politics, but our substantive knowledge falls far short of our needs and intellectual capabilities, and I think that we can still gain.

I must plead completely guilty to Heinz's major point.   Many very important methodological advances have been made in the field of American politics, and I have not focused my paper on them.   If I had done so, it would be presumptuous; my special field is not American politics, and I assume that if Professor Charlesworth had wanted mainly a paper on methodological advances in the field of American politics, he would have asked for Robert Dahl or Robert Lane or any of the other leaders in this field, who are at universities around the country, to do this.   Since around this table there are Hans Morgenthau and Harold Guetzkow and Vernon Van Dyke, people in the international field, and Fred Watkins in theories, with a strong comparative inclination, I thought that what was wanted was a comparison where the theory could be primarily cross-national.

But I would agree that there is a very strong body of evidence in the American government field which should be taken into account.   Indeed, many of the recent advances have occurred in comparative politics, for instance, by adopting methods developed originally in observing the American political system and taking them abroad.   This seems to me to be related to the observation that people in most countries have much more basic expertise in understanding the politics of their own country than in understanding foreign policy, international relations, and data on foreigners.   In this sense, drawing on this American competence in domestic politics is highly desirable and to the good.

I should like to add, however, that a considerable number of lesser innovations have come out of fields other than American politics.   On the whole, American political scientists analyzing domestic politics have made very inadequate and imperfect use of aggregate data.   They were so impressed by the early controversies between the pollsters and the census-takers that they switched entirely to one type of evidence and deprived themselves of the very substantial opportunities of getting the other type. The so-called ecological fallacies have now been amply discussed; one now knows to some extent how to deal with them.   One can take these matters into account, and I do think that there is a real future also in the study of the American political system in using several streams of data rather than just the one. There is a story that if you give a little boy a hammer he will go around and look for everything that can be hammered. When you give political scientists interview techniques and survey methods, they will go around and interview. But now we can perhaps afford a chest of tools. Content analysis, aggregate data, and mathematical modeling should all be used increasingly to supplement the evidence of interviews.

A very major, to my mind, and very frequent point made by Heinz is the relating of matter in microanalysis and macroanalysis. Here we oscillate quite often in our present state of ignorance between two extreme attitudes. The one attitude is that the small system is so fundamentally different from the big system that one may need quite different methods. The other notion, which is as old as Plato, is that the human personality is a miniature republic. As suspected, both of these statements are true, namely, that there are important similarities at different system levels. I have observed myself the similarities that seem to prevail between the big suburbs who defend themselves against the metropolitan authority and the sovereign state which will be opposed to a regional federation. On the other hand there are very significant differences between system levels, and this seems to me one of the most fruitful fields in political science: to ascertain what, exactly, is comparable and similar and what is not.

There is one other perennial step in the aforementioned minuet. A dancer says, "I have found some data which bear on an interesting problem." To the same rhythm of the music, someone steps back two steps and says, "How accurate and reliable are your data?" Now, at least, we can go on to the next figure in the minuet. We have tried to find out what the error margin on the data could be. Let us say there could be an error margin of plus-or-minus 15 per cent. Well, then, the next step in the minuet is to state the hypothesis that if a certain condition will be present, the frequency of this behavior will double. If the difference in the frequency of the behavior, as predicted by the theory, is 100 per cent, then a 15 per cent error in the data will not do any serious harm. In other words, we can become aware of the concept of permissible error. If a theory says that a certain change is to be expected as being of a certain order of magnitude, and this order of magnitude is the same as or smaller than the error margin on the data already given, then these data are not suitable for testing the theory. If, on the other hand, the change expected by the theory is very substantially larger than the error margin of the data, then the inaccurate data will suffice to confirm or disconfirm it, within the limits of their relevance. We must never forget that all data between heaven and earth are inaccurate. What you always have to know are two figures if you can possibly get them— what is the margin of change that is relevant for the theory and, what is the margin of inaccuracy which is inherent in the data that you now have. If possible, the data get better, and then you can test the old theories with a more sensitive test, and you can extend your testing procedures to new and more sensitive theories.

For instance, take Pareto's statement that income distribution is the same in all societies, that, fundamentally, the distribution between rich and poor will be the same in all societies and, therefore, that political and social change is substantially powerless to produce really significant differences in distribution. With all the weaknesses of modern income statistics, it is quite clear now that that theory is false, that the coefficients of equality and income given, for instance, in the use of others, show various substantial differences—something, of course, that many political scientists who have had the good sense to look at Switzerland and Bolivia could have told them. But, nevertheless, we can say now, and we can say it because it is simply really true, that income distribution can be made quite different. The range of differences is not unlimited. Pareto could come back, therefore, from a second position and say that there is still some similarity in the income curves between the more unequal and the more equalitarian countries. We can answer, yes, but the differences are also very considerable and clearly worth paying attention to. We can, in other words, even with imperfect data, add something that is not perennial to our understanding of politics—something related to secular change.

This applies not only to classical theorists. Let me take, for example, a modern theorist whom I have found fascinating and interesting, Louis Hartz. What makes those Australians, he asked, into Australians? What makes the Americans and Canadians, what they are? His approach is, to my mind, creative. It is nice to see that theory can be creative again, and I would say that quite a good deal of this could generate some very interesting work by people simply looking at some attitude tests again, and looking at content analysis. Some people think that one does not have to prove a statement if one can get it out of literature, but I think that it could be shown that what comes out of literature and history can also be tested by detailed and reproducible evidence. I know, for instance that one can test certain statements on German national character by looking at the mass opinion responses as to what German subjects, two thousand of them, will name as their main virtue. You guessed it— diligence. In other words, one can find out to what extent the traditional image of the character of a people is shared by large numbers of the population themselves. And in survey research, as in market research, one can often test to what extent actions correspond to attitudes.

I must differ from Heinz in his view that propositional inventories are not worth doing if the proposition should turn out to be disjointed. The histories of many fields show that a middle level of theory, a special theory, simply an if-then statement or proposition, can later on become embedded in a grand theory, but I would not wait until I had a grand theory before finding whether a certain if-then proposition was true or false. To be sure, when I say that a certain proposition is not trivial, I am already saying, by implication, that I have some big unformulated theory in terms of which this particular proposition appears nontrivial to me.

One theory has it that if people are ranked very high in one value, they are also very high in other values, such as deference, power, and so on. This agglutination theory, as it is stated, can, of course, be given different meanings. If one assumes that the correlation is very high indeed—90 per cent or 99 per cent or the like—one ends up with the theory of the power elite of such theorists as C. Wright Mills. If one takes that as one's premise, as Dahl does in *Who Governs,* one can show that the top one-quarter of one per cent of income-receivers in New Haven do not, in fact, dominate the Republican and Democratic nominating committees, the city-planning board, and the city committees.

One can then say that one concludes that C. Wright Mills is refuted.

The next step, of course, is to agree that the theory is interesting and the proposition meaningful in several ways, but to test it by mapping it in numbers. For instance, let us take, on the vertical axis, income-receivers from the top one per cent all the way down to the bottom. Let us plot our supposed dependent variable on the horizontal axis. If we use the number of people on the Republican nominating committee, we would get a curve that would show how many per cent we have to go down the income scale before we get a majority of the nominating committee. My suspicion is that the C. Wright Mills theory—that the top one per cent fill the committee—is clearly false. But, on the other hand, the notion that correlation to income is random probability is also false. It may turn out that by the time one gets through the top fifth of income-receivers in New Haven, one may have packed both nominating committees of both parties quite nicely. I do not know whether this is true, but we can find out and some day someone will.

In other words, we can begin to shift from a yes-or-no question to a how-much question. We can get an agglutination profile, and we can then find what the agglutination profile is between power, let us say, and reputation, between power and well-being, and between power and other similar entities. We can, in other words, begin to look at correlation evidence and answer some questions. We can now say something like this: that one-half, let us say, of the variance in a person's position in one value could be predicted from his position in another, but not more than one-half; the other half would come from something else. And in doing this, we might get a better image of political reality.

What bothers me about many theories is that they are clumsy; they are formulated in either-or terms; they are formulated in terms of noncausation, and the cause is then supposed to explain either everything or nothing. It is more interesting to formulate, or reformulate, a proposition in terms of probability and to say about *how much* of the outcome could be accounted for by one element and how much of the outcome could be accounted for from other elements or is autonomous and free.

And here I would like to come back to a more general point,

namely, the confrontation of data streams. We can use this in many ways precisely to deal with some of the perennial problems of using attitude data as indicators of probable behavior. We can take all the opinion statistics and then also ascertain how people actually cast their votes, and we can find what the difference is between attitude data and actual voting. Or, when we ask Germans in an attitude poll how many of them sent parcels to East Germany last year, we get an answer; then we can check it against statistics of actual parcel-post mailings and make a tally of this. The market researchers, of course, do not spend their money on asking people's attitudes about buying tooth paste. The people put up their money actually to buy tooth paste, and we gratefully begin to get aggregate data, quite often of what people actually did.

Indeed, I would be quite happy to get data, as Heinz has mentioned, where, for instance, it turns out that voting attitudes are only very loosely correlated with the representative votes presented in a roll call. We might find that 16 per cent of the roll-call vote could be predicted by not paying any attention to the representative and looking only at voter opinon back home. That would leave 84 per cent of the roll-call votes to be accounted for from something else.

Here again, what we are interested in is not the complete determination. We are interested in the contribution of different variables, and for this, for the assessment of correlations, I would say that the typical pattern that I would like to see in research would be for researchers to get some mass-attitudinal aggregative data, if they can, and get some interviews, if they can, with the relevant elite. The relevant elites may differ, depending on whether it is a cultural question or whether it is an agricultural question, but there are relevant elites, and there are people in key positions who are supposed to know, who ought to know, and who are reputed to know. And researchers can find out what they say. Then we could get a content analysis of what is stated in the mass media, or what is stated, if we can get samples, in letters, correspondences, diaries, historical letters, and the like. If Max Weber says that Protestants are money-minded, let us find out whether there are more frequent references to money and money symbols in Protestant correspondence than in Catholic correspondence from particular times and places. This can be found out, and using these things together, let us see whether the results are consistent enough that we can build some kind of theory, or model, or some kind of coherent plan on them.

The last point which you [Eulau] did not mention in your paper—you should have—is this: if one gives a medical doctor an X-ray machine, a gadget for making blood counts complete with a laboratory technician, an electrocardiogram, and other research tools, including gadgets in which he may take a childlike enjoyment, the quality of his diagnosis will then still depend, quite critically, on how many sick people he has looked at with how much understanding in the course of his medical practice. In this sense, the whole bag of tricks, the modern methodology, can be taught only at extreme risk to people who have no clinical experience. There is a real risk that the universities may produce extremely competent technicians with a quite inaccurate knowledge and understanding of politics. Now, in a pinch, I would rather put myself into the hands of a very well-experienced and good doctor who had never seen an electrocardiogram than into the hands of a laboratory technician who was not much of a doctor. But I hope that I would not have to settle for either of these two poor alternatives. We may end up with good experienced doctors who can get men with an electrocardiogram machine to help them. I think that at Harvard they try to train their doctors first, while at some other places they try to teach people more about the gadgets, and I think that, at some places, they strive, probably not very successfully, to teach them both.

As for the question which Harold Guetzkow raised toward the end, I will accept the point that the simulation of attitude changes is under way.

As for the point raised by David Spitz, if there is anything to the systems theory approach, we ought to be able to distinguish between a system that destroys itself and a system that does not, just as one can distinguish between a destructive cycle and a reproduction cycle. One ought to be able to distinguish it as clearly as one can see whether a certain machine will shake itself to pieces or whether it can work without speedy breakdown. One can look at a traffic pattern and see if the thing will break down at 5 P.M., and also detect some imperfect pattern that will function after a fashion. One can distinguish which are viable and which are nonviable systems. I believe that we can do this in politics. I believe that it is the obligation of the political scientist to identify nonviable systems—the death traps and fire traps of political theory and practice. The political theory of the international system of 1914, let us say, was a fire trap, and a competent political scientist could conceivably have forecast what would happen if they began to put the armies of those days into the troop trains and mobilization plans of those days and how the situation would get out of control. But I think it is our obligation now, in the nuclear age, to see such things, and we can see certain theories, systems, or behavior patterns that seem to us viable or not. Here we are normative; we must be normative; we have a professional obligation to tell people that we think that this will not work or that we think it will cause an opposite reaction from that expected.

SPITZ: Suppose you get a mass of data that would enable you to say—I do not know whether this can be done, but suppose it is possible—that a totalitarian system can be established on such principles as to be viable, that is, not self-destructive, and that a democratic system can also be rendered viable. How would you then determine the position to be taken by a political scientist?

DEUTSCH: Now, the first part is a gross distinction, is a normative one; there is the viable system again versus the suicidal system. The Nazi system in the 1930's was a suicidal system.

MORGENTHAU: But could we know it was that? We know it now, obviously, but how could we know it in 1942?

DEUTSCH: Yes, I would argue that, with all the Nazi system's weaknesses, it could be shown from 1937–1938 on that that system was sure to do two things. First, it was sure to run into war; second, it was sure to produce a self-closure in the minds of its government which would make it extremely unlikely that it would succeed in estimating realistically the force that it was mobilizing against itself.

MORGENTHAU: Could we not have concluded on the basis of subjective data that we had available in 1938 or 1939 that the Allies would run into war, but not necessarily a victorious war?

DEUTSCH: No, I do not think so, because in that case we

could have counted noses. I am glad you mentioned the year 1942 in your previous question. Statistics show that from 1939 to 1941 the total tonnage of ammunition produced by the Axis outweighed considerably the tonnage of ammunition produced by the Allies. In 1942, for the first time, the tonnage of ammunition produced by the enemies of the Axis greatly outweighed the tonnage of ammunition of the Axis. This is the mathematical equivalent to what Churchill called the "hinge of fate," that is, the population numbers, the square miles, the industrial resources of the United States, of Russia, and of Britain were, in the end, decisively superior to any industrial resources that the Nazis could develop.

The other point, which was available from 1938 on, was that no non-German people in Europe felt any great enthusiasm for the Nazis. The idea that fascism could make enthusiastic converts beyond the German national group in really large numbers turned out to be wrong. If it had been possible for the Nazis to make fanatical Nazis just as unlikely to surrender in a fight out of the rest of the Europeans as they did out of the Germans, the chance of Nazi victory, again, would have been greater. But from 1938 on, it became clear that the Nazis could not trust the occupied Czechs. It became clear in 1939 and 1940 that the Nazis could not trust the Poles, the French, and the Belgians. It became clear that, in the end, the Nazis would have neither enough men nor enough ammunition. By late 1942, only a near-miracle could have saved them from defeat.

MORGENTHAU: By the same token, one could probably have made in 1756 a similar negative quantitative assessment of the chances of Frederick the Great to win the Seven Years War against all of Europe, if one had counted resources, popularity, and the like. But one could not have assessed quantitatively the moral stamina and the political and military genius of Frederick the Great. If I can make just one other comment, I am reminded of the attempts that were made in the eighteenth century to quantify the balance of power, giving numerical weights to industrial capacity, population, and the like. Frederick the Great is reported to have said when he was confronted with this scheme: "How do you assess the influence which a mistress has upon a prince?"

Deutsch: Well, there is an answer to this question, and the answer is the one which we know from the game of chess. If two players have roughly the same number of pieces, the individual quality of a player makes a big difference. If one player has both rooks and queen ahead of the other, however, then a considerable difference in skill may no longer influence the outcome. We cannot find out how big the difference is. Even if I agreed with you that Frederick the Great was a very able ruler, one cannot by that explain the Seven Years War completely. We can quantify the military participation rate in Prussia at that time, when about 5 per cent of her population was in arms, and hers was a military participation ratio which was quite unique for that epoch. It showed what that state and that administration could accomplish, but even then we must say that even at that Frederick was probably lucky. It was a very near thing.

In other words, let us not try to make the world more determinate than it is. When one observes it, one can see that, to a point, it was a matter of chance which side won the Seven Years War. One can only say in the Nazi case that it was clear that the Nazi regime was going to run into more and more enemies, and seeing how few Germans there were in the world and how many people there were in the rest of the world, one could see that the likelihood of the Nazis coming to grief was overwhelming and the likelihood of their conquering the world was very, very small indeed, and there was no way, no mechanism in the Nazi system to make them stop short of this.

Charlesworth: How about positing a war between China and Russia? We do not know the answer there. How would we go about that?

Deutsch: Nobody knows that, and I would assume at the moment that war between the two is very unlikely to break out.

Morgenthau: I would agree with you on a nonquantitative basis. Let me ask you another question. I was intrigued by your reference to the interpretation of the Protestant ethic. You say that we could compare the references to money in the Protestant and Catholic correspondence. This implies the philosophical and psychological presupposition that one's interest in money can be determined by content analysis.

DEUTSCH: This is Martin Luther's theory: what man's heart is full of will overflow from his mouth.

MORGENTHAU: If I had used that as an example I could be forgiven, but I cannot forgive your using that example. I am serious. Let me say that it is quite possible, considering modern psychology, that the exact opposite is true—that people who are very much interested in money will make it a point to talk about religion or anything else but money.

DEUTSCH: Yes, you are right. The Freudian psychology has reached such a level of perfection that psychologists can rationalize any kind of observed outcome, but luckily we do not depend only on deductive reasoning: we have the data. That is to say, a UNESCO experiment was telling——

MORGENTHAU: Which experiment?

DEUTSCH: UNESCO sponsored an experiment in which Harold and Gladys Anderson told an unfinished story involving the loss of a sum of money in a school class. School children—10,000 fifth-graders in 25 cities in 11 countries—were consulted. The unfinished story was told, namely, that money had been collected for some kind of art paper and put in the drawer of the teacher's desk. During a mathematics exercise, the teacher discovered that the money was gone. What did the teacher think and what did he say, what did the children feel, what did the children say, what happened? The children were asked to finish the story. The answers of these 10,000 children were coded by coders and put on IBM cards, and any number of things were noticed about them. For instance, it turned out that the American children of Knoxville, Tennessee, and Benton Harbor, Michigan, 1,700 of them, felt, first, that they were sure that the money had not been stolen, but only lost and would be found again, second, that the children would tell the truth to the teacher, and, third, that the teacher would believe the children even if they did not tell the truth, and hence nobody would be punished. The European children, unlike the American children, were sure that the money had been stolen, that it would not be recovered, that the teacher would not believe the children, that the children would lie to the teacher, that the teacher would not believe the children even if they did not lie, and that surely somebody would be punished.

The exciting thing was how many of the children took the trouble in completing the story to tell what actually became of the money. The eleven cities came out in a sequence on this, and the Andersons asked me what I thought could explain this. They did not have a theory. I said that I did not have a theory either, but Max Weber had one; let us see whether it fits. Well, in Helsinki, Birmingham, England, and Stockholm, over 90 per cent of the children accounted for the money. In the rest of the cities, all the high percentages accounting for the money came from Protestant countries. The lowest of the Protestant countries was Germany, where Hamburg showed 67 per cent and Karlsruhe, 57 per cent. The highest Catholic country in terms of accounting for money was, again, Germany (Munich, 47 per cent). Then came Italy, and below came Vera Cruz, Mexico, and San Juan, Puerto Rico—32 and 34 per cent, respectively. Max Weber was being confirmed out of the mouths of fifth-graders and by means of IBM cards.

MORGENTHAU: Well, I would doubt that. The low percentages came from Catholic regions which are also agricultural regions. When you talk about Munich, you are talking about people who largely came from agricultural families or from families who had strong agricultural connections.

DEUTSCH: The area is three-quarters industrial.

MORGENTHAU: Yes, but not southern Bavaria. Southern Bavaria is predominantly agricultural in its outlook.

DEUTSCH: That does not help, because Finland is certainly more agricultural.

SPITZ: Not Helsinki.

DEUTSCH: Yes, but I mean that Helsinki is certainly not less agricultural than Munich.

MORGENTHAU: I really do not think that one can prove or disprove the Weberian thesis by testing school children in different parts of Europe. It seems to me unconvincing. The results are interesting, in fact, fascinating, but still not conclusive.

DEUTSCH: You are quite right—they are not conclusive.

YOUNG: You do not buy them?

DEUTSCH: They are obviously not conclusive; there is much more, naturally, but the present evidence of this kind is worth considering.

Morgenthau: This is very interesting, because you see, Jacob Viner, for instance, has been trying for years to disprove the Weberian thesis by reading the religious literature and the sermons, all the sermons he could lay his hands on, and I think that his kind of comprehensive investigation of the written testimonies is, to me, at least, much more convincing than this kind of limited mechanical undertaking.

Deutsch: You may find that Max Weber's theory was too primitive.

Spitz: Professor Deutsch, there is a pre-Freudian theory about the man who wanted to join the Quakers because he had heard that the Quakers were a God-fearing and money-making people, and he wanted to be one of them. How do you measure that?

Deutsch: Well, it depends on what you want to measure it by.

Spitz: Yes, well why would the man want to become a Quaker —because they are a God-fearing people or because they are a money-making people?

Deutsch: I would say that a close observation of the individual man would probably show which of the two is more serious to him. I just remembered the statement which Beatrice Webb made in her memoirs, in which she said that her mother said that anybody who sells goods below price displeases God. I think that such a statement is much more illustrative and illuminating than this kind of limited empirical investigation. I cannot well imagine that a Catholic mother anywhere would have made such a statement to a child.

Guetzkow: The problem of your sample is that if she is the only mother who says that then we are in luck again.

Deutsch: Then we have to find other mothers.

Guetzkow: That is right.

Spitz: And then we are making a survey.

Guetzkow: I tend to take a position that is a little different, and I want to have some help from David on this with respect to the immorality of positivist techniques.

Spitz: I was not arguing that. Let me tell you what my concern here is. I have no objection, in principle, to data accumulation and to the use of data wherever possible. What has interested me in many discussions with the empiricists, however, is the ease with which they themselves leap from factual to nonverifiable or even normative statements. I will cite the case of a scientist, a colleague and a professor of chemistry, who laid out certain tenets of his credo in scientific terms—one, two, three, four, five, six—and then jumped from these verifiable statements about the nature of the universe to the proposition that *therefore* God exists. Now, how can you go from one to the other? In the same way, when I read Karl Deutsch's paper, for thirty-four pages I read about data—how data are gathered, used, ordered, and so on—and suddenly I found myself reading about freedom and slavery, freedom and peace, and the like.

PALMER: He had to end some way.

SPITZ: Yes, he did. So my question is: How do you go from one to the other? Obviously—to use a doctor as an example—performing an operation can save a life or destroy one; Karl says, however, that you can only do one. But which one? And on the basis of what scientific principle or empirical datum is that decision made?

GUETZKOW: Now, where do we go to spell out these value problems other than reading what relevant predecessors have said of these things? Is there new knowledge that we should be putting on our agenda as political scientists? Are there any new directions here? What are we to do in this area as political scientists?

SPITZ: Well, that is just the question that I was putting to Karl, because this is his paper, and just as Heinz refused to discuss his research, so I do not want to go into my research. I am simply asking how somebody who is committed throughout thirty-four pages to this kind of empirical work can suddenly jump in one sentence or two to the other. How—in terms of what empirical principle—would you, as teachers and writers in political science, instruct me to utilize these data in the service of freedom and peace rather than slavery or war? How do you emerge with humanistic ends other than viability? Now, viability is, in a sense, an empirical matter. I accept that, but there are other things than viability, because mischievous systems can also be viable. Oligarchy has persisted for a great many centuries. The Chinese, the Indian, and the Egyptian systems lasted a long time.

It may be that you want to insist on a longer period; you may want to say that they have to be viable for three hundred years instead of one hundred years. I do not know.

Let me take a man like John Stuart Mill, for example. He argues that the true test of a political system is not whether it works, but what it contributes to the quality of the individuals inhabiting the country. In these terms, I want to look at something like education, not merely at the viability of a system; I must look at the values that people hold. I see, for example, in the modern American university, that the overwhelming number of the students do not seem to care very much for the values that I associate with a humane society and a humane civilization. They are there largely for vocational and social purposes. They crowd into the colleges of business and agriculture and engineering; they come to a university not to become civilized men, but to learn a trade or a profession.

But if the purpose of education is to produce better men, what can we do to create the kind of society in which they will value the right things? Now, maybe you will say that this is not our business as political scientists. But when we see that there are certain children (and adults) who are not educated, and when we consider the contention of a man like Edward Bellamy, for example, in his book *Looking Backward*, that education is necessary not simply for the quality of the person but to assure that the person who is born has parents who know how to deal with him, and that the society in which we live has citizens who know how to treat other citizens, then we realize that education cannot be left to the chance whims of economic powers, hence the state moves into the realm of education.

Now, these are the kinds of values that I have in mind; they include but go beyond the idea of a political system geared to the service of freedom or peace or viability. There are a whole group of values that turn on the quality of human existence and on the conditions—adequate housing, adequate medical care, and the like—that enable men to make choices. I have always assumed—and perhaps this is why I am labeled a normative political theorist—that one of the functions of political science is to chart lines that make possible the attainment of such values, to anticipate the needs of a good society, to try to spell out what governments ought to do, and not simply to describe what governments do. I am not talking now in Utopian terms. Clearly, we must always be aware of the historical limitations within which we operate; we must know what we can do as distinct from what ideally we would like to see done. Nevertheless, to me, as a political scientist or political theorist, this notion of what governments ought to do has always been crucial. Now, as I read your paper, Karl, there was no such concern in it for thirty-four pages, until suddenly on the thirty-fifth page, there you are, and I want to know how you got there.

DEUTSCH: Do you want me to write another paper?

SPITZ: No, I want you to tell me how pages one to thirty-four warrant those three sentences on the thirty-fifth page, and I shall be a happy man.

DEUTSCH: You have asked the question, but you have not given me much time to answer it, because you have restated it every time that I have tried to answer it. You can try to evaluate a system in two ways—does it destroy itself, does it destroy other systems from which it draws nourishment, for instance, a larger system in which it exists, or does it destroy smaller systems which are its components? Is it a system which will not only survive itself, but is also kind to its own ecology in which it grew, and to the larger system within which it exists? A cancer cell is viable, all too viable, but it destroys its host.

On the other hand, I would expect a system not to destroy its subsystems. This is the difference between a type of organization where a subsystem is really getting simpler but limited and a social organization of human beings where the individual is becoming richer and more complex. In operational and in normative terms, I prefer a system that has three properties, that is, it does not destroy the larger community, the larger system in which it exists; it can coexist with other systems on its own level; and it is solicitous of its components. This, of course, is a complicated way of saying that a nation-state should be a good citizen in the world, and it should be respectful of the personalities in the group or people which constitute it, but one can use stated empirical research methods to see whether a particular government professing to do such a thing, does it in fact.

For instance, if one follows the nineteenth-century idea of minimal government, which was applied in the twentieth century to certain colonies, one will find that the education, health, and welfare sectors are so scandalously neglected, as in many African colonies in the 1940's and early 1950's, that, in fact, a government which professed to be solicitous of individuals and freedom was, in effect, making many colonials lead lives of considerable degradation.

It may be argued that many of the unstable and unviable governments in the developing countries and the other far less developed societies are underserviced and undergoverned, and it is quite true that these societies will be poor for quite a while under any political system. It is still possible that they have made their government somewhat more responsive to their needs. For instance, we find that even under the government Indonesia now has, education, as you mentioned, is available to many more children than when Indonesia was governed by the colonial Dutch. As it is, we can ask for an operational study of this type of question: Which governments do make available which values to what groups of the citizens? And, in this sense, the data, the reproducible data, which we try to find, do have some use in distinguishing between the professions and the performance of governments.

For this last point that you raise, you are perfectly right: economics began in the days of Thomas Aquinas, if you wish, as a moral science with the search for the just price. When it was half-grown, it became a dismal science, that is, one which codified its half-knowledge into an extremely tough image of the world in which mercy and pity became, in a way, the preserves of muddle-headed imbeciles who really did not know hard-boiled economics. And, at that level, when applied to policy, economics did a limited amount of good in getting rid of some unreasonable tariffs, but it also brought about a considerable amount of harm and a good deal of suffering. It was also called a dismal science at that time. Later on, the economists came to learn still more and began to learn about propensities to save, propensities to invest, consumer behavior, and many other things. Economics became more differentiated, more subtle, and more applicable to action, including action toward a more humanistic and more

humanitarian set of norms behind it—the full-employment policies of the modern welfare states.

Political science may be going through a similar sequence.
From Plato to Thomas Aquinas, it was mainly a moral science
concerned with justice. If I may say so, from Machiavelli to
Hans Morgenthau, it has concentrated on the scientific analysis of
power, and I think that Hans has considerably more moral concern
than Machiavelli, although Machiavelli, too, should not be under-
estimated. In Hans's case, his willingness to stand up for his
values is very conspicuous in this country, but I do think that the
next step will be that if one treats politics as a pure analysis of
power, it has to many of us a bit of the aspect of a dismal science,
of a hard-boiled science. I would say that this does not happen in
Hans Morgenthau's hands because he knows far too much history.
It becomes more nearly that in the hands of such strategists as
Herman Kahn. I am thinking of Heinrich Heine's poem of his
dream in which a hangman walked behind him through the streets
of Cologne saying: "I am the action to your theories." I hope
that you, Hans, do not see the shadow of Herman Kahn behind
you. I see him behind you sometimes, but I do not think that you
want his shadow because you have taught the importance of mod-
eration and of good sense and of a sense of balance in these
matters.

But I do think, in addition to hoping that we have more balanced political scientists, that we do need a much better political
science, and that means that, in addition to the power value—
which is indeed a part—we may eventually need a model which
can deal, at least, with the equally important values that are less
readily quantified, such as the values of respect, affection, and
physical well-being. In other words, we may have to deal with
politics as a study of using limited capacities for influence and
enforcement in order to guide communities on paths of action
which will increase their position in a universe of many, not few,
values, in such a manner as to produce a significant increase in one
value, without destroying any other major value, whichever it
might be. Wealth, power, and enlightenment should not be
bought by intolerable damage to any other of the essential things.
This, to me, is a condition of legitimacy. If a policy is actually
legitimate, it increases one value without imposing intolerable

harm or damage on another value. And I think that this political science of legitimacy might eventually bring together many of normative concerns and indirect empirical concerns.

MORGENTHAU: I am grateful for what you have presented, and I have learned a great deal from it. Certainly, one point has been made in favor of the quantitative approach, and that is its ability to prove the correctness of, and to refine, certain assumptions that one makes impressionistically and on the basis of what is called common sense or the traditional wisdom. However, that approach is not applicable to one of the central political issues: requiring the preservation of values, that is, a choice. We are faced here with the problem that one cannot preserve all values equally which one regards as worth preserving. In other words, one is faced with a political or moral decision. One has to sacrifice one worth-while value in order to preserve another which one believes to be more worth-while, whereas other groups in the population believe that the sacrifice ought to be the other way around.

So we have political conflict, and these political conflicts are the very heart of political life. They operate within a dimension which is not accessible to quantitative analysis, for which that analysis is irrelevant. For one must say at one point that a certain portion of freedom must be sacrificed for the sake of order and authority, but this is the same type of decision, on a collective basis, which an individual must make at the great turning points of his life. He must decide what is most important for him, and, however painful and morally ambiguous it may be, he must sacrifice another value.

Furthermore, and finally, I have to come back to the issue of optimism versus pessimism. There is, of course, a belief in progress in your whole philosophy. Let me give you a quotation presenting the extreme of a pessimistic approach. John Bassett Moore once said that nothing new has been discovered in political science since Aristotle, with the exception of the nation-wide presidential primary. This is certainly an exaggeration, but it points to a profound truth, that is, that the fundamental issues of politics are not subject to historical change. In the field of morality, there has been no progress, at least since the beginning of Western civilization.

DEUTSCH: There is some evidence that there has been progress in the development of human civilization in general. Let me talk about Western civilization from the Greeks and Rome onward. Let us think of the treatment of women, the treatment of children, the treatment of animals and criminals, and many other things. The kind of cruelties which Greece and Rome committed publicly, particularly in Rome, had to be concealed even by the Nazis, even from their own adherents. In many cases, I am sure that the moral climate has, in a significant way, changed.

MORGENTHAU: But look at the treatment of prisoners of war in Vietnam.

DEUTSCH: I do not think that these pictures are going to appear on American columns of triumph, as they would have in ancient Rome.

But I would like to come back to another relevant point. It is perfectly possible that, in an extreme situation, a group of people may think that they must sacrifice a major essential value "A", such as freedom, in order to preserve a new "B", such as order, and that another group will say that they do not want to sacrifice the value freedom to the value order. Then we have one of those horrible, memorable situations where they have to shoot it out. I should argue that we are here dealing with a breakdown of politics. Much of the politician's art consists in avoiding intolerable choices. He must avoid them not only for himself but also for his community and often even for his adversaries. The usual political process in the community uses whatever abilities of influence and enforcement it has to find a pathway which may fall back on convention, as well as on interest goals, but which, in any case, is a pathway that keeps sacrifices of any one thing tolerable, so as to sacrifice marginal increments of one value which are valued lower in order to get marginal increments of another value which is valued at a higher point.

Now, the need for these values is nonlinear. In other words, if we are very free, we are quite willing to take an infringement of our freedom, such as rationing in wartime, let us say, in order to preserve some other value, but there comes a point in most value continua where the curve becomes very steep, and a further deprivation of this value becomes very critical. This is essentially an argument extending marginal-utility analysis. If I have lots of water, I do not mind giving up one drink. If I am almost dying of thirst, depriving me of the last drink of water is torture, and may kill me.

It is the fundamental error of totalitarianism to overlook or to pay insufficient attention to this characteristic of the human need for values. The totalitarians assume that a particular value can be sacrificed completely, or almost without any attention to how much one takes away from it in order to achieve another one. The constitutional approach to politics does imply that there are limits to the deprivation of any one of the major value dimensions that you can impose upon people. A more enlightened humanitarianism will take more people into account, but the basic difference between the totalitarian and the constitutional way of thinking, I believe, is that the constitutional way assumes from the beginning that there are limits to the deprivations that one can put upon any people in any major value dimension, and that these limits are not only normative but also a matter of stubborn empirical fact.

Now, just as an economic process can break down and family life can break down and marriages can break down, a political process can break down, and, in fact, as political scientists, we are responsible for studying when this is likely to happen, what happens when it does, and how the pieces get picked up, and by whom, after it does happen. But in the end of such a period, there is always an integration. By its very nature, a totalitarian phase of political behavior is extremely impermanent. Now, we can get different images concerning how it will end, whether it will be overthrown from outside as the Nazi totalitarianism was or by erosion from within or, to some partial degree, become an authoritarianism which is slightly more tolerant of minimal spheres of privacy. Here, again, our empirical approach is consistent with the normative approach. One of the most fruitful things to happen in the future is more dialogue between the wisdom of normative political science and the questions that can be asked empirically if the evidence can be found.

CHARLESWORTH: Gentlemen, I regret that we did not allocate more time. This has been a most useful, fruitful, and stimulating conference. On behalf of the American Academy of Political and Social Science, I want to thank all of you for your trouble in coming here, for your care in preparation, and for your earnestness in participation.

Some Thoughts Relating to the Present Dimensions and Directions of Political Science

By James C. Charlesworth

WHAT follows does not pretend to be a summary of the papers and discussions published in this monograph, since the reader can easily reach his own conclusions concerning the collective effort. Nor does this article presume to analyze and appraise the present scope, objectives, and methods of political science, whether the discipline is looked at as it ought to be or as it is. The purpose of this paper is, rather, to pose a number of questions which came out of the conference and the thinking that led up to it. In putting these questions I hope I shall not be considered offensive if I exercise my academic right to suggest answers.

QUESTIONS RELATING TO SCOPE

(1) The first question is an old one: *Why do we adhere to the self-conscious and inaccurate term "political science"?* As Einstein said, our subject is more difficult than physics. The econometricians are making it more difficult than economics. The more abstract, the more diffuse, the more normativistic, the more historical, and the more philosophical we are the less we can ape the real sciences and the less we can lay claim to being scientific. We can be scientific, if we severely limit the scope of our discipline, but if we did would we not excise its most valuable parts? And we are scientific, in some corners of our subject, but in other corners our subject is heavy with values and prescriptions, which can never be scientific.

Why must we be scientific, anyway? Art, literature, religion, and philosophy are not scientific, and their professors and expositors render a service and enjoy a prestige at least equal to ours. The Germans of the opening years of this century never really understood government, as distinguished from administration, law, and philosophy, hence it would be a long delayed but wholesome thing to discard *Wissenschaft* and declare our independence of the founders of the American Political Science Association who fortuitously had come under the influence of the German abstractionists. We could then call our subject "government," or "politics," which is not unheard of in respected academic circles, and we would no longer face the arched eyebrows of our fellow students of social subjects, and no longer damage our best political formulations by forcing them into laboratory shapes.

The present growing emphasis on quantification, observation, and behavioral recordation threatens to determine the scope of our subject. As a prominent commentator on mass communications said recently, "The medium is the message." If our medium, or vehicle, is to be confined to methods dictated by the physical laboratorians, the face of our discipline will indeed be altered. I am afraid that some of our confraternity think that because the scientific method is good in some quarters of our subject, no other method is good in any other quarter. We must not be like the Christian Scientist who believes that because his therapy is good for psychosomatic diseases, no other treatment is good for cancer.

(2) *Is political philosophy the queen of our discipline, and, if so, what is it?* How, in particular, does it differ from ideology, and theory, and political expression?

Theories may be said to be systematic analyses and explications of phenomena. There are theories to explain many things —internal combustion engines, business cycles, the best way to shave, relativity in light and gravity, the causes of wars, and the function of local governments, among others. Also there are theories about sovereignty, constitutionalism, democracy, political pluralism, nationalism, and every other conceptual aspect of government.

Ideologies represent the thinking—or feeling—characteristic of recognized groups, hence they are identified as being adjectival and predictable rather than substantive.

Political philosophy is more comprehensive than theories and ideologies combined. It is usually formal, relatively abstract, reasoned, thorough, synoptic, and authoritative. Consequently, it is not plentiful, and cannot be said to reflect adequately or currently the evolution of a period.

Political expression, however, is plentiful enough, for it is continually appearing in plays, poems, statutes, party platforms, speeches, riots, resolutions, and demonstrations, as well as in systematic books and articles. Hence, the student of political philosophy cannot capture the mood or temper of an era if he confines himself to documents penned by a small number of outstanding thinkers. By so doing he makes a useful excursion into literary biography and personal philosophy, but he does not thereby get to know the thinking and feeling of masses of the people and their political representatives and spokesmen (for we must remember that it is democratic government we are studying).

We have tried to answer the first part of our question by trying to answer the second part first. If what we have just said is sound, political philosophy is not the queen of our discipline, and should be considered to be part of the more inclusive, the more current, the more vigorous, and the more meaningful disputation we can call political expression.

(3) Another question arises—about the *internal unity and coherence of our subject*. At a meeting of our Association we see in the same hotel an expert on sixteenth-century monarchomachism in dubious rapport with an expert on municipal refuse disposal. Also, there are authorities on public finance, international government, corrupt-practices acts, American constitutional law, village life in India, regional planning, nationalism and international power politics, methodology in general political research, community power structure—these make up only part of the list. Yet these professionals are all called political scientists, and they all have the same merchantable Ph.D. If this is what a political scientist is supposed to be, how can one train him? Is any other subject so extended, even sociology?

At one time economics suffered from a similar spread, but that discipline has now been made tenable and viable by a process of fissiparation. Economics proper embraces the history and mathematics of economics, comparative systems, economic theory, and the like, and separate departments and faculties have been created for business law, finance, marketing, accounting, industry and management, private and social insurance, and transportation.

There is much to be said for a division of our discipline into three disciplines—government, administration, and international relations. "Government" would embrace theory, American and comparative government, political development, planning, parties, constitutional law and civil liberties, and cognate subjects. "Administration" would include public administration, public personnel administration, local and metropolitan government, most of state government, comparative administration, and the like. "International relations" would cover diplomacy, international law and government, power politics, and their related history, demography, and economics.

(With the reader's indulgence, I shall pretend throughout the rest of this essay that this tripartite division exists, and I shall use captions accordingly.)

(4) *Should the study of government have a limited scope?* Does art, or religion, or law? Government touches everything and is affected by everything. If *quod omnes tangit ab omnibus approbetur,* we cannot set bounds to government, which is the approving and sanctioning as well as an initiating element. This does not mean, of course, that political scientists are totalitarians; it means that when a thing affects more than one family it is a public matter, and is *ipso facto* a part of the context of government.

It is true that the wider the scope of our discipline the less we shall know about it, but unless we are to contract our subject as rigorously as the economists have reduced theirs, we shall have to sacrifice depth to breadth. If one elects to study outer space, one cannot limit it to what one can measure; likewise if one chooses to study the limitless ramifications of human political relationships one must be reconciled to its infinite boundaries.

One may even make the bold statement that the student of government should study and write about whatever seems to him to be important—whether or not such inquiry currently is considered to be part of our discipline. If he persuades enough other people that his topic *is* important, it perforce becomes part of our discipline.

(5) Another question relates to *the advisability of curtailing the scope of international relations*. Would it be desirable to teach the principles and methods of diplomacy, the geographical, ethnic, religious, linguistic, economic, and other ecological factors affecting it, and stay away from the *haut commérage* of current power politics? How does one know whether Mao is in power, and, if so, what he is thinking? (We have had presumptuous and self-appointed functionaries in the past, especially during the Middle Ages, who pretended to reveal the mind of God, but the artifice never advanced human understanding.) It is well known, to people who know it, that highly placed public figures do not reveal to sources leading to the general public their reasons for decisions and their plans for future decisions.

One cannot deny, however, that continued or imaginary exercises in role-playing, in which exciting international characters are the protagonists, are a strong lure, hence we are not likely to see a confinement of the subject of international relations to the mere ecology of international relations. Presumably the professor of international relations knows as much about the reasons for a foreign statesman's actions as the professor of American government knows about the reasons for a President's actions (even when the President states them) or a professor of constitutional law knows about the reasons for an Associate Justice's vote. But it would be helpful if we all talked less about things we cannot demonstrate. (This is not to say that the professor should not contend about what is good for the country, in which endeavor he can be as scientific as possible but need not be scientific at all; it means that we should not presume to translate the minds of persons we do not know intimately.)

(6) *Does the study of government pertain to public and legal governments only, or does it also embrace nongovernmental systems?* Should we study not only governmental regulation of stock markets, railroad systems, and the examination of candidates for admission to the bar, but also study stock markets as effective, parasovereign power clusters themselves, which control (not merely influence) their own world of activities and persons?

It would seem that any system which *controls* people should be studied as part of the total governmental process, and that we should not confine ourselves to institutions called states, which are created by constituent assemblies and described by things called constitutions. The academic term "government" should not, therefore, be limited to "sovereign" government.

In this connection one may notice the difference between government as conceived of as a tangible sovereign, with tangible pronouncements, or as an interplay (or, as the physicist would have it, an equilibrium) among forces exerted by parapolitical and nonpolitical groups—see Bentley and Truman. (The same difference has been clearly revealed in the field of jurisprudence, by Maine and Austin.)

Just as we insist that the political pluralist must demonstrate plural controls, as distinguished from plural pressures, so we may conclude that the interaction of political processes does not constitute government until it results in controls intrinsically generated.

(7) *Should we place greater emphasis on political development theory?* (This question does not refer merely to the development of government in primitive societies; it also relates to the adjustments made in advanced, highly sophisticated systems to accommodate the government to developing needs and conditions.) The answer to the question would seem to be yes, if we are to be useful in interpreting government to an ongoing society and are to be something more pertinent and important than mere antiquarians.

As between the primitive (nowadays euphemistically called "developing") and the advanced systems, there is evidence that we are paying too much attention to the underdeveloped countries. After all, the story of faltering constitutionalism in recently liberated country X is essentially (although not locally) the same as that for recently liberated country Y; it would seem that our discipline will be enriched more certainly and in greater measure if we study the more intricate adjustments and developments in our most advanced societies.

(8) *Is the study of government part of sociology?* It is fashionable among some of our younger set to call themselves politico-sociologists and to agree with the position of men like Giddings, who held that sociology is generic and political science is one of the specifics, and Ross, who said that the state is only one form of social control, and the pluralists, who asserted that

the state, or the government, is only one of the associations which dominate our lives. But if we are to agree that our discipline is to be a subclassification of sociology, we must first know what sociology is. If we dismiss the wag who said that sociology is what they teach in university departments of sociology, and if we study the graduate school bulletins and the latest books, we discover subdivisions called the family, power structure, functionalism, criminology, demography, the community, race relations socialization, and the like. How can we fit our subject into this salmagundi? To consolidate the two subjects would be like mixing two quantities of odd lots.

There are, of course, many differences between sociology and the study of government, but the essential one is that government has to do with overriding power, which demands compliance by all groups, whereas sociology deals principally with pertinent influences on pertinent groups. Government, therefore, is intrinsically different from society, and, therefore, a consolidation of the two academic disciplines would hardly be a fruitful one.

QUESTIONS RELATING TO METHODS

(9) *Are methods primarily related to the subject, or primarily related to the scholar as a person?* Thomas C. Wolfe (whose writing was not all autobiographical) would ride all night on subways and learn about people by seeing things in their faces which other observers were not able to discern. One of Jack London's methods of developing plots was to buy fourteen from Sinclair Lewis for $70. Ernest Hemingway periodically would deny himself sleep and gin and "mortify the flesh" until he had pounded out the message he felt was in him. Anyone sophisticated enough to read this monograph knows dozens of methods of work associated with famous creative authors, but what does this have to do with the study of government?

It has to do in the respect that there are creative writers in the field of government too. One can write a book on congressional government without visiting Congress. Another can tell more about City Hall by talking to all kinds of people, including bootblacks, than by painstakingly going through the records. Still another can rhapsodize about the "moods" of his computer. One can interpret politics after studying mental deviants. Another can better predict the next posture of the Supreme Court by studying congressional politics than by projecting the stream of published decisions. Still another could tell us more about Secretary Lansing's World War I actions if he knew more about Colonel House.

But here, too, in the field of government we need not multiply examples to indicate that in the innovative, the creative, the controversial, and the influential parts of our literature, there are no appropriate rules of methodology. In the minuscule, the pedestrian, the predictable, and the common-pattern type of writing, it is clear that procedure governs both matter and form.

If this is true, it would seem that we should divide our students into the inner- and outer-directed, and encourage the one group to be themselves and the other to learn a routine.

(10) *Should the newer approaches to the study of government be synthesized, or will they be more rewarding if they are pursued independently?* Scholars who separately emphasize behavioralism, mathematics and quantification, functionalism, decision-making, systems theory, communications, game theory, and development theory, understandably concentrate in their own specialty, and make little effort to relate their findings and theories to other new developments. They are pioneers, mastering particular sectors, and do not pretend to be synoptic mapmakers.

If it is true that the medium is the message and that the scope of a discipline is determined in the long run by its methodology, it would seem that adherence to new and highly particularized approaches to the study of government will result in a series of highly limited, not to say distorted, images of the same government. It would also seem, therefore, that protagonists of these newer and more highly specialized approaches should take time to see how their findings may be reconciled and fitted together with the findings of other specialists. Should we not seek the harmony of Aristotle rather than the harmony of Plato?

(11) *Can concepts be reified?* It will be remembered that in the long dispute between the nominalists and the realists, the nominalists contended that the existence alleged by the realists was merely *flatus vocis* (a sound in the throat) and that man could create something by inventing a name for it. Plato was

the first great mind to attribute objective reality to ideas (or ideals), and despite our rigorous epistemology and our trend toward quantification and physical measurement many of our word-mongers persist in the practice.

What is a political fact, anyway? Does it mean anything that has actually happened, and does it exclude relationships between things that have happened unless those relationships can physically happen? Is something knowable if it has never happened?

Every knowledgeable reader knows that one could go on for pages asking questions relating to epistemology, logic, and metaphysics, and he also knows that despite centuries of intense cerebration such questions have never been answered.

Would we not, then, be well advised to stay away from the reification of concepts? Too many corners of our discipline are only too dimly lighted now; we need not bring in new areas of esoteric, recondite, neological, and unreal products of wandering imagination.

(12) *Should we develop a more precise terminology?* In the field of physics, "speed" and "velocity" do not mean the same thing. In the field of political philosophy, Spencerian "liberalism" means something quite different from New Deal "liberalism." The words "democracy" and "justice" are protean. Examples of imprecise usage in our profession can easily be extended into a long list, as I discovered recently when I developed a small dictionary for my students.

It has been one of our satisfactions that we use the language of the street. And may the Lord spare us from the imposition of an arcane vocabulary devised by a group of mandarins!

Nevertheless, there is frequently a failure of communication in our exchanges, especially in confrontations and polarized discussions.

I modestly submit that our Association should constitute a group to prepare a brief dictionary, which would exclude proper nouns and deal only with lower-case words. It would not be ridiculous for us to have a supreme committee, like a minuscule French Academy, to rule on usage from time to time.

(13) *Should we emphasize the actuarial approach?* Some of our careful and precise writers are disposed to question

Aristotle's rule that things which are generally true are true. In civil rights cases, for example, the performance of a jurisdiction as a whole might be excellent, but in an exceptional case, where justice misfired, the particular individual suffers total injustice. The employment rate, for example, may be 96.8 per cent, but a particular man who is unemployed is totally unemployed. Housing starts across the country may be up, but how many houses have been started in the Watts section? The Supreme Court has ruled that the safety of the members of a society does not transcend the rights of a single individual accused of a crime.

These precision people hold that a person cannot be made into a statistic, and that the happiness of one person can properly be equated with that of a hundred.

But, nevertheless, we must remember that it is a pragmatic, real government we are dealing with, and that we are not moral absolutists, or theologians thundering that every single human is cast in the image of God, and must be accorded the appropriate care and dignity. A perfectionist can never be a statesman.

Consequently, I recommend that we teach our young that things which are generally true are true, and that philosophies should not be built on exceptions. In doing so we should make the point that the beginner in a science tends to notice and stress differences in phenomena, for example, no two grains of sand are alike, whereas the mature scientist tends to notice and stress similarities, for example, although no two grains of sand are more like other grains of sand than they are like anything else, consequently we can make generalizations about sand.

(14) *Should we encourage greater use of the case method?* It is well known that we have case books in law, corporation finance, public administration, business management, and the like, and that we do not have case books in jurisprudence, Keynesian economics, and the anatomy of governmental and business leadership. In the field of constitutional law the case method becomes less and less apropos as the string of cases lengthens and the reversals accumulate. In the field of public administration the cases collected a few years ago were too few, too long in text, and too simple. The business of training a public administrator calls for written and oral messages with many subtle nuances,

whereas the few large items in the case books create a configuration like that of separated boulders on a beach.

When we train people, we develop skills in identifying and solving separate problems. When we educate people, we synthesize data and try to get our charges to see things whole and in perspective.

Some parts of our discipline, especially public administration, emphasize training rather than education. But it is one of the theses of this essay that the study of public administration and international relations should be separated from that of government. Subsuming such a separation, it seems to me that the case method has little to recommend it in the field of government.

(15) *Can computers analyze the content of prose?* Many of us are familiar with the school-boy howlers produced by computers put to the task of translating language. They, of course, fail to detect the idiom, just as Mark Twain's wife, trying to shame her husband by imitating his cursing, produced "the words but not the music."

Authors of elementary spellers and readers for decades have been counting the occurrences of words in literature of the pertinent levels, so as to drill on the ones most commonly encountered. This is, of course, a very elementary exercise, and it remains to be demonstrated how this method can contribute to sharp scholarship in our field. A machine can faithfully record the recurrence and recurrence of a theme or fact, and yet miss the meaning of one subtle sentence, which gives the overlying character to the whole document.

It would seem that we should not trust the computer except as a mass selector, eliminating the dross, so that we may examine that which the computer can not comprehend. We must not forget the well-worn question, "What would have happened if the apple which fell on Sir Isaac Newton's head had fallen on a computer?"

Questions Relating to Objectives

If it is true that government is affected by whatever it touches and that it touches everything, it must follow that students of government cannot delimit the scope of their discipline in advance. If it is also true (as contended earlier in this essay) that methodology is more clearly pertinent to the student as an individual than to his subject, it must follow that the only way we can *identify* our discipline is by its *objectives*.

(16) The leading question *concerns our principal purpose in studying and teaching government*. Is it to acquire and impart a mental discipline, which could also be achieved by pursuing an ancient Greek adverb through the centuries of an evolving language? Is it mainly to adorn the mind, as is the case with much of literature? Is it to make good citizens? Is it to master operating skills, one of which is to deal effectively with the government as an adversary? Is it to learn substantively what is "good" for society, and procedurally how to achieve it? Is it to acquire new knowledge about a subject, with such acquisition being accepted as an end in itself?

(Lest someone say that we try to do all of these things, let me remind that in the initial sentence in the preceding paragraph I used the word "principal.")

It would seem that professors of government have not settled on a principal objective. Most of them are doing ham-and-eggs work in basic courses which are taught because they have "always" been taught. A favored few enjoy the luxury of selecting a small area of study and of deriving the comfort of knowing more about that area than anyone else. Few professors are concerned with a grand design for the study of government.

When Benjamin Franklin founded the American Philosophical Society and later joined it with the Junto, he adhered to the title "Society for Promoting Useful Knowledge." Some of our academic brethren profess to be displeased if it is suggested that what they do should be useful. Now it may not be immediately or even remotely useful for a liberal arts student to study astronomy, medieval Spanish, or the chronology and dimensions of the third ice age, but how can the study of government be justified if it is not to be useful? It would seem, therefore, that the student of government should first study society and then see what government can do to improve society. If, then, the purpose of the study of government is normativism, there will be more controversy in our academic halls than there is now. (Despite all protestations to the contrary, the principal purpose of architecture is to keep the rain off, but within that over-all mission there is a great deal of controversy about how best to combine utility with beauty.) Controversy—and more of it—should be welcomed in our discipline, even about why we are studying government.

Suggestions about public policy are made freely by labor unions, authoritarian churches, manufacturers' associations, ward committees, Parent-Teacher Associations, farm federations, and veterans' and patriots' organizations, but it appears to be unseemly for a professor of government to advocate a specific course. (This statement is not weakened by the occasional appearance of China experts and the like before Senate committees; they are called to provide information.) Who, indeed, should be better qualified to recommend public policy than a detached and presumably intelligent man who has studied it all of his adult life and has no axe to grind?

For these and other reasons which cannot be elucidated here for lack of space, I believe that our fraternity should assume a bold posture, and presume to tell society what is good for it. This does not mean that history, quantification, theory, observation, and documentation should be discontinued; it means that they should be subordinated to the main objective of prescribing governmental goals and designing governmental programs.

If this posture were adopted, our meetings would pass resolutions, our journals would carry trenchant editorials, more of our writers would write books which take positions, and more of our professors would run for public office and tell students how the government should be operated. Our organization would lose its tax-exempt status, but we would all be more responsible, more masculine, and more adult. The country would be better off.

(17) *Should professionals in our field be expected to predict?* Should a seismologist be expected to announce in advance the next earthquake in Japan? Can anyone predict the behavior of the pound? Who can tell whether women's skirts will become shorter or longer? How many automobiles will be sold in the United States next year? What will the New York stock market do two months from now? How and where will World War III start?

Alas, in 1948 we spent a great deal of money and could not even predict who was to be elected President!

If we are well advised to stay away from predicting, we need not be so chary about projecting. It seems that we know enough to say that a neighborhood is going to degenerate into a slum unless remedial action is taken. There is no great mystery about the reciprocal effects of budgets, tax rates, public debts, and inflation. Rises and falls in the morale of public employees and resulting recruiting and quitting rates can be charted pretty accurately. Highway construction and highway congestion can be studied *pari passu.* (Further examples need not be cited here.)

But it is risky, on the other hand, to project the crime rate, or the rate of unemployment, or the persuasions of marginal members of political parties.

Consequently, it may be concluded that we should eschew prediction, but that we should project where we may, by extending or repeating history, using factor analysis, comparisons, polls, and the like.

(18) *Should our teaching and writing place a heavier emphasis on political values and moral relativism?* Unfortunately our personal codes are hodgepodges of precepts and prejudices learned from parents, professional societies, business chambers, labor unions, sectarians, and commercial journalists. Why should not a professor of government instruct his charges on the moral relativism of regressive taxation? Who among the vocal elements just mentioned has a *moral* right to speak on the subject? If the professor of government carefully stays away from predestination and the immaculate conception, may he not ask the clergyman to stay away from birth control and divorce?

It seems to me that on these matters we have been too self-effacing, too scientific, and too diffident.

It is not enough, however, to summon the courage to take responsible positions; we must develop a methodology and discipline of study so that we may know how to formulate values logically and without emotion.

(19) Other questions *relate to writing and teaching about public administration and international relations.* Should public administration be an esoteric, literary subject? Should the administrator be frequently reminded that he is part sociologist, part social psychologist, and part executive, and that his

organization should be studied as a special society, which shapes him but which he does not shape?

I believe that I must make a blunt reply to this question. The teacher of public administration should do two things— show his charges how to *identify* problems and then how to *solve* them. If he has not been a public administrator he should not be teaching the subject. He should act as a football player, not as a spectator at a football game, and he should deal in exercises, problems, and methods to achieve administrative objectives, and his teaching materials should be rigidly exoteric. How does a man like Max Weber, who died in 1920, and whose milieu was middle European sociology, economics, religion, and law, have any place in a class in public administration assembled in the United States in 1967?   (He does, of course, have a proper place in classes in political theory, both in Europe and America.)

We all recognize that public administration is a huge and obtrusive factor in our present culture, and that therefore anyone seeking a liberal arts education must learn about the nature and importance of public administration in his way of life. The presentation of this aspect of the subject has nothing whatever to do with the training of public administrators, however. They should be trained as surgeons are trained, that is, by showing them how to remove an appendix, and the like. The difference is the same as the difference between teaching the piano and teaching music appreciation by playing records and giving lectures.

There are three kinds of governmental attachés, so far as decision-making is concerned—the researcher, who collects enveloping data on an assigned subject, the adviser, who makes recommendations to a superior, and the executive, who makes decisions in a manner which is currently pertinent to the subject. Professors of public administration should show their students how to make decisions, even though young graduates entering the field will not be permitted to exercise such authority at the outset of their careers.

(20) *Should government be shaped by the behavior of citizens, or should it shape behavior?* This question resembles somewhat the *expressio unius exclusio alterius* dialogue in the heredity-environment dispute. (Reasonable people agree that it is never

altogether the one or the other, but they also agree that it is principally environment that shapes the race and heredity that shapes the individual.)

If government were to be merely the response-resultant of popular behavior, we should have to dismiss the factor of progress. But this cannot be dismissed, if the history of Western civilization means anything. Can things like compulsory inoculation, public education, traffic laws, and the like arise spontaneously from the masses? Can invention, industrial direction, and public welfare programs have any source but a minority of higher-minded members of society?

We all know that good public servants try to educate their "pertinent publics," so as to make enforcement easier and programs more beneficial, but we also know that, by and large, the citizenry must be compelled to comply with directives intended for its own good. Accordingly it seems that behavioral studies should be advisory and procedural; they should not pretend to make governmental policy conform to the current predilections of the people.

It has always seemed to me that the history of civilization is the history of institutions rather than of individual persons or masses of persons. If this is so, it would seem that students of government should emphasize governmental institutions and programs, and leave to the social psychologists the business of justifying studies of individual responses as ends in themselves.

(21) *Should the student of government make bold to criticize society and the government?* If he is to adopt the role of a strong normativist, as advocated above, he must indeed be a critic. But he need not have a critical attitude stronger than is suitable for a clergyman, a journalist, or a civic leader. He should, of course, be a constructive critic, and should strive directly to help make governmental and related programs work. As one of the contributors in this symposium said, he should not hesitate to be a social engineer.

(22) *Should we challenge the wild claims of the demophilists?* The word democracy has, of course, acquired a halo, and what is called democratic government is supposed to be defended and even extolled by our confraternity whether it is completely defensible or not.

(I hasten to make a distinction here between what I call anabolic and katabolic democracy. A broad democratic base for a welfare program can readily be defended, whereas a highly pervasive procedural democracy could easily wreck the nice adjustments in our intricate society.)

But we must remember that democracy has been a brief minute in the long hour of history, and that it requires a most highly favorable ecology for its introduction or survival. The plain truth is that we are presently trying to introduce it among people—inside as well as outside of the United States—who cannot appreciate its fine nuances and exercise its subtle restraints.

One can make the generalization that through the ages political systems break down largely because they overextend their central principles—oligarchies become too closely oligarchical, dictatorships too dictatorial, and democracies too democratic.

Many people will disagree with this, and many of them will be sincere, for they believe that democracy is ennobling, and is its own complete justification for being. Many who agree will not have the courage to flout the strident doctrine of the market place. Those who agree recognize that democracy, although ideally desirable, is never for long a viable form of organization, and that a good thing will last longer if it is not pushed to extremes. One of their views is that there is no valid reason for having more democracy in government than in industry, commerce, labor organizations, organized religion, education, and society in general.

It would seem to me that more of us who are intellectually committed to this point of view might advance the cause of good government by saying so.